Frederick Wright

Scientific aspects of Christian evidences

Frederick Wright

Scientific aspects of Christian evidences

ISBN/EAN: 9783337124540

Printed in Europe, USA, Canada, Australia, Japan

Cover: Foto ©Lupo / pixelio.de

More available books at **www.hansebooks.com**

SCIENTIFIC ASPECTS OF CHRISTIAN EVIDENCES

BY

G. FREDERICK WRIGHT
D. D., LL. D., F. G. S. A.

PROFESSOR OF THE HARMONY OF SCIENCE AND REVELATION
OBERLIN COLLEGE

AUTHOR OF THE LOGIC OF CHRISTIAN EVIDENCES
THE ICE AGE IN NORTH AMERICA, ETC.

ILLUSTRATED

NEW YORK
D. APPLETON AND COMPANY
1898

PREFACE.

AMONG well-founded beliefs, Christianity is not peculiar in being incapable of *demonstrative* proof and in being open to a variety of objections which are difficult to answer. Of the misleading tendencies in modern thought, one of the most serious is that of setting up an unreasonable standard of proof as the necessary basis for active belief. Indeed, in a vast number of instances, the insistence upon experimental or demonstrative proof is so unreasonable that it amounts to a species of insanity. Many who yield themselves to this tendency come to distrust ordinary evidence just as a certain class of insane persons do their best friends. Their condition of mind is like that of those who are so afraid of poison that it is with the utmost difficulty that they are persuaded that anything is free from it, while life is too short to admit of a preliminary mathematical demonstration of the fact.

Not only has the prevalence of this tendency induced in the specialists who have yielded themselves to it lamentable poverty of religious faith, but it has blinded them to the higher significance of their own fields of investigation; for modern science is far more than a record of sensations and experiments. It is itself in every department a system of thought in which the facts of sense-perception are combined, comprehended, and interpreted by the higher reasoning powers. The true man of science is also a man of faith. He, as well as the Christian believer, walks in the light of the evidence of many things unseen, and satisfies his mind with the substance of many things hoped for.

At the same time it is recognised that our defence of Christianity must be more than negative. In order to serve as a satisfactory basis for religious hope and activity, the facts of Christianity must be proved beyond "reasonable doubt." The Christian apologist must cheerfully accept the responsibility of adducing such proof. But in this respect the present volume contents itself mainly with the preliminary discussion of numerous fundamental assumptions which vitally affect the argument, and with the elaboration of the important new lines of evidence which have come to light during the closing quarter of the nineteenth century. The evidences of the historical truth of the foundations of Christianity have always been ample. In the providence of God they have now become superabundant. It can but be profitable for all to go over the ground afresh in the light of recent investigations and discoveries.

PREFACE.

As this volume is an elaboration of the Lowell Institute Lectures delivered by me in Boston during the latter part of 1896, I am glad of this opportunity to express my deep obligation to the managers of that course for the facilities they have afforded me of reaching the general public with a presentation of views which are the result of many years' earnest thought and studious investigation.

G. FREDERICK WRIGHT.

OBERLIN, *November 1, 1897.*

CONTENTS.

CHAPTER	PAGE
I.—LIMITS OF SCIENTIFIC THOUGHT	1
II.—THE PARADOXES OF SCIENCE	28
III.—GOD AND NATURE	62
IV.—DARWINISM AND DESIGN	89
V.—MEDIATE MIRACLES	115
VI.—BEYOND REASONABLE DOUBT	172
VII.—NEWLY DISCOVERED EXTERNAL EVIDENCES OF CHRISTIANITY	201
VIII.—THE TESTIMONY OF TEXTUAL CRITICISM	244
IX.—INTERNAL EVIDENCES OF THE EARLY DATE OF THE FOUR GOSPELS	279
X.—POSITIVE RESULTS OF THE CUMULATIVE EVIDENCE	328
INDEX	351

LIST OF ILLUSTRATIONS.

FIGURE   PAGE
1. Section of raised beach and "head" . . . 150
2. Village de Santenay 152
3. Section across Sugar Loaf Hill, Gibraltar . . . 153
4. Section across Middle Hill, Gibraltar 153
5. Map of Bay of Palermo 155
6. Diagram section across the Island of Guernsey . . 160
7. Sections from La Motte Islet to Mont Ubé, Jersey . . 162

SCIENTIFIC ASPECTS
OF CHRISTIAN EVIDENCES.

CHAPTER I.

LIMITS OF SCIENTIFIC THOUGHT.

THE prevailing anxiety concerning the bearings of the scientific discoveries of this age upon the foundations of religious belief is largely groundless; for from a philosophical point of view, modern science is more superficial than it is popularly represented to be. Startling as have been the scientific discoveries of the nineteenth century, and profoundly as they have changed certain aspects of modern civilization, they have in reality but slightly touched the true basis of religious hope and aspiration. In fact, the realm of mystery has not been appreciably encroached upon by modern scientific discovery. It is still as true as ever that "what we know is as nothing to what we know not." There is still as much call as ever for a positive revelation of things which it is both important for us to know and impossible for us to extract from the diffused designs embodied in the material universe.

In pursuing our inquiries concerning the foundations of Christian faith and hope, it will be profitable at the start to take stock of our ignorance. We will therefore begin by making a partial inventory of the things which we do not know. By this means we may be able to clear the field of some of the arrogant but false assumptions which are put forth by many as if they were established facts, and which interfere with that freedom of investigation which is essential to correct conclusions.

<small>Inventory of our Ignorance.</small>

The importance of making this inventory of our ignorance is readily seen when we consider to what extent our ordinary reasoning is affected by the underlying assumptions with which we approach the consideration of specific questions. No amount of evidence will convince us of what we presume at the outset to be an impossibility or an absurdity. Much is gained, therefore, when we are brought to admit concerning the thing to be proved that we do not know *but* it is true.

An agnostic is one whose mind is in a state of suspense. He does not know that there is a God; but, if he is a pure agnostic, he should not affect to know the contrary. The pure agnostic does not know that there is not a God.* The pure agnostic is as careful about denying as he is about affirming. Unfortunately, however, this is not the case with all agnostics. Some of the most prominent among them confound the unknown with the unknowable. Like Herbert Spencer, they are ready not only to affirm that God is unknown to men, but to go further and affirm that he can not be known except in a negative way.

<small>True and False Agnosticism.</small>

Upon this point we may profitably quote a few

---

* See Romanes, Thoughts on Religion, p. 107 *et seq.*

discriminating statements from the late George J. Romanes:

The modern and highly convenient term "Agnosticism" is used in two very different senses. By its originator, Prof. Huxley, it was coined to signify an attitude of reasoned ignorance touching everything that lies beyond the sphere of sense perception—a professed inability to found valid belief on any other basis. It is in this its original sense—and also, in my opinion, its only philosophically justifiable sense—that I shall understand the term. But the other and perhaps more popular sense in which the word is now employed is as the correlative of Mr. H. Spencer's doctrine of the Unknowable. This latter term is philosophically erroneous, implying important negative knowledge that if there be a God we know this much about him—that he *can not* reveal himself to man. *Pure* agnosticism is as defined by Huxley.*

The object of this chapter will be to clear the ground of some of these current misapprehensions concerning the limitations of knowledge, that we may have a freer field for investigation than we should otherwise have.

The Origin of Matter.

We naturally begin with the state of our knowledge concerning the origin of matter. Is matter a created product, or is it eternal? It requires but little consideration to convince one that we do not know that matter is eternal, but are at liberty to believe that the universe in all its parts is the product of design. The ordinary doctrine concerning matter is that it is a cre-

Matter not necessarily Eternal.

---

* Thoughts on Religion, pp. 107, 108.

ated product; that, unlike the Deity, it had a beginning and may have an end. The bearing of this upon the doctrine of design in the universe is apparent. If the Creator in his work is dealing with intractable matter already in existence, the freedom of his designs is interfered with from the start. But the doctrine of the creation of matter has not really been touched by modern science. Our increased knowledge of the attributes of matter has done nothing to establish its eternity or to throw doubt upon its creation.

Something, indeed, must be eternal; but it is not necessarily matter. On the contrary, it is far easier to believe that that which is eternal has the attributes of free, intelligent spirit than it is to believe the contrary. Instead of being a hindrance in this respect, modern science is a positive help; for, so far as science speaks at all, it favours a spiritual conception of the universe. While, in the light of present knowledge, it is by no means impossible still to think of matter as the product of mind, it is still as impossible as ever to think of a free spirit as emerging from matter. In fact, matter, when we come to get near its elementary condition, is seen to be nothing but a mode of motion. The universe, as we have come to regard it in the light of modern science, is but a limited combination of correlated forces. To the scientific eye the elements of the material world resolve themselves into invisible atoms of inconceivable smallness combined into molecules whose qualities are chiefly determined by the motion of atoms arranged in clusters far more wonderful and complicated than those of the solar system. The individual

Matter can not produce Mind.

atoms of water are doubtless as hard as are those of iron; but their orbital motion in the molecules of iron is inconceivably swifter than that in those of water. A jet of water rushing with its full force from a hydraulic pipe under high pressure is impenetrable by an iron bar. In this respect it presents the phenomena of a solid. In their ultimate analysis, atoms do not exhibit the attributes of eternal self-existence, but rather, as Herschel has said, those of manufactured articles. The doctrine of definite atomic weights and of multiple proportions in all chemical combinations, so far as it indicates anything, indicates the design of a Creator. On scientific grounds, therefore, we can neither assert the eternity of matter nor deny its creation and the beginning of its existence in time.

The Origin of Life.

It has not been proved that life is a development of matter. The mystery of life is still as great as ever it has been. Apparently no progress has been made toward explaining its origin. On the other hand, the theory of spontaneous generation has been shown by a great variety of experiments to be without foundation; for, wherever all germs have been known to be destroyed, it has been impossible to produce a living organism. Prof. Huxley,[*] indeed, affected to *believe* that somewhere in infinite time, and amid the infinite series of changes through which matter has been called to pass, life with all its possibilities did somehow originate from mate-

Prof. Huxley's Robust Faith.

---

[*] See Encyclopædia Britannica article Biology.

rial forces. But this was an object of faith on his part pure and simple, as much so as any theological dogma which is held by the Church. If he had consistently adhered to his agnosticism, he never would have published that belief, but would have been content to say, "I do not know." In publishing the belief, he abandoned his professed ground of pure agnosticism and joined the ranks of philosophic believers. Such robust faith in the power of material forces fairly puts to shame the halting belief of many theists.

THE ENDLESS EXISTENCE OF THE PRESENT ORDER OF THINGS.

We do not know that the existing physical conditions have continued indefinitely or that they are to continue so. On the contrary, evidence accumulates that the universe is perpetually changing, and that these changes compel a constant migration of organic life from one place to another. Induction deals only with the changes which take place in a system already established. It has no means of inference respecting the absolute beginning of the system.

There has been in this respect much misapprehension concerning the range of inference attempted by Darwin. It should be noted that his method differs very widely from that of Spencer. Spencer is pre-eminently an *a priori* philosopher attempting, like the spider, to spin a universe out of his own bowels. Beginning with the simplest possible conception of matter and force, he tries to show that all things will evolve in necessary order from a beginning so simple that,

Limitations of the Darwinian Argument.

though not absolutely nothing, it is next to nothing. With him evolution "is an integration of matter and concomitant dissipation of motion, during which the matter passes from an indefinite, incoherent homogeneity to a definite, coherent heterogeneity, and during which the retained motion undergoes a parallel transformation." *

Darwin, on the other hand, taking organic Nature as he finds it, attempts by experiment and observation and reasonable inference from effects to causes to learn the actual course of development. By assuming continuity in the past, he endeavours to see how far back by study of the marks still remaining the development can be traced. For the initiation of the forces whose effects in the marvellous phenomena of plant and animal life are unfolded before us, Darwin has no explanation other than that of the theologian, but assumes that in the beginning the Creator breathed into the original elements all the powers and potentialities which have since appeared.

An interesting illustration of the helplessness of inductive logic in the presence of ultimate facts appears in the efforts of astronomers and physicists to explain the continuance of the solar system, and to estimate the length of its career. According to all the principles of modern philosophy, the solar system is but a passing phase of history which can not repeat itself, and whose beginning can not have been many hundred millions of years ago, and can not be conceived of except as the product of a designing will. Of this the late Mr. Croll

The Universe is running down.

---

* First Principles, p. 396.

has given a most powerful statement in his little volume on Stellar Evolution.

Mr. Croll, as the propounder and defender of an astronomical theory of the Glacial period which made great demands upon geological time, encountered the startling calculations made by Lord Kelvin, Prof. Tait, George H. Darwin, and others, going to show that the solar system is running down so fast that geological history must be compressed into what seems to some an incredibly short space of time. Whereas geologists had been in the habit of assuming that many hundred million years were at their command, these physicists came in with their demonstrations that if all things have continued from the first as they now are, the solar system would part with its heat by radiation in less than one hundred million years, leaving only a fraction of that brief time fit for the development of plant and animal life.

Indeed, if, as physicists are pretty well agreed in assuming, the heat of the sun is nothing but transmuted gravitation, it can be demonstrated that the total supply furnished by the system could not last more than thirty million years. Some method for replenishing the supply must therefore be devised. Partial relief was obtained by the theory that additions to the heat of the solar system were constantly made by showers of meteors which are pouring in both upon the sun and upon the planets. But even this involves a limit to the system; for if this process continued indefinitely, the supply would be exhausted, and the bulk of the solar system would become so great as to disturb its harmony.

Limitations to Geological Time.

LIMITS OF SCIENTIFIC THOUGHT. 9

In despair of any other way to keep up the supply of heat as long as his theory of geological time required, Mr Croll supposed that the amount furnished by gravitation was at the outset augmented by that of the arrested motion of two dark worlds which came in collision. But this collision, with all its beneficent consequences, could not be supposed to be the result of chance. So productive a blow must have been aimed by an all-wise and all-powerful hand. The ultimate idea to which the theorist came is therefore none other than that to which Newton gave expression long before—namely, that a designing will must be postulated at the beginning of the present order of events—thus confirming the conclusion of Clerk Maxwell, that all systems of materialism require a God to make them work. But we have no evidence that such systems are eternal. On the contrary, it would appear that not only is it true that

Impossible to exclude Design from Nature.

> Our little systems have their day,

but that the same is true of the whole material universe. That which we see is but one of Nature's endlessly passing phases.

THE CONTINUITY OF NATURE.

Science has not proved the absolute continuity of Nature. The continuity of Nature may be an object of scientific faith, but it is far from being a demonstrated conclusion. The belief in a free will whose choices are not determined by outside forces, but are self-determined, stands upon as solid a basis as it has ever had.

In this is involved the whole question of the possibility of miracles and of a providential control of Nature. Physical science which by the argument of progressive approach proves the natural conservation of energy and correlation of forces, does not thereby rule out the higher law of providential interferences. For from our own experience we know that new combinations of forces and new directions to it are given by our own self-determining wills, which are not physical forces at all, but only spiritual entities, having neither length, nor breadth, nor height, nor depth, nor gravity, nor any other physical properties.

The system of Nature abounds in instances of unstable equilibrium, into which, without adding any physical force, thought can enter and give new direction to a large circle of connected forces, and bring about results which do not lie in the system as a simple causally connected concatenation of events. In other words, knowledge is power. If one only knows how and where to penetrate the system of natural forces, he can enter it and mould it to his will.

Critical Points of Unstable Equilibrium in Nature.

"Behold, how great a fire a little spark kindleth!" After years of patient mining beneath the tumultuous waters of Hell Gate, in the channel connecting Long Island Sound with New York harbor, a complicated mine is prepared with its chambers filled with dynamite. Connected with this highly explosive compound thus skilfully distributed is a copper wire coming up above the surface and running out an indefinite distance upon the shore. So far everything remains as it was, with the exception of the small amount of rock which has been removed by human hands. But there has been

LIMITS OF SCIENTIFIC THOUGHT. 11

method in the removal, and method in the preparation of the mine. Everything will remain, however, as it is unless a spark is transmitted to those caverns beneath the water sufficient to ignite the explosive compound. Everything now depends upon knowing how to produce the explosion.

The engineer's daughter, a girl of tender years, is to be the agent employed to complete the plan and bring the catastrophe to a culmination. The electric batteries are arranged so that by simply pressing a button the connection will be made which will send the electric current upon its destructive errand. The father speaks the word; the impression is conveyed through the auditory nerve to a point in the brain where there is such absolutely unstable equilibrium that a thought of the child directs the pent-up force in her brain through the nerves and muscles of the arm and hand, and presses the button which releases and directs the electricity that is to explode the dynamite in the chamber of the mine, and remove forever the rocks that have so long obstructed navigation in this dangerous channel.

But in all this complicated operation of causes there has nothing been added to or subtracted from the forces of Nature. Had the mine not been made, and the wire not been laid, and the button not been pressed, the potential forces in operation would have remained unchanged, and would have continued to exert themselves in the production of those peculiar molecular conditions which characterize their original state. But the thought of man has entered in to *direct* their energies to the accomplishment of a specific purpose for man's behalf. The correlation and conserva-

Mental Acts not subject to the Law of Conservation.

tion of force is preserved whether the mine is exploded or whether it is left inaccessible to the electric spark. But great material results have been produced by the intervention of a thought, which has no material qualities, and which is incapable of being retained in the chain of correlated forces. However much like a paradox this may sound, it is a kind of fact of which we may be conscious every waking moment of our lives.

Nothing is more interesting than to trace out the possible consequences of diverse choices of the will when turned upon these apexes of unstable equilibrium along which it moves at every instant. Much has been written concerning the Two Ocean Pass in the Yellowstone Park. This is a swamp at the summit of the watershed between the Yellowstone and the Snake River, the one a tributary of the Missouri and the other of the Columbia. Along this ridgepole of the continent there flows a small stream which divides upon the very crest, part turning toward the distant Gulf of Mexico and part toward the Pacific Ocean. It almost takes one's breath away to think of the delicacy of poise of the fluid thus balanced upon this mountain height between the two quarters of the globe. To the right, particles may bear messages and transmit force to the plains of Oregon; to the left, to the sugar plantations of Louisiana! But at an infinitely higher poise is the unstable force in the highly organized brain of the man, be he savage or civilized, who sits at this fountain-head of power, and by his will determines whether to commit his message to the one or the other.

A still more striking illustration of the delicate poise of the forces to be set in motion by a thought appears in the influence of a word fitly spoken at a critical point in the world's history. In rebuke of those who fain would have prevented the broken-hearted woman of Bible story from pouring, in token of her affection, the box of precious ointment upon her Saviour's feet, Jesus said: "Let her alone; why trouble ye her? She hath wrought a good work on me. For ye have the poor with you always, and whensoever ye will ye may do them good; but me ye have not always." It has been truly said that all the artistic development of the Christian Church was dependent upon the utterance of these words. They consecrated forever the "altar of sacrifice." All along the ages since their utterance they have fallen upon the ears of devout worshippers who have longed to give artistic expression to their love, and the world has in consequence been covered with stately buildings of exquisite form and delicate architecture adapted to quicken the thought, raise the aspirations, and console the sorrows of all successive generations. The cathedrals of Europe sprang up from the seed that was sown in the utterance of these tender words of the Founder of Christianity. The determining cause was not material, but spiritual and imponderable. Yet the course of material Nature has thereby been interrupted and diverted, and made to bear fruit from germs which were not inherent in her own powers.

Science can not exclude the influence of mind upon Nature, even should it demonstrate the conservation of energy; for it requires no more physical force to utter a kind word than to speak an unkind one: the same strokes of the pen will sign a declaration of war or a treaty of peace; the same amount of waste of phosphorus in the brain which determines the

Mystery of Man's Power over Nature.

policy of a government in promoting internal improvements whereby commerce will be facilitated could be made to determine a policy of isolation which should make a hermit nation of a people. Knowledge is power. If we only knew how to unlock the manifold resources of Nature so as to utilize her reservoirs of energy which are in unstable equilibrium, there is no limit to what we might do. With so much command as we have over these powers of Nature, it is absurd, therefore, to affirm that the Creator is as limited in his direct power over Nature as we are. That miracles are credible and answers to prayer possible are things which science can not deny, except in a fair field of induction where inferences are uncertain in proportion to ignorance and to the uncertain limitations of the data from which they are drawn.

The Possible Immortality of the Soul.

Science does not know that the soul is not immortal. It is true that many would say that we do not know the existence of the soul. But, on the contrary, no one can intelligently deny its existence. The one supposition is certainly as allowable as the other. That the power of thought does not continue after the dissolution of the body is a proposition which no wise man of science would dare maintain in a dogmatic manner. He may say that he does not believe it will continue. But in that case he has passed from the realm of certainty to that of speculation, and is on common ground with the theologian. He may say that he can not conceive how there can be thought

The Continuance of Life less mysterious than its Origin.

without the brain. To which it can properly be answered, neither can he conceive how there can be thought with a brain.

We do not know as there is any necessary limitation of thought to such an organized compound as we find in the brain. The man of science may say that it is inconceivable that thought should not cease with the death of the body. To which it may properly be answered that it is inconceivable that thought should begin with the organization of the brain. Or, if he attempts to disprove the continuance of the individual power of thought after death by appealing to experience, he has then abandoned certainty and taken refuge in the sphere of faith which he so much derides. Besides, he has no experience from which to draw a conclusion. Death is that bourne from which no traveller returns. What the soul can do in connection with some other organization is beyond the power of man's ken to determine.

It is not without reason that minds of the greatest capacity have loved to speculate upon the possibilities which are before us in the union of the soul with a more subtile material organization than that which we now possess, and its consequent entrance upon a wider field of exploration. After remarking upon the imperfection of our five senses and of man's "terrestrial imbecility" in endeavouring to interpret their deliverances, and of the many intimations that sensations may be "much extended" in a delicate and sensitive organization, the late Prof. Benjamin Pierce is but expressing the feelings of most great minds when he gives way to speculation in the following words:

Inviting Field for Speculation.

... That the immense extent of unheard and unseen vibrations with which the universe is palpitating should never become available to the soul, is contrary to the analogies of Nature. It is far from unreasonable to suppose that there will be a corresponding variety of ways of knowledge, and of opportunities for scientific study, for the development of strange inventions for re-enforcing the senses, and for the creation of wonderful, grand, and lovely forms of fancy and imagination. In the exquisite organizations of the celestial substance, the range of sensible vibrations may be increased immeasurably; and the ultimate limits to which future perception and education may advance is possibly a mystery, transcending the powers of research even of archangels.

The increased possibilities of future inquiry may not only arise from increased capacities of sensation, but also from better conditions for exact and delicate observation. No quickening of the senses can relieve the astronomer from our flittering and obscuring atmosphere; nor can the carpet of the good fairy lift him above its influence; nor can he by any art sweep the skies clear or quiet their ceaseless twinkle. . . .

Do we need a nearer approach to the planets and stars? There is Halley's comet, upon which we might be conveyed through the whole extent of the solar system; and there are other comets which might carry us out to the home of the meteors or to the most distant regions of space.*

Mysterious Relations of Mind to Body. All this is rendered credible by the fact that we can not close our eyes to the familiar experience of often losing the power of thought in sleep and swoons and under the influence of drugs and disease, and afterward acquiring it again. If it be said that the analogy is not here complete, because the organization

---

* Ideality in the Physical Sciences, pp. 191–193.

of the brain still has remained intact, we answer that the analogy does not need to be perfect to prove the main point. It is as inconceivable that the thinking identity should remain amid the changes through which the brain is known to pass during a single lifetime as that it should retain its identity while passing into a more subtile organization. Science has made no progress in identifying matter and mind. There is no more resemblance between the processes of secreting bile and that of creating thought than there is between bile and thought. Bile, though a secretion from the liver, is still a material product, while thought has none of the properties of a material product. Pure agnosticism maintains not merely that it does not know that the soul is immortal, but that it does not know that it is not immortal. To go further is to enter the field of unsupported dogmatism.

The Existence of Evil perhaps not Inconsistent with the Benevolence of God.

It is not within the province of science to say that the existence of evil in the world disproves either the benevolence or the omnipotence of the Creator, for the darkness of the problem of the existence of evil has not been lightened, but rather deepened, by scientific discovery. The problem, however, can be freed of some of its difficulties by correctly defining our terms and exercising consistency in using them.

The omnipotence of God is his power to do everything in the range of possibility. It is not within the range of omnipotence to do absurdities—that is, to do things which in their very statement are self-contradictions. Such are the childish puzzles: Can God make a stone so heavy that he can not move it? Can God make two hills without a valley between them? Can God add two and two together so that the sum shall be five? A teacher once asked a pupil if she supposed God could make a plane triangle the sum of whose angles would be more than two right angles. The unsuspecting pupil replied "Yes." Whereupon the teacher asked, "What kind of a triangle would that be?" Only the wit of a young lady could have saved one from utter confusion at such a time. But this pupil was equal to the occasion, and triumphantly answered, "I think it would be an omnipotent triangle." And so it would.

Omnipotence defined.

The answer to all such questions is that they are in their very statements absurdities; they are mere collocations of words without any real meaning. They do not signify things, but *no*things. In answer to the objections brought against the doctrine of the divine power and goodness based on the existence of natural evil, it is sufficient for us to show that possibly the objectors make as absurd demands upon the Creator as are involved in the foregoing puzzles. The defence of divine power and goodness is sufficient which maintains that in creating and sustaining the present universe the Divine Being, for all we know to the contrary, secures the highest *attainable* good of the whole. In order to make the proposition a component part of our faith, it is only necessary for us to be made to see the superior worth of certain classes of joys which are logically connected with incidental evils. Perhaps there

Absurdities set aside.

is a logical contradiction in the choice of the higher good without these incidental evils. If so, it would be neither wise nor benevolent to decline the higher good because of the accompanying evils, though they do subtract somewhat from the absolute value of the whole. In order, therefore, to justify the ways of God in creation, it is necessary, first, to take a proper measure of the various orders of beings which may come into existence, and of their various susceptibilities to pain and pleasure. Such a view must consider also the permanence of the system, and must keep in mind the possibilities of the future as well as the embarrassments of the present.

According to the true doctrine of theism, there was no absolute necessity for the creation of the universe. The universe is not a mere emanation from the Deity. That is pantheism. The world was created by a free act of the Almighty. So far as the necessities of his own nature were concerned, God could have continued to exist forever without creating anything. For his own part, the Creator could have taken as great satisfaction during the last half of eternity as he did in the first half of it without the society of man and the angels. When God created man he had no counsellor, but created according to the discretion of his own benevolent and all-wise mind. The universe itself is the record of the Creator's wisdom. From this record we properly infer that there are inherent difficulties in the way of realizing the highest conceivable good.

Creation a Free Act.

It is clear, for example, even upon a superficial examination, that the highest satisfaction of finite beings can not consist in a dead level of experience. If finite beings would enjoy the sweet to the fullest extent, they must also have tasted the bitter. If they would appreciate the sunlight, they must also see the shadows. But it is far better to possess the sweet with an admixture of bitter than not to have the sweet at all. It is better to have light *and* shadow than never to rise above the gloomy shades of nonexistence.

<small>Liability to Pain an Incidental Good.</small>

If we are asked why God should not have endowed his creatures with the capability of highest bliss without the encumbrance of such liability to suffering, we need not hesitate to answer that we do not fully know. We are not bound to know all the reasons for the actions of a superior personal being in whom we trust. As finite creatures, we are limited in our capacity of knowledge, and can more readily discern the grounds for confiding in the character of a superior being than we can discern the principles on which that being would justify his conduct. It is a necessary incident in human experience, and indeed of all finite intellectual existence, that its knowledge should be limited, and that the secrets of the Lord should be reserved for future unfolding. But while this is all true, it is no small satisfaction to direct our vision to the farthest extent of its penetrating power, where we can dimly discern the deep foundations upon which our structure of faith and hope reposes. While we can not hope fully to explain the mystery of God's permission of evil, we can show by way of illustration the direction in which a solution may be possible.

If the philosophic sceptic will go with the geologist to Canada, he will there behold some of the oldest fossiliferous rocks in the world, and will have pointed out to him that the little cells in the tubular masses composing the limestones of that region are the skeletons of something like the coral-building polyp,* whose low form of life manifests itself not in highly organized centres, but in a general sensitivity pervading the whole mass. In very early times the whole bottom of the Laurentian Sea, stretching from Lake Huron to Labrador, and from the St. Lawrence River far up toward Hudson Bay, was covered with this slimy, gelatinous sort of jellyfish, whose life was centred nowhere, but, like the gray twilight, was diffused through the whole mass. If the winds and waves tore off a part of it and floated it away from the main body, this part would still continue to live and grow. If this nondescript animal was capable of pleasure or pain, it was only in the lowest degree. No ordinary enemy could do it harm, and nothing but a sweeping change in the general conditions of the period could destroy its life.

A Geological Illustration.

But if even a Hottentot should be asked if he were willing to be absorbed into such a life as that, he would answer in the negative, rightly insisting that there was more joy beneath the shelter of a single Hottentot's hut than in an oceanful of jellyfish. If reminded that he was subject to headaches and rheumatic pains, to bruises and sores, to hunger and thirst, to the ravages of fever and pestilence, to the hazards of war, the oppression of enemies, and the cunning guile of crafty neighbours, he would still answer, and answer correctly, that the well-being of a single tribe of his fellows was

---

* Eozoon Canadense.

of more worth than that of the whole animal creation. That morbid state of mind which pronounces life not worth living, and leads the victim to leave the ills he has and rashly fly through suicide to encounter others that he knows not of, is a product of civilization and of sin.

A high state of civilization simply presents a still more forcible illustration of the truth of the proposition we are now considering. As the moun- *Superiority of Civilization.* tain peaks grow higher, the valleys between them grow deeper; so, with the increased capacities for happiness produced by civilization, there is incident to them an increased liability to failure and to the existence of incorporate evils. The civilized man is more sensitive to suffering than the barbarian is. Yet who in his right mind would not choose to be a civilized man, with all the attendant disabilities of civilization, rather than to possess the impassive nature of a barbarian?

<blockquote>
Better fifty years of Europe
Than a cycle of Cathay.
</blockquote>

THE UNKNOWN CAPACITY OF THE HUMAN MIND.

Science does not know but that the mind of man is the greatest thing in the world, and that its wants are so various and complex that it *Man's Superiority to Nature.* is impossible to create a mechanical universe which shall fully supply them. Thus the man of science can not deny the fundamental assumption of Christianity, which is, that man is so much greater than Nature that he needs a special revelation. The man of science can not intelligently deny that to give full expression of the Creator's regard for the creature made in his own image he may be compelled to break through the veil of Nature and reveal himself directly to the highest objects of his creative power. This assumption of Christian theism remains undisturbed amid the din of scientific progress. Indeed, the inadequacy of a mechanical universe to satisfy all the wants of a human mind may be a part of its perfection. Otherwise Nature might be forever a veil separating man from personal intercourse with his Creator. It is by no means certain that the best system for man is one in which no remedial agencies and no personal intervention on the part of the Creator are required. But of this more will be said at a later stage of the discussion.

In most of the reasoning against the supernatural facts of the Christian system the whole ground of objection disappears when the relative capacity of the human mind is properly realized. Butler was right in insisting that the mere "possibility" of the immortal life and of a connection between its untold interests and our development here, rendered nugatory all *a priori* objections to the Christian system on the ground of its introducing supernatural remedial agencies in man's behalf.

It is interesting to record also in the same connection the frank confession of the late Prof. Romanes:

When I wrote the preceding treatise [the Candid Examination], I did not sufficiently appreciate the immense importance of *human* nature, as distinguished from physical nature, in any inquiry touching Theism. But since then I have seriously studied anthropology (including the science of comparative religion), psychology, and metaphysics, with the result of clearly seeing that human nature is the most important part of Nature as a whole whereby to investigate the theory of Theism. This I ought to have anticipated on merely *a priori* grounds, and no doubt should have perceived had I not been too much immersed in merely physical research.*

Significance of these Negative Results.

At this stage of our inquiry we would be careful to say that we are not intending to make any extravagant claims for negative evidence or to foreclose further discussion, but are simply aiming to clear the field of misapprehensions arising from exaggerated estimates of the extent of scientific discovery. Modern science prides itself on being inductive; but the nature and limits of inductive science are so largely misunderstood, that many inductive philosophers when dealing with religious problems unconsciously surrender their fundamental principles, and are led to limit their knowledge in this field to the certainties attainable only in what are called complete inductions, where there is a direct and exhaustive examination of all the facts. But such an examination should rather induce a state of positive humility respecting everything beyond. Being certain only that there are as many fish in the sea as have been caught in his net, the fisherman should not deny that there are other, and other kinds of fish in the illimitable ocean which he has left unexplored. In respect of religious questions, modern science is in the position of one who has spent a single season upon St. George's

The Freedom of Faith.

---

* Thoughts on Religion, p. 154.

LIMITS OF SCIENTIFIC THOUGHT. 25

Bank and comes home laden with a varied and valuable cargo. No one will begrudge him the price he can obtain for the products of his skilful and laborious efforts; but if he proceeds to exact a return for his commodities on the representation that the broad expanse and the profound depths and varied conditions of the ocean provide no other kinds than those which he has secured in this limited area and within the limited depths of his lines, we may rightly enter a caveat and demand liberty to believe that there are many things in the universe not dreamed of in his philosophy.

In considering objections to Christianity it is important for us not to overestimate the light shed upon spiritual things by modern physical science. To this end it is profitable to keep in mind the long list of most eminent scientific discoverers who at the same time maintain their unshaken belief in the supernatural facts of Christianity. It is not strange that this array exercised a powerful restraining influence upon such a mind as that of Mr. Romanes. He could not but be deeply impressed during his years of unbelief with the fact that so many of his eminent associates pursued their extended investigations in physical science without any disturbance to their religious faith. Thus he says:

The Great Leaders of Science ordinarily Men of Faith.

> If we look to the greatest mathematicians in the world's history, we find Kepler and Newton as Christians. . . . Or, coming to our own times, and confining our attention to the principal seat of mathematical study, when I was at Cambridge there was a galaxy of genius in that department emanating from that place such as had never before been equalled. And the curious thing in our present con-

nection is that all the most illustrious names were ranged on the side of orthodoxy. Sir W. Thomson, Sir George Stokes, Profs. Tait, Adams, Clerk Maxwell, and Cayley— not to mention a number of lesser lights, such as Routh, Todhunter, Ferrers, etc.—were all avowed Christians. . . .

Now it would doubtless be easy to find elsewhere than in Cambridge mathematicians of the first order who in our own generation are or have been professedly anti-Christian in their beliefs, although certainly not so great an array of such extraordinary powers. But, be this as it may, the case of Cambridge in my own time seems to me of itself enough to prove that Christian belief is neither made nor marred by the highest powers of reasoning apart from other and still more potent factors.*

It is profitable to note that the greatest physicist of our own day joins with the greatest mathematical genius of all times in confessing his absolute ignorance of the ultimate constitution of Nature. Sir Isaac Newton, at the close of his career, compared himself to a child on the seashore who had succeeded in picking up only a few of the pebbles which spread themselves in endless succession along a boundless shore. In similar strain, Lord Kelvin, at the jubilee celebration of his professorship at Glasgow, said:

Great Knowledge leads to Positive Humility.

> One word characterizes the most strenuous of the efforts for the advancement of science that I have made perseveringly during fifty-five years. That word is failure. I know no more of electric and magnetic force, or of the relation between ether, electricity, and ponderable matter, or of chemical affinity, than I knew and tried to teach to my students of natural philosophy fifty years ago in my first session as professor.

---

* Thoughts on Religion, pp. 137, 138.

LIMITS OF SCIENTIFIC THOUGHT. 27

Without committing ourselves to all the inferences which have been drawn from them, we may, in conclusion, quote with general approval the following well-known and piquant paragraph from Sir William Hamilton:

The highest reach of human science is the scientific recognition of human ignorance: "*Qui nescit ignorare, ignorat scire.*" This "learned ignorance" is the rational conviction by the human mind of its inability to transcend certain limits; it is the knowledge of ourselves—the science of man. This is accomplished by a demonstration of the disproportion between what is to be known and our faculties of knowing—the disproportion, to wit, between the infinite and the finite. In fact, the recognition of human ignorance is not only the one highest, but the one true knowledge, and its first fruit, as has been said, is humility. Simple nescience is not proud; consummated science is positively humble. . . .

The grand result of human wisdom is thus only a consciousness that what we know is as nothing to what we know not ("*Quantum est quod nescimus*")—an articulate confession, in fact, by our natural reason of the truth declared in revelation, that "*now* we see through a glass darkly." *

---

* Philosophy of Sir William Hamilton (D. Appleton & Co.), pp. 517, 518.

CHAPTER II.

THE PARADOXES OF SCIENCE.

There is a somewhat general impression abroad in the world that whatever is scientific is clear and free from doubt and difficulty. But such an opinion is as far as possible from the truth. The mysteries of existence, though seeming to be progressively solved by science, are never more than partially solved. Indeed, in the strict sense of the word, they are never solved at all. The attempted explanations of science, instead of being real solutions of mystery, are merely substitutions of one mystery for another, or, what is more frequently the case, of several mysteries in place of one.

The Theory of Gravitation.

The Newtonian theory of gravitation is far from being so simple as it seems, and this its author clearly saw and was free to acknowledge. In reality, Newton's law of gravitation is simply a mathematical statement of facts established by observation. The statement that all material objects act as if attracted toward each other by a force which is directly as the product of the combined masses, and inversely as the square of

Newton's Early Views.

the distance, has been verified as completely as any matter of human experience. Newton's hypothesis as to the cause of this uniform action of law is, however, incapable of absolute verification, while its acceptance impales us on one or other horn of a dilemma from which it is not easy to be extricated. We must either believe that bodies act upon each other from a distance through a vacuum or that matter is continuous in space, so that there is no such thing as a vacuum. In his third letter to Bentley, Newton declared that it was to him "inconceivable that inanimate brute matter should, without the mediation of something else which is not material, operate upon and affect other matter, without mutual contact." And again, "that one body may act upon another at a distance, through a vacuum, without the mediation of anything else by and through which their action may be conveyed from one to another, is to me so great an absurdity that I believe no man who has in philosophical matters a competent faculty of thinking can ever fall into it. Gravity must be caused by an agent acting constantly according to certain laws; but whether this agent be material or immaterial, I have left to the consideration of my readers."

So keenly were the difficulties of this paradox felt that many of Newton's eminent contemporaries, especially upon the Continent, refused to accept the theory of gravitation, thus delaying its final triumph for a century. Huygens declared the theory to be absurd; John Bernoulli, that it was "revolting to minds accustomed to receiving no principle in physics save those which are incontestable and evident"; while Leibnitz called gravitation "an incorporeal, an inexplicable power."

Philosophical Objections.

To the contemporaries of Newton, and, indeed, as we have seen, to Newton himself, that one material body should act upon another at a distance seemed not only inconceivable but absurd.

The philosophical statements of this difficulty are easily understood and incapable of refutation. A material body can no more act *where* it is not than when it is not. According to the Newtonian hypothesis, matter in itself is inert and motionless. Its sole office is to receive and transmit or transform such motion as is imparted to it from the outside. The impartation of motion to a mass of matter is always from behind: it is by a push, and not by a pull. With reason did Newton's contemporaries assert that his theory of gravitation seemed to compel the readmission of occult forces to the realm of science; whereas, it had been the great mission of scientific men up to that time to banish such conceptions from the universe.

Nor have the difficulties of Newton's theory disappeared since his day. The acceptance of the law as a fact has taken place in spite of the paradoxes which his theory involves, and mathematicians and physicists are as much puzzled as ever to find any ultimate explanation of the law.

Gravitation not Analogous to other Forces.

The swiftest rate of transmission of an action with which we are familiar is that of light, which speeds at the rate of one hundred and eighty-five thousand miles per second, and crosses the space separating the sun from the earth in eight and one quarter minutes. But the astronomers have shown that, if the force of gravitation be not transmitted instantaneously, it must cer-

1. Acts Instantaneously.

tainly be at a rate which is fifty million times greater than that of light—that is, it can not be more than one one hundred thousandth of a second in passing from the earth to the sun.* If its rate were less than this, it would have been detected by the careful observations which astronomers have already made. From the nearest fixed star the light reaches us, travelling at the rate of one hundred and eighty-five thousand miles a second, in three years; but the force of gravity, if it requires any time at all to cross that space, can not take more than two seconds. Astronomical calculations are based upon the assumption that the action of gravitation is instantaneous across all distances of space.

A grain of sand exerts its gravitating influence upon another grain upon the opposite side of the globe. The intervention of the earth neither augments nor abates the action of the mysterious power. Sound is obstructed in various degrees by the objects intervening between the centre from which it is propagated and the listening ear. The rays of light are utterly unable to penetrate many substances, and are interfered with to some extent by those which are called transparent, while the Roentgen rays, though more penetrating than those of light, are arrested by many substances. But to gravitation everything is transparent.

2. Is Absolutely Indifferent to all Intervening Objects.

The gravitating power of a mass of matter appears to be unlimited in capacity. The energy expended by the sun in holding the planets in their orbits does

---

* Smithsonian Report, 1876, p. 212.

not to any degree exhaust its power. The planets might be multiplied indefinitely, and the sun would continue to attract each addition to the family with a power which is directly as the product of the two masses, and inversely as the square of their distances apart.

<small>3. Is Inexhaustible.</small>

This apparently unlimited capacity of the attractive force of gravitation perplexed and confounded Faraday to such an extent that he thought it to be in flat contradiction to the important and well-established modern doctrine of the conservation of energy. To Faraday, indeed, it seemed that a gravitating body possessed the mysterious power both of annihilating and of creating force. If, for example, a ball be projected to a height of ten miles from the centre of gravity of another body, the attraction at the point at which the projectile force was overcome by the force of gravitation is only one one hundredth as great as it was at the distance of one mile, while, in returning again, the force of the gravitation in the mass increases a hundredfold.

<small>Faraday's Difficulty.</small>

To Faraday this seemed like an alternate annihilation and creation of force. When the bodies are removed from each other by ten units of distance, their mutual force exerted upon each other is only one one hundredth of what it was at the distance of one diameter. But it possesses now what the physicists call an energy of position one hundred times greater than before. When the bodies are permitted to fall through this space and collide, this potential energy manifests itself, first, in augmenting the velocity of the fall, and, finally, in the transformation of its energy of position into an energy of heat, which dissipates in space. The mass becomes cold when the heat is all radiated, but it does not lose any of its attractive power. Unlike heat, the power of attraction is not scattered by radiation. It continues its activity forever in its new position, reaching out its mysterious arms of influence instantaneously, and through all time, to the remotest realms of space.

Ever since the days of Newton unceasing efforts have been made to explain gravitation by some theory of the impact of material elements upon each other, and by that means to avoid the difficulty of supposing action at a distance or the action of a body where it is not. Newton's theory was that, as gravitation is merely constant stress, it was produced by the steady pressure of ethereal matter filling all space, but being much rarer in the dense bodies of the stars and planets than it is in the empty celestial spaces, growing denser and denser perpetually in passing from them to greater distances, "thereby causing the gravity of those great bodies toward one another, and of their parts toward bodies, every body endeavouring to go from the denser part of the medium toward the rarer." * But as this involves an increase of density up to the point of infinity in the outer circles, it could scarcely be entertained; while, as it would also tend to retard the planetary movements, he concludes that, as "there is no evidence for its existence, therefore it ought to be rejected. And if it be rejected, the hypothesis that light consists in pression, or motion, propagated through such a medium, are rejected with it." †

[margin note: Attempted Physical Explanations.]

---

* Optics, bk. iii, appendix. Query 21.
† Ibid., Query 28.

So great are the difficulties of this theory, that Newton at last came back to accept the position which, twenty-four years before, he had declared to be so absurd that no competent thinker could ever fall into it, and despairingly asks, "Have not the small particles of bodies certain powers, virtues, or forces, by which *they act at a distance?* . . . What I call attraction *may* be performed by impulse, or by some other means unknown to me. I use that word here to signify only in general any force by which bodies tend toward one another, whatsoever be the cause." *

<small>Newton's Later Views.</small>

In 1692, in Newton's third letter to Bentley, he had expressed himself similarly to this effect, averring that "gravity must be caused by an agent acting constantly according to certain laws; but whether this agent be material or immaterial I have left to the consideration of my readers." Again, in the Principia, at the conclusion of the third book, he writes: "Hitherto I have not been able to discover the cause of those properties of gravity from phenomena, and I frame no hypothesis; for whatever is not deduced from the phenomena is to be called an hypothesis. . . . To us it is enough that gravity does really exist and act according to the laws which we have explained."

The recognition of this paradox by John Stuart Mill, and his confident acceptance of the facts which involve it, is even more remarkable than in the case of Sir Isaac Newton. Where the great discoverer halted and wavered, the logician marches boldly forward and cheer-

<small>Can a Body act where it is not?</small>

---

* Optics, bk. iii, appendix. Query 31.

fully impales himself on one horn of the destructive dilemma. "No one now feels," says Mill, "any difficulty in conceiving gravity to be, as much as any other property is, 'innate, inherent, and essential to matter,' nor finds the comprehension of it facilitated in the smallest degree by the supposition of an ether; nor thinks it at all incredible that the celestial bodies can and do act, where they, in actual bodily presence, are not. To us it is not more wonderful that bodies should act upon one another 'without mutual contact,' than that they should do so when in contact; we are familiar with both these facts, and we find them equally inexplicable but equally easy to believe." *

But, notwithstanding the ease with which Mill disposes of the paradox, it still remains true that the greatest leaders in modern science are perplexed by it as much as Newton was, and efforts to explain gravitation by some theory of impact or of pressure, and thus to avoid the apparent absurdity of an attraction which is felt at a distance and through a vacuum, are as prevalent at the close of the nineteenth century as they were in the latter part of the seventeenth. Prof. Tait † still maintains that the theory of Lesage is "the only even apparently hopeful attempt which has yet been made to explain the mechanism of gravitation." Lesage's theory was that all space is frequented by innumerable minute particles of matter moving with great velocity in every possible direction, and that the onward motion of a portion of these particles is intercepted by the masses

Theory of Lesage.

---

* Logic, Harper's ed., N. Y., 1867, pp. 461, 462.
† Lectures before the British Association, 1876, at Glasgow.

of matter with which they come in contact. But where the course is free in both directions, the effect of these impacts is neutralized by the impact of those from an opposite direction. When, however, two bodies are in line, each would protect the other from a certain number of impacts upon the sides which are facing each other, and so give rise to a mutual attraction; in other words, two bodies produce between them a shadow of protection from the impinging molecules as they do from rays of light.

But, ingenious as this theory is, it involves more than one apparent absurdity as great as that which Newton perceived in action at a distance. The most patent of these is that urged by Clerk Maxwell, who shows that the impact of molecules which would suffice to produce gravitation would generate such an amount of heat that they would in a few seconds raise not only the body, but the whole material universe to the melting point.*

The other direction in which physicists have been looking for a rational conception of the force of gravitation is to the possible effects of waves of transmission through an all-prevalent ether, such as is hypothecated to account for the phenomena of life. The most carefully wrought-out theory of this class is that of Prof. James Challis,† an eminent mathematician of

Theory of Prof. Challis.

---

* Encyclopædia Britannica, article Atoms.

† Smithsonian Rep., 1876, pp. 247–254; Principles of Mathematics and Physics (Cambridge, 1869, pp. 750). A theory somewhat resembling this has been carefully wrought out by Mr. J. H. Kedzie in his interesting volume on Solar Heat, Gravitation, and Sun Spots (Chicago, 1886, pp. 304).

THE PARADOXES OF SCIENCE. 37

Cambridge, England, who assumes that the universe is pervaded by an ether which is defined to be "a uniform, elastic fluid medium pervading all space not occupied by atoms, and varying in pressure proportionally to the variations of its density. The theory recognises no other kinds of force than these two, the one an active force resident in the ether, and the other a passive reaction of the atoms." *

This ether is supposed to be all-tremulous with vibratory waves of different lengths, each order of length giving rise to various exhibitions of force—waves of a certain length producing heat; those of another length, light; those of other lengths, molecular attraction; and of still another length, gravity.

But, since heat manifests itself as a repulsive force, separating the particles from each other, while gravity is an attractive force, drawing the particles together, we have ethereal vibrations producing exactly opposite results—that is, while some of the vibrations are forcing the particles of matter toward each other, other vibrations are separating them from each other. Prof. Challis undertakes to solve the difficulty by supposing that waves of different magnitude may produce opposite results—those of large length producing attraction, and those of extremely small length producing repulsion.

Some of the most interesting paradoxes involved in this supposition will appear later in connection with remarks upon the atomic theory of matter. But here it is sufficient to say that the ceaseless vibrations of the

---

* Smithsonian Report, 1876, p. 247.
4

all-pervading ether involve an omnipresent activity which is absolutely without any scientific explanation. Prof. Challis's carefully elaborated theory makes the atoms themselves the cause of those indefinitely minute vibrations involving repulsion; while the vibrations of greater wave length, producing gravitation, must come from the outside, and be produced from some independent and inexhaustible source of energy. In short, this theory, like all others, in its attempt to account for gravitation, ends in a paradox. It is, scientifically speaking, absurd. But the facts, nevertheless, remain to warn us against making the limit of our conceptions the measure of the truth.

Implied Omnipotence of the Atom.

The Atomic Constitution of Matter.

In close connection with these difficulties concerning the Newtonian theory of gravitation are those of the modern scientific conception of the constitution of matter. By numerous well-established scientific methods of proof, matter, according to the new chemistry, consists of sixty or seventy kinds of minute atoms which are collected into molecules and masses, or volumes, and held together by the mysterious force of molecular attraction, and kept apart to various degrees of distance by certain repulsive forces connected with the vibrations of an all-pervading ether. Under this view a molecule, like a solar system, is simply a body of atoms in motion, like a swarm of gnats in the air; while the larger masses of matter represent more comprehensive systems of motion compounded

THE PARADOXES OF SCIENCE. 39

with centripetal and centrifugal forces of mysterious origin.

According to the well-established results of modern science, the difference between the three forms of any particular kind of matter—namely, the solid, the fluid, and the gaseous—is produced by the presence of heat, which is a mode of wave motion in matter and in the all-pervading ether. As a result of an increased intensity of heat, the molecules of matter are separated from each other and thrown into larger ranges of vibration or orbits of revolution. We are familiar with this fact in the innumerable instances in which heat is transformed into motion, as in the cylinder of the steam engine, and in the contrary process, where visible heat is produced by the arrest of motion. A few smart blows from the blacksmith's hammer, for example, will raise a slim bar of Swedish iron to a red heat. Water, however, furnishes us the most familiar illustration of the three forms of matter in their relations to heat. By the addition of a certain amount of heat, water is changed to a gas, in which condition the particles become so separated that they are invisible, and any amount of tension can be produced by confining them in an inclosed space and subjecting the volume to increased degrees of heat. The theory of the steam engine is that the heat applied to the boiler produces tension by increasing the vibratory motion of the ether in which the gaseous atoms are floating, thus imparting increased velocity to the ultimate particles of water confined in the piston. It is the impact of these infinitesimal atoms against the end of the piston which pushes it along. It is the law of

The Three Forms of Matter.

all gases that the volume is increased proportionally with the increase of temperature; but, as already said, this increased volume is merely increased activity of motion on the part of the ultimate atoms. With twice the temperature the motion of the inclosed atoms is twice as rapid. In other words, the application of twice the amount of heat to a gas doubles the orbit of atomic revolution in each instant of time.

But in connection with this theory several paradoxes arise. Newton supposed that the ultimate particles of matter were impenetrable and inelastic—that is, that they were absolutely hard. To use his own words, "These primitive particles, being solids, are incomparably harder than any porous bodies compounded of them; even so very hard as never to wear or break in pieces; no ordinary power being able to divide what God himself made one in the first creation." * But this supposition of the impenetrability and consequent inelasticity of the ultimate atoms involves a paradox. On this supposition the collision of atoms which is constantly supposed to take place in gaseous bodies would produce a loss of motion where we know there is perpetual motion; for nothing is more certain than that a volume of gas confined within definite limits, in a room of constant temperature, maintains its character without change. The molecular energy of gas does not become dissipated in space; its machinery

Is the Atom Indivisible?

---

* Optics, 4th ed., p. 375; quoted in Stallo's Modern Physics, p. 41.

THE PARADOXES OF SCIENCE. 41

does not run down by reason of the friction of its parts.

To escape this paradox of the perpetual motion and collision of absolutely solid atoms, a class of physicists (of whom Lord Kelvin and the late Clerk Maxwell are most eminent representatives) have invented atoms which are absolutely elastic. These atoms can collide indefinitely without losing any motion. When followed out to its full length, this conception leads us back again to the Cartesian theory, which so long withstood Newton, and delayed the acceptance of gravitation—namely, that there is no such thing as vacuous space, but that all space is full of a fluid which is absolutely continuous, and whose particles, if we can speak of particles, are infinitely divisible. In this inconceivable fluid, possessing qualities which in any form of statement are absolutely irreconcilable, there are supposed to be an indefinite number of inconceivable vortices or whirlpools producing the phenomena which on the other theory are thought of as impenetrable atoms. Maxwell's treatise on the dynamical theory of gases is in large part a discussion of the "motions and collisions of perfectly elastic spheres"; while Lord Kelvin says, "We are forbidden by the modern theory of the conservation of energy to assume inelasticity or anything short of perfect elasticity of the ultimate molecules, whether of ultra-mundane or mundane matter." *
Thus, upon this theory, we have the absolute creation of something out of nothing. The whirling motion of particles of fluid which are no particles produce all

Marginal note: Something out of Nothing.

---

* Stallo's Modern Physics, p. 42.

the effects of the indestructible atom of definite weight and of all the properties which are supposed upon the other theory. This, however, is but a single illustration of the readiness of scientific men to accept in succession contradictory explanations of facts revealed to them by experience and mathematical calculation.

The Mystery of Life.

So far we have dealt with facts and theories of a purely physical character. But the forces of animate nature are even more perplexing, recondite, and paradoxical, if indeed it is proper to speak of more or less degrees of inconceivability where all is absolutely mysterious. The Darwinian theory of evolution, for example, is based upon the observed fact that in general the progeny is like the parent. This is the law of heredity, without which there could be no such thing as species. If the progeny was not in general like the parent, utter confusion would everywhere prevail in the animate world, and we could form no calculation of what the harvest would be from the seed which had been sown. Without this law there would be no warrant that hen's eggs would produce chickens, or that grapeseed would not produce thorns, or figs thistles.

The Principia of Darwinism.

At the same time this transmission of qualities from parent to offspring is not perfect: there is a limited range of variation, such that no two individuals are absolutely alike; contrary to the common belief, one pea is always distinguishable from another pea, and in more complex organisms the variations are still more marked.

The complexity of the problem which the scientific evolutionist endeavours to solve is so great that every attempted explanation of the theory leads one to the verge of absolute incredulity. Indeed, nothing can better illustrate the limitations of human thought in its endeavour to compass the nature of ultimate causes than the efforts of our leading philosophical naturalists to explain the law of heredity as displayed in the actual history of the vegetable and animal kingdoms; for not only are all these explanations manifestly incomplete in themselves and founded upon ultimate assumptions which defy explanation, but they are all so far unintelligible, or perhaps we should say inconceivable, that none of them can be made clear to anybody, not even to their own authors.

Biological Perplexities.

Not to attempt an exhaustive catalogue of these theories, it is sufficient to refer to a few which have attracted most attention by reason of the eminence of their advocates.

From Buffon and Bonnet of the eighteenth century we have inherited the theory that the original germs from which the whole succession of plants and animals have been evolved included within them miniatures of the whole succession. This has often been illustrated to the popular mind by the supposition that the bud of the oak contained in it a miniature tree, and that behind the bud was a still smaller miniature, and so on *ad infinitum;* so that the process of evolution was but an unfolding of real forms impressed upon the germ at the original creation.

Theory of Incasement.

Herbert Spencer's theory is that " germ cells are

essentially nothing more than vehicles, in which are contained small groups of the physiological units in a fit state for obeying their proclivity toward the structural arrangement of the species they belong to." * By "physiological units" he means "vitalized molecules" in "all of which there dwells the intrinsic aptitude to aggregate into the form of that species." † These vitalized molecules possess a mysterious polarity which he accepts as an ultimate fact.‡

Polarized Units.

Mr. Darwin's theory was named by the author Pangenesis, and, at first, was thought by him to have some resemblance to the foregoing theory of Mr. Spencer; but from one of Darwin's letters * we learn that Mr. Spencer was unable to see any resemblance between the two theories, which, Darwin confesses, greatly relieved his mind, since he himself had utterly failed to be sure what Spencer meant by his polarized physiological units, and "so [to avoid charge of plagiarism] thought it safest to give my [Darwin's] view as almost the same as his [Spencer's]," while Spencer, it seems, returned the compliment by saying that he was not sure that he understood Darwin; yet, says Darwin, "I took such pains, I must think I expressed myself clearly." But that there was some difficulty with the theory Darwin was compelled to fear, since so few of his friends acknowledged their ability to understand it; for, he writes, " Bates says he has read it twice, and is not sure that he understands it "; while " Old Sir H. Holland

Pangenesis.

---

* Biology, vol. i, p. 254.   ‡ Ibid., p. 183.
† Ibid., p. 181.   * Vol. ii, p. 260.

says he has read it twice, and thinks it very tough, but believes that sooner or later 'some view akin to it' will be accepted." Still Darwin declares that he feels " sure if Pangenesis is now stillborn it will, thank God, at some future time reappear, begotten by some other father, and christened by some other name."

The intellectual difficulties into which one is plunged by attempting " to connect by some intelligible bond " the facts of heredity may be best presented by giving a somewhat detailed account of Pangenesis and of the wonderful feats which it is supposed to accomplish in Nature.

Briefly stated, the theory is that organic bodies are composed of cells and colonies of cells which, though organized into unity by some mysterious power, are themselves units possessing a remarkable degree of independence, and " propagate themselves by self-division or proliferation, retaining the same nature." * In a mysterious way some of these cells are made to contain the potentiality of the whole organism. In the lower forms of life every cell contains this power of reproduction, while in the higher forms the power is only partially limited. From any small section of the leaf of a begonia, for example, a perfect plant may be grown. Some fresh-water worms when cut into forty pieces arise again to life in forty perfect animals. When the limbs of some of the lower animals are amputated, new and perfect limbs grow out to replace the old. Nor is this power wholly absent in the highest animal forms. Without this power of self-reproduction on the part of the cells, there

The Cell Theory.

---

* Animals and Plants, vol. ii, p. 448.

would be no such thing as the healing of a wound in the human body or the joining together of fractured bones.

But it is in the reproduction of plants and animals in connection with sexual processes that the profoundest mysteries are forced upon our attention. In these organisms the species is perpetuated only through the agencies of special cells, and that ordinarily when those of different sexes are united. The mystery is only appreciated when we consider both the minuteness of these cells and the burden which is laid upon them. To begin with, they are microscopical objects ordinarily invisible to the naked eye; yet upon them is laid the burden of receiving from all parts of the body or of the plant the potentialities which shall reproduce the individual in its entirety and continue to transmit specific characters to future generations.

In his efforts to connect the facts by "some intelligible bond," Mr. Darwin supposes that every cell in the body of the plant or animal "throws off minute granules or atoms, which circulate freely throughout the system, and when supplied with proper nutriment multiply by self-division, subsequently becoming developed into cells like those from which they were derived." * To these atoms he gives the name of gemmules. The "gemmules are supposed to be thrown off by every cell or unit, not only during the adult stage, but during all the stages of development." Lastly, he assumes "that the gemmules in their dormant state have a mutual affinity for each other, leading to their ag-

Marginal note: Darwin's "Gemmules."

---

* Animals and Plants, vol. ii, p. 448.

gregation either into buds or into the sexual elements.

The smallness of these gemmules did not escape the notice of Mr. Darwin, nor did it stagger his belief in them, for he says:

> As each unit, or group of similar units throughout the body, casts off its gemmules, and as all are contained within the smallest egg or seed, and within each spermatozoon or pollen grain, their number and minuteness must be something inconceivable. I shall hereafter recur to this objection, which at first appears so formidable; but it may here be remarked that a codfish has been found to produce 4,872,000 eggs, a single ascaris about 64,000,000 eggs, and a single orchidaceous plant probably as many million seeds. In these several cases the spermatozoa and pollen grains must exist in considerably larger numbers. Now, when we have to deal with numbers such as these, which the human intellect can not grasp, there is no good reason for rejecting our present hypothesis on account of the assumed existence of cell gemmules a few thousand times more numerous.*

The strength and precision of the elective affinity displayed by these prolific gemmules is illustrated by Darwin in the case of the Compositæ, the species of which number about ten thousand; yet "there can be no doubt that if the pollen of all these species could be, simultaneously or successively, placed on the stigma of any one species, this one would elect with unerring certainty its own pollen." † The precision is still more wonderfully shown among animals when different varieties are crossed. For example, if a short-horned cow is

Elective Affinity of Cells.

---

* Animals and Plants, vol. ii, pp. 453, 454. † Ibid., p. 455.

crossed with a long-horned variety, the progeny shows the effect in the horns, and not in the horny hoofs, which are of the same material; while the " offspring from two birds with differently coloured tails have their tails, and not their whole plumage, affected." * Still further he concludes that each particular feather of a bird " generates a large number of gemmules " which are possibly aggregated into a compound gemmule, for, complex as is the structure of a feather, " each separate part is liable to inherited variations." †

Having shown that sexual and asexual generation are fundamentally the same, Parthenogenesis seems no longer wonderful to Mr. Darwin; " in fact, the wonder is that it should not oftener occur." ‡ But while " the reproductive organs do not actually create the sexual elements," but " merely determine or permit the aggregations of the gemmules in a special manner," these organs do still have " high functions to perform." " They give to both elements a specific affinity for each other. . . . They adapt one or both elements for independent temporary existence and for mutual union." At the same time it is significant to be told that " what determines the aggregation of the gemmules within the sexual organs we do not in the least know." # Finally, after saying that " the power of propagation possessed by each separate cell determines the reproduction, the variability, the development, and renovation of each living organism," and that " no other attempt has been made to connect under one point of view these several grand classes of facts," Darwin frankly confesses that

---

*Animals and Plants, vol. ii, p. 455.   ‡ Ibid., p. 459.
† Ibid., p. 458.   # Ibid., p. 459.

"we can not fathom the marvellous complexity of an organic being; but, on the hypothesis here advanced, this complexity is much increased. Each living creature must be looked at as a microcosm—a little universe, formed of a host of self-propagating organisms, inconceivably minute and as numerous as the stars in heaven." *

The force of this concluding remark will be lost if we do not pause for a little to bring before our minds some of the facts concerning the principle of reversion which Darwin declares to be " the most wonderful of all the attributes of inheritance"; for, as he truly says, "what can be more wonderful than that characters which have disappeared during scores, or hundreds, or even thousands of generations, should suddenly reappear perfectly developed." So that "we are led to believe that every character which occasionally reappears is present in each generation . . . ready to be evolved under proper conditions." †

<small>Mysteries of Heredity.</small>

With many of the facts underlying these statements we are all so familiar that we cease to be impressed by their marvellous character. We know, for example, that a child oftentimes resembles his grandparent more than he does his parent, and indeed we are not much surprised when, through the law of reversion, the child reproduces the peculiar attributes of some even more remote ancestor. So strong is this tendency to reversion that the preservation of an improved variety of plants or an improved breed of animals can be maintained only at the price of constant vigilance on the

---

* Animals and Plants, vol. ii, p. 483.   † Ibid., p. 447.

part of the horticulturist or the breeder. It is doubtless true, as Darwin says, that "by the aid of a little selection, carried on during a few generations, most of our cultivated plants could probably be brought back, without any great change in their conditions of life, to a wild or nearly wild condition." *

When one adds to these facts the marvels concerning the metamorphoses through which the individuals of many species constantly pass, as when the caterpillar changes to the butterfly, and when peculiar instincts and mental characteristics develop only after a series of alternate generations or at particular stages in the life of the individual, one does not wonder at the difficulty experienced by some of Darwin's most eminent friends in seeing just what he meant by his theory, and in failing to find that "positive comfort" in it which the author himself professed to experience. It is not strange that "Hooker . . . seems to think that the hypothesis is little more than saying that organisms have such and such potentialities," † or that Huxley failed "to gain a distinct idea" "when it is said that the cells of a plant, or stump, include atoms derived from every other cell of the whole organism and capable of development"; but preferred to say that "a single cell of a plant, or the stump of an amputated limb, have the 'potentiality' of reproducing the whole—or 'diffuse an influence'" ‡ toward the accomplishment of this result, even though these words could give Darwin no positive idea.

Pangenesis Incredible.

---

* Animals and Plants, vol. ii, p. 45.   ‡ Ibid., p. 264.
† Letters of Darwin, vol. ii, p. 262.

At the present time the theoretical point most under discussion relates to the inheritability of acquired characteristics. It was the theory of Lamarck that variation in animals was mainly produced by the effort of individuals to attain objects which were a little beyond the reach of their present capacity; and this principle was not wholly ignored by Darwin, who believed that the use or disuse of organs had much to do in producing transmitted variations. Still it puzzled him to see, on his theory, how this could be. "Nothing," he says, "in the whole circuit of physiology is more wonderful. How can the use or disuse of a particular limb or of the brain affect a small aggregate of reproductive cells, seated in a distant part of the body, in such a manner that the being developed from these cells inherits the character of either one or both parents?"

Lamarck's Theory.

Weismann answers this question by absolutely denying the influence of external conditions on heredity. On the other hand, he affirms that acquired characteristics are not and can not be inherited. In his view, variations originate wholly apart from the external conditions. He believes that immortality is an attribute of the cell, or what he calls the germ plasm, and that there is absolute continuity in the development of this hypothetical basis of life. Wallace is in substantial agreement with Weismann, and these two leaders are supported by a large following of eminent younger naturalists who are designated as neo-Darwinians. The late Prof. Romanes devoted the last years of his life largely to the defence and development of Darwin's

Weismann's Theory.

views upon these points, and to answering the arguments of Weismann and Wallace.

The many criticisms to which Weismann's theory has been subjected have drawn out from him at last not only a defence, but an explicit statement of what is involved in his views, which is both exceedingly instructive, and significant of the close connection between scientific theories concerning the origin of things and metaphysics.

The theory of Weismann with respect to the origin and development of species from germ plasm was originally closely akin to the necessitarian theological systems which rested everything upon foreordination, and left nothing for free will. This, however, was seen to overburden the material particles of germ plasm upon any mechanical theory of their action. The great objection to his theory lay in the fact that variations in plants and animals are not haphazard; for, if they occurred at haphazard, definite varieties could not be maintained, even on the highest view of natural selection. To maintain a variety the selector must have something definite to select. Weismann meets the difficulty by throwing the principle of variation and of selection back into the unknown realm of germinal activity, supposing that in that realm, which is out of sight, if not beyond the realm of thought even, there is a struggle for existence going on analogous to that of which we hear so much in the visible realm of natural history. There is a survival of the fittest among the particles of Weismann's germ plasm. Thus he says:

Inadequacy of Natural Selection.

The struggle for existence takes place at all the stages of life between all orders of living units from the biophores recently disclosed, upward to the elements that are accessible to direct observation, to the cells, and still higher up, to individuals and colonies.* If . . . there is any solution possible to the riddle of adaptiveness to ends—a riddle held by former generations to be insoluble—it can be obtained only through the assistance of this principle of the self-regulation of the originating organisms. . . . Selection of *persons* alone is *not sufficient* to explain the phenomena; *germinal* selection must be added. . . . It is true it leads us into a terrain which can not be submitted directly to observation by means of our organs of touch and by our eyes, but it shares this disadvantage in common with all other ultimate inferences in natural science, even in the domain of inorganic nature: in the end all of them lead us into hypothetical regions.†

Ultimate Mysteries.
Earlier in this same address Weismann had confessed that " we can not penetrate by this hypothesis to the last root of the phenomena "; and that " all our knowledge is, and remains throughout, provisional "; expressing surprise that " any living being could have the temerity to pretend even so much as to guess at the *actual* ultimate phenomena in evolution and heredity "; " for," he avers, " the whole question is a matter of symbols only, just as it is in the matter of ' forces,' ' atoms,' ' ether undulations,' etc., the only difference being that in biology we stumble much earlier upon the unknown than in physics." ‡

The appropriateness of these last-quoted phrases

---

* Germinal Selection. An address delivered before the International Congress of Zoölogists at Leyden, September 16, 1895; translated from MS., by T. J. McCormack; published in the Monist, January, 1896, pp. 250–293; especially p. 291.

† Monist, January, 1896, p. 292. ‡ Ibid., p. 286.

from Weismann is made even more clear when we consider the theory of life units and of living fluid as it is defended by Prof. Minot,* who maintains that Darwin's theory of Pangenesis and of Gemmules is untenable, and that Spencer's conception of "*physiological units,*" although an advance on Pangenesis, is still insufficient; while the plastidules of Haeckel and the biophores and determinants of Weismann " have made a gay tournament of hypotheses," thus † leaving no theory so probable as his own—namely, that life is perpetuated not by hypothetical life units, but by means of a living fluid which he thus describes:

The Foam Theory of Life.

The physical basis of life is protoplasm; protoplasm consists of two fluids, intimately commingled, yet separate, and which may include various granules of solid organic substances, more or less complex, and also include globules of various liquids. This theory in its best form has been termed the foam theory, because foam offers the most familiar illustration of the kind of structure conceived by this theory as characteristic of living matter. As in foam, air and water are commingled, so in protoplasm are cell sap and the proteid or albuminoid fluid commingled. The latter it is which, when coagulated by our so-called preserving reagents, gives under the microscope the familiar appearance of a network of solid threads. This theory I consider by far the best theory of the nature of protoplasm yet advanced. . . . It seems to me [he says further] that we have now reached a point when we need no longer divide

---

* Article, Microscopical Study of Living Matter, North American Review, May, 1896, pp. 612–620; On Heredity and Rejuvenation, American Naturalist, January and February, 1896, pp. 1–9, 89–101.

† North American Review, p. 618.

protoplasm into its living and not living constituents. It is all living, the water and salts as much as the proteids and other organic compounds. Its phenomena are displays of energy resulting, so far as we at present know, from chemical actions, the possibility of which is given by the commingling of substances in the foam structure. . . .

The conception of protoplasm above advocated seems at first to involve a complete materialism [he continues], but against this conclusion I must protest, for I hold that an opposite interpretation of life best accords with our knowledge—namely, that since there appear to be vital phenomena, which do not occur without life, it is legitimate to assume that there is a special vital power, which is not necessarily identical with any form of physical energy, though it may be conceived to cause the transformation of energy. Indeed, it is perfectly thinkable that the universe would come to rest, were not the balance of the forms of energy disturbed by the life power.*

Prof. Minot's Explanation. In the article on Heredity and Rejuvenation, Prof. Minot is more precise, holding "that the hereditary impulse is distributed in very different cells, and is probably distributed equally through all cells." † Rejecting germ plasm in Weismann's sense, which he affirms does not exist, Minot holds that "the development of an organism does not depend upon a substance stored in special cells, but on a special condition (stage) of organization." ‡ Rejecting Weismann's theory of the "continuity of germ cells," and Darwin's conception of Pangenesis, he adopts the conception of Nussbaum of "the continuity of the germinal substance." The problem, according to Minot, therefore, now is, what " is the ex-

---

* North American Review, pp. 619, 620.   ‡ Ibid., p. 93.
† American Naturalist, p. 95.

planation of the germinating power and the propagation of this power." *

This is indeed the problem, and has been from the beginning. But it is difficult to see the fundamental distinction between these various theories, or how any of them avoid materialism and the paradoxes into which all forms of materialism eventually run. How can a cell carry in it a pattern of all that is to come, unless there is some physical substratum for it, and on any theory the process of subdivision as we recede from germ to parent germ leads us to the contemplation of elements smaller than the very atoms out of which the physicist makes the world.

Complexity of the Cell Theory. The mysteries involved in the cell theory appear in the following representation of it by Prof. G. C. Bourne, of Oxford:

It was Prof. W. K. Clifford, I think, who first drew a graphic picture of the molecular forces which are at work in any chemical compound, by describing the atoms as linked to one another and dancing a sort of merry-go-round within circumscribed limits. We may carry on the illustration, which, fanciful though it may seem, is supported by physical and mathematical considerations. A biont is a great organized war dance, performed by a whole army corps. The individuals composing each company are the atoms; they are linked to one another by companies and each company dances its own figure. Every company is a molecule, and every company dance is but a part of a larger dance, in which the companies act in relation to one another, as the individuals act in the company dance. The larger dances are regimental dances and every regiment is a micella. The

---

*American Naturalist, p. 91.

regimental dances are but parts of still larger brigade dances, and the brigade dances are but part of the great dance of the whole army corps, which, taken as a whole, is a biont. The illustration is not quite exact, for each company must not be considered as consisting of like individuals, but of many individuals of all arms, some like and some unlike, linked in such various ways that no two companies are the same, partly because of the proportions of different kinds of individuals composing them, partly because of the way in which those individuals are linked together. Nor must we imagine that individuals are permanently attached to companies, nor yet companies to regiments, but that in the course of the dance individuals are passed from company to company, and companies from regiment to regiment, each conforming temporarily to the particular figure of that part of the dance to which he or it for the time belongs. Further than this the individuals engaged in the whole dance are never long the same; there are bystanders who for a time do not participate in the dance but are caught up one by one, whirled through the figures, passed from company to company, from regiment to regiment, and brigade to brigade, and are eventually passed out of the dance again, after having participated in some or all of the figures as the case may be. Every individual in the dance is at some time passed out of the dance, becomes a bystander, and may again be caught up and whirled along in the dance once more.

The illustration is fanciful, if you please, but it is of the same kind as illustrations used to depict the play of molecular forces in the inorganic world. It serves a purpose in that it gives the imagination something to work upon, and it enables one to conceive of the immense complexity which is possible in a chemico-physical process. The army dance which I describe is capable of any number of combinations, a number amply sufficient to satisfy the needs of those who insist so strongly on the marvellous complexity of life. Let anybody imagine an army to be composed of four brigades, each brigade of four regiments, each regiment of ten companies, and each company to contain a hundred individuals of the eight kinds, carbon, oxygen, hydrogen, nitrogen, sulphur, phosphorus, potassium, and iron, in varying proportions, and let him work out the possible combinations. I think he will be satisfied with the complexity.

What then of heredity and of the capacity which I have mentioned for acquiring historic qualities?

Believing as I do that the vital processes must in the end be attributed to a particular mode of molecular motion, I believe that it is the form of movement which is transmitted. Returning to my illustration, I would say that it is the figure of the whole dance which makes up the species, and that it is the figure—the mode of motion—which is inherited, clearly not the individuals engaged in the dance, except in a very small degree, for they are constantly coming into the dance anew and as constantly being passed out of it. Under certain circumstances there may be an excess of one or more kinds of new individuals pressing into one part of the dance which will affect the figure of the company dance which they crowd into, and this will affect regimental figures and ultimately, in decreasing degrees, the whole army figure. In this way we may picture to ourselves the action of external influences in bringing about variation.*

<small>Life still as Mysterious as ever.</small>

The truth is that every effort so far made to discover what Darwin calls "an intelligible bond" harmoniously connecting together the incalculable diversity of facts exhibited in the life of plants and animals becomes not only a mystery, but a paradox, and brings all investigators to a precipice facing a boundless metaphysical fogbank. The theories of the

---

* Article, The Present Position of Cell Theory, in Science Progress, for June, 1896, pp. 321-323.

nineteenth century are not pre-eminently clearer than were those of the eighteenth. It is easy to show that Bonnet's theory of "incasement" rested on expressions which contained utter vacuity of meaning. He indeed supposed an evolution which was real—the pattern of the progeny having a real existence in the parental germ, supposing that the pattern of the whole development was really "incased" in the original created germ. "But," he says, "it is not necessary to suppose that the germ has all the features which characterize the mother as an individual. The germ bears the original imprint of the species, and not that of the individuality. It is on a small scale a man, a horse, a bull, etc., but it is not a certain man, a certain horse, a certain bull, etc." * As another has well expressed it, " in organs conceived as infinitesimal, shape, size, proportions, signified nothing." ."The ears, for example, in the germs of the horse were supposed to preexist as actual ears, but in what shape and proportions Bonnet never undertook to say. . . . They must have shape, but not the particular shape presented in the adult state." †

Careful study of more recent theories shows that in their ultimate analysis they are each as paradoxical as was their great predecessor. It is easy for Weismann to show that Spencer's theory of "physiological units" involves an incomprehensible complexity of molecular motion in every organic variation for which no cause is assigned, thus leaving his theory to rest on nothing. It is equally easy for Minot to show that Darwin's

---

* Quoted by C. O. Whitman, Monist, April, 1895, p. 423.
† Ibid., pp. 422, 423.

"gemmules" and Weismann's "biophores" are too clumsy to go through with all the evolutions demanded of them, but it is difficult to see how his own theory of "foamy germ plasm" has any physical basis at all to stand upon.

The moral of this discussion may be stated in a few words. Religious philosophy does not by any means possess a monopoly of all the mysteries of existence. The truths of religion are not the only truths which apparently rest on paradoxical statements. All verbal statements of ultimate truth are paradoxical; but this arises partly from the essential infirmities of language. It is no less true in science than it is in theology that the whole truth is too complex to be compressed into single statements. The human imagination does not give us the full measure of the truth which we are compelled to believe.

No Science has a Monopoly of Mystery.

These conclusions at once clear the field of a great mass of current objections to Christianity, since they show us that our knowledge of Nature even at the close of the nineteenth century is entirely too superficial to give any weight to *a priori* objections to the central facts of the Bible. Nothing which we have learned of the constitution of matter or of the universe renders the conception of a miracle impossible, or materially increases its improbability. The worst foes of Christianity are not physicists, but metaphysicians. Hume is more dangerous than Darwin; the agnosticism of Hamilton and Mansel is harder to meet than that of Tyndall or Huxley; the fatalism of the philosophers is more to be dreaded than the materialism of any school of science. The sophistries of the Socratic philosophy touching the freedom of the will are more subtle than are those of the Spencerian school. Christianity, being a religion of fact and history, is a free-born son in the family of the inductive sciences, and is not specially hampered by the paradoxes which are connected with all attempts to give expression to ultimate conceptions of truth. The field is free for the reception of such moral evidence of the truth of Christianity as it has pleased the Creator to afford us.

CHAPTER III.

GOD AND NATURE.

ROUGHLY speaking, there are three ways in which God's relation to Nature has been viewed by Christian philosophers.*

1. Nature is looked upon as having been so endowed by the Creator with forces at the beginning of time that all the subsequent phenomena are the products of its mechanical evolution. On this view the suggestion of any need of interference with the operations of Nature is regarded as derogatory to the Creator's power and wisdom. This is the deistic view.

2. The phenomena of Nature are regarded as "the immediate, orderly, constant, but infinitely diversified, action" of an ever-present and intelligent supreme cause. This is the theory of divine immanence so much in vogue at the present time.

3. The operations of Nature are thought of as in the main going on by virtue of forces communicated at the beginning, but subject to insulated and systematic interpositions in which the Creator puts his hand afresh to the work for the sake of more perfect adjustment to the wants of his creatures, and of more demonstrative

---

* See Asa Gray's Darwiniana, pp. 158, 159, from which this classification has been taken in a modified form.

manifestation of his presence. This is the view more generally entertained by Christian philosophers. These will now be taken up in their order.

THE DEISTIC VIEW.

The deistic view of the universe is an attempt to bring everything down to the level of mechanical principles. It can not be denied that there is a grandeur in its conceptions which is overpowering and, in certain aspects, extremely attractive. If the universe is indeed a pure mechanism whose phenomena are all reducible to combinations of matter and motion, it would be a mark of perfection that it should go on forever in all its parts without interference—that is, that it should be self-regulative. It is truly said that a timepiece is perfect in proportion to its capacity to run indefinitely and correctly without intervention of the clockmaker. Just so far as the clock has to be corrected and regulated, it discloses imperfection and shows the limitations of the original maker.

Mechanical Perfection of Nature.

Thus it is held that the power of the Creator is displayed in the mechanical perfection and sufficiency of the material universe. It is indeed said to be a first principle of philosophy that the universe is nothing but a series of causally connected sequences with which there is no intervention from the outside; that in the beginning every grain of sand was weighed in the balances and assigned its part in the unfolding drama of universal being. It is not uncommon to hear it affirmed that had there been a single grain more or less, or had a single grain been placed in a different position, the whole history of the universe would have been changed thereby. By the man of science both matter and motion are looked upon as constant quantities in the universe. Motion which is lost by one body is supposed to be gained by another. When the onward motion of a mass of matter is arrested, the same quantity of motion remains in the molecular agitation produced by the impact. By many Christian believers this view of the universe is supposed to receive the indorsement of the Saviour when he says "the hairs of your head are numbered," and "a sparrow does not fall on the ground without your Heavenly Father."

The only way in which such a material universe can be adjusted to the realities of the spiritual world is upon the theory of pre-established harmony, such as was advocated by Leibnitz. Upon this theory, the universe of matter and the universe of mind are supposed to move along together independently of each other, but with perfect harmony in their developments. It is as when two clocks are so delicately adjusted that they shall keep time forever without variation. Thus Leibnitz supposed the movements of man's physical organism to be merely a pantomime of the spiritual. According to this theory, the universe is like Babbage's calculating machine, developed to perfection and set to turn out, in objective form, all the material symbols expressive of the infinitely complex movements of the spiritual world.

Theory of Pre-established Harmony.

Upon this theory, which is supposed by many to represent the truly scientific conception of the universe, there is no real connection between finite mind and matter, and the providence of the Creator is so exalted

GOD AND NATURE. 65

that all the wants of the universe are met by prearrangement. On this view, foreknowledge and foreordination are pushed so far into the front that God ceases to be a very present help in time of trouble, and retires to the position of a bountiful and all-powerful Provider who has done his work and left his stores of provisions where his needy creatures could find them and feed upon them, while he himself is never at hand to dispense the bounty in person.

It would be improper altogether to disparage this view of divine providence; since there is no question that it correctly represents man's relation to the larger part of the bounties which he receives from the Creator's hand; for it can not be denied that God with infinite forethought has through the mechanism of the material universe provided for most of the exigencies of his spiritual creation. The gold and the silver, the coal and the iron, were hidden away in the mines countless ages before they were to be appropriated by man. The stores of oil and gas, the qualities and characteristics of the vegetable and animal kingdoms, and the chemical condition of the soils were prepared for the use of man long before he appeared to make use of them. Nor does the lapse of time wholly shut us off from the perception of God's personal presence. The standard question of philosophy, How can a thing act where it is not? is properly met by the counterquestion, True; but where is it? Is not the thing wherever its effects are felt? Are we separated wholly from our benefactors even when they are absent and unseen? Is not the parent in a very real sense in the fortune which his children inherit? Is

The Theory Sublime, but Inadequate.

not the thought of the friend in the message which is borne to us in the beleaguered city on the wings of a carrier dove?

But this mechanical view of the universe which leaves no connection between mind and matter except that of a pre-established harmony, and which provides for the human heart no communion with the Creator but that which comes down along the lines of motion instituted at the primeval act of creation, is incomplete and unscientific, because, as will be shown later, it is not comprehensive of all the facts of human experience and history.

The Theory of Divine Immanence.

At the opposite pole from the mechanical view of the universe stands the conception, now so prevalent, of the divine immanence—a doctrine which exaggerates the sustaining activities of the Creator while unduly limiting his creative power. The advocates of this view are so unwilling to surrender the belief that God is ever present amid the activities of the universe that they go to the extreme of denying that he has produced any self-acting forces at all. On this view the universe is nothing but a succession of constant divine activities. Second causes are ruled out of the problem. The uniformities which we are accustomed to attribute to the efficiency of second causes are attributed by this theory to the constancy of the divine purpose in process of continual execution.

It is certainly easy to believe that in God's actions, as in those of man, there are varying degrees of constancy. Accepting Butler's definition that a law of

Nature is simply an expression of that which is stated and uniform in its occurrence, the advocates of the divine immanence would say that these natural uniformities are but the temporary expression of divine ideas in successive uniform acts. Some classes of divine acts are much more constant than others, just as in the case of human acts some are repeated much more persistently than others, though all are the acts of a free will.

The Action of a Free Will may be constant.

For instance, a business man in going to and from his office may for years be as regular as the stars are in their courses, while he may be utterly irregular in most of the actions of his daily life. On this view, the laws of Nature may be compared to those uniformities provided for in governments by a constitution, which by a choice of the people protects them from the temporary fluctuations of public sentiment, as shown in annual elections or even in the departments of legislation which are less directly amenable to temporary influences. Constitutions are not, indeed, like the laws of the Medes and Persians, absolutely unchangeable, but they secure a reasonable degree of uniformity in laws touching the more fundamental principles of national prosperity. In constitutional provisions the people provide for stability as well as freedom in the regulative principles of the government.

The theory that Nature is but a continuous manifestation of "immanent Deity" differs from pantheism in that it affirms the personality of God. But in denying any independence to second causes it encounters the conscious sense of responsibility in man, which affirms that at least the sin of each man is his own. Man certainly is to some extent an independent force in the world. He is, at least, the architect of his own character. God is not the direct author of sin. The actions of man are not altogether automatic. Prof. Huxley laboured in vain to convince the world that he was himself an automaton.* But there was too much method in his pugnacity to admit of such an easy explanation. He was himself too good an illustration of the adjustability of free will to permit his verbal arguments to have any permanent weight. Whatever may be done with the reality of the material universe, the fact of free will can not be ruled out of the problem of existence. This will appear still more clearly in considering the grounds for accepting the third method of stating the relation of God to Nature.

Sidenote: But Man is more than an Automaton.

The Theory of Created Secondary Causes which are still under the Control of the Creator.

The advocates of the doctrine of the divine immanence are indeed free to say that the Creator's wisdom binds him to that degree of constancy in action which we really find in Nature. But in taking this view of the case no difficulty is really avoided, while by adopting it we have both unduly limited the ability of the Creator to produce self-acting secondary causes, and have ignored the plainest testimony of the human mind to its own independent powers. In any scientific view of the case the freedom of the human will, its power to choose between good and evil, to merit praise, and to

---

* See Science and Culture, lect. ix.

incur guilt can not be left out of sight or denied to be an actual fact.

Man is a responsible, self-acting unit of force. No theory of the universe which denies or overlooks this fact can be scientific. Whoever denies it commits scientific suicide at the outset by denying one of the plainest and most fundamental of all the facts of observation and consciousness. But recognising this fact of the responsible, self-determining power of the human will, there is no difficulty in accepting the realistic view of Nature in general—that is, that the Creator has bestowed properties upon matter which are inherent and independent. Theologically, this might be expressed as the segregation into material forms of a certain portion of the eternal force residing in the Creator's will. The independence both of matter and of finite mind rests upon both a dictate of the divine wisdom and a fiat of the divine will. The constancy of natural laws may be said to depend upon the determinate creative fiat in which God in his wisdom withdrew his immediate activity from the ordinary control of the specific points of concentrated force which appear in the universe of mind and matter.

Reality of Secondary Causes.

Thus, whether we take the view of the deist or of those who advocate the doctrine of the divine immanence need make little difference with our reasoning upon the facts of existence. In the one case uniformity is the product of a single act of divine wisdom at the beginning; in the other, it is the product of continuous acts determined by the same wisdom. On either theory we could practically deal with matter and mind as real forces, and hold that the material elements of which the universe is made have been endowed with permanent properties. We could contend that the positive amount of matter and motion in the universe is, as scientific men affirm, a stated amount incapable of addition or diminution, except by a fiat of the Creator; while at the same time we could hold that the doctrine of the conservation of force is consistent with any amount of interference with the direction of the motion. It is here that the relation of the immaterial creation to the material comes to view in its most important consequences.

Mind and matter occupy opposite poles of existence. Neither can be defined in terms of the other. It is true that language is full of figures of speech drawn from one side or the other and applied to the factors at the opposite poles. On this account there is great danger of confusion of thought. For example, from the physical side of existence we derive a large proportion of the words descriptive of purely mental facts. We speak of a "weighty argument," of "a pointed conclusion," of "an upright character," of "a straight course of conduct," and so on without end, describing moral conduct by material figures of speech. On the other hand, we speak of the "affinity" of chemical atoms or molecules, and of natural "selection" when describing the adjustments of varieties to the conditions of life, and of "adaptation" and of "design" in Nature when we are thinking wholly of the physical results, and not at all of a mental factor in the problem.

Thought more than a Mode of Motion.

Miracles and Free Will.

The question of miracles is intimately connected with our views concerning the relation of God to Nature. We shall make best progress in our efforts to understand this relation if we first carefully consider that of finite mind to the material universe and its power to control the activities of matter.

To a certain extent finite mind is manifestly dependent upon material forces, and so far is their servant. But every one in full possession of his mental powers knows that he is not absolutely dependent upon his material environment. In certain conditions the material forces are in such unstable equilibrium that man can disturb it and direct the motion of the forces to the service of his own free will. Those conditions of absolute instability exist somewhere in the human body, where there is a limited region in which the human will reigns supreme. I hold in my hand a pencil. In my body there is stored up a definite amount of physical force at the command of my will. Unused, this force will be dissipated through the automatic movements of my body. But I can direct a certain amount of this force to various ends of my choice, changing the character of its effective work. I can throw it to the right or to the left, accomplishing different purposes, and, while making no addition to the absolute expenditure of force and production of motion, can modify the motions of every material particle in the universe. If it falls to the right, the force of its position will be communicated to a definite combination of moving bodies upon that side; if to the left,

Laws of Nature violated by Free Will.

to a different combination upon the other side. The absolute former equilibrium will never be restored. Only the fact that the amount of the disturbance is relatively infinitesimal prevents a catastrophe.

Fortunately the universe is so balanced, and the road to the centres of powers so concealed, that man is not able to produce widespread catas-trophes. But knowledge is power. There are innumerable stores of physical energy ready to exert themselves for him who knows where they are and how to unlock their secret chambers. Indeed, the whole history of the human race, and especially of the higher forms of civilization, is that of man's increased knowledge concerning the stored-up forces of Nature and the means by which they may be appropriated to his use. Through knowledge of a certain class of these forces man creates a steam engine, he learns the qualities of iron, he discovers methods of separating it from the ore and of giving to it the forms which enter into a locomotive. He discovers the expansive power of steam, and searches out the hidden places where coal was stored in the early geological ages. By a combination of these forces, which represents an amount of mental capacity that is inconceivably sublime, the locomotive is set upon the track, the fires are kindled beneath its boiler, the pressure of the steam is hissing out its readiness to obey the behests of man. The engineer sits in his place with his hand upon the lever. Shall the force move forward or shall it move backward? Motion in either direction will satisfy all the requirements of the law of the conservation of energy. Action and reaction will be equal in either case. But if it moves forward

Limited Sphere of Man's Free Will.

it may be to destruction and death, while if it moves backward it means the safety of all the interests committed to the engineer's charge.

It is not, however, a physical force which determines the direction in which the stored-up energy shall move: that is determined by a thought, by an act of will, which, as already remarked, has neither length, nor breadth, nor thickness, nor weight, and, in fact, is not a material thing at all. Somewhere in the marvellous mechanism of the human body there is an adjustment of physical forces which is in absolute unstable equilibrium. There the mind mysteriously but really lets loose the forces according to its will. From these infinitesimal movements communicated by the mind to the gray matter of the brain, and by that to the nerves which cause the contractions of the muscles which push or pull the lever, the throttle is opened on one side or the other, and there follows an avalanche of definitely directly physical forces whose final effects are so vast as to be utterly inconceivable to the human mind.

Mind does move Matter.

The illustrations of the truth of the aphorism that "knowledge is power," and that it is more than a figure of speech, abound on every hand, and multiply with our advancing civilization. When we know how to utilize the forces of Nature, we can speak directly with our friends though separated from them by the whole width of the Atlantic, and we can transform Niagara into incandescent lights to illumine the streets and houses and mines scattered over the length and breadth of the continent. If we but know how we can make from the mud of our streets a shining metal which rust can

Knowledge is Power.

not corrupt, we can build palaces in which to cross the sea independent of wind and tide, and construct machines which shall possibly enable us to excel the birds in flying through the air. Or, again, if we know how, we can store up explosives which will rend the mountains asunder, and make war so destructive that it will cease to be a pastime or the measure of a nation's patriotism. Doubtless if we but knew how we could tap the interior of the earth and draw thence directly the heat which we now obtain by roundabout processes through the consumption of coal and oil and gas.

The human will accomplishes nothing by main strength. There is no evidence that it can impart its power directly to any ponderable object. Its work is wholly done by indirections. It unlocks the unstable equilibrium provided in the body with which it is connected, and directs the automatic machinery there provided so as to unloose the vast stores of force which are in unstable equilibrium through Nature. Yes, knowledge *is* power, and, whatever may be said about the lower orders of the animal creation, man is not a *mere* automaton. As scientific men, we are bound to accept this as a fact, even though we can not explain it. In this respect it is simply of a piece with the many other ultimate facts into whose presence scientific investigation has led us and left us. For we have already seen that the theory of gravitation, the theory of the atomic constitution of matter, the theory of the origin of species through natural selection, and every other scientific theory, all lead us to the shore of a boundless ocean forever encompassed with clouds and darkness. On this shore such great leaders as Sir Isaac

True, though Mysterious.

GOD AND NATURE. 75

Newton, Faraday, Clerk Maxwell, Asa Gray, and Lord Kelvin stand in reverential awe, bowing before the wisdom of an absolute Creator.

This point is forcibly emphasized by one of the leading comparative anatomists of America in the following words. Speaking of the universal instinct to refer motions in Nature to an original personal source the late Prof. Cope pointedly says:

The Power of Mind over Matter a Scientific Fact of Observation.

Its essence is the fact that we control our own bodies in a great degree, and that our material organs obey the behests of our mind. We do things for, to us, satisfactory reasons, and for satisfactory reasons we leave many things undone which we could readily do. What has science done toward explaining this most ordinary phenomenon? We may truthfully say, absolutely nothing. It remains a fact that a majority, if not all animals, move their bodies in their entirety or in part, because they have sensations. In the lower animals these sensations are merely either sense impressions from without, or they are from within, being produced by their physical condition. We rise but little in the scale when effects of memory are evident, for we find that many actions are due to experience of the results of former actions. With still higher development, mental organization becomes more apparent, and the reasoning and emotional states have more and more distinct outcome in intelligent acts. But the mechanism by which the act is called forth by the mental state has never been explained.

The difficulty lies here. A sensation, or a state of mind, weighs nothing. A material body, let it be a cell or a mass of cells, as a muscle, weighs something. How then can the former move the latter? From a mechanical point of view it can not be done. For that which has no weight to set in motion anything which has weight is to violate the law of the conservation and correlation of energy.

And this law is not only an *a priori* necessity, but it has been demonstrated *a posteriori* in so many cases that exceptions can not be thought of. So a school of physiologists say that *it is not done*. No animal eats because it is hungry, or drinks because it is thirsty. The man does not direct the muscles of his arm when he writes nor those of his tongue when he speaks. But it is easy to see why such a school of physiologists include but an infinitesimal part of mankind.*

MIND AND MATTER.

The truth that there are in the universe two distinct modes of existence—namely, mind and matter—the one possessing the power of thought and independent choice, the other possessing the qualities of inertia and motion, is no less a scientific fact than a philosophical dictum.

Not commensurate.

The observation is as old as Plato and Aristotle that science is more than perception. A series of sensations is not knowledge. Knowledge is produced by the combination of separate perceptions, which is brought about by a distinct entity, standing outside of the material mechanism producing the individual sensations. The eye perceives the beauty of the apple, the nostrils take in its fragrance, the tongue tastes its sweetness; but there is something higher than all these which combines these sensations with a thousand others to furnish the total concept of the apple. Indeed, the very sensations themselves are infinitely higher than the mechanical vibrations by which they are produced. The feeling, perceiving, reasoning subject is a thing

---

* Monist (July, 1893), vol. iii, pp. 624, 625.

by itself incapable of being comprehended in terms of mechanical motion. This is true even of the lower affections of mind. Mr. Spencer's "peculiar discharge of undulatory motion between cerebral ganglia that uniformly accompanies a feeling" does not explain the feeling. These discharges must be received and translated by a permanent entity which is independent of the ganglia in order to become feeling of one kind or another. The interval between the material vibrations of the smallest dimensions and the sensation of a living subject is absolute and impassable. This is most clearly seen in the higher feelings and sentiments by which the human mind is moved. As Tyndall has well said, no reason can be imagined why a right-hand spiral motion in the nerve cells of the brain should produce the sensation of love, and a left-hand spiral motion the sensation of hate.

To the same effect, Le Conte says: *

Thought more than a Secretion of the Brain. Suppose we exposed the brain of a living man in a state of intense activity. Suppose, further, that our senses were absolutely perfect, so that we could see every change of whatever sort taking place in the brain substance. What would we see ? Obviously nothing but molecular changes, physical and chemical; for to the outside observer there is absolutely nothing else there to see. But the subject sees nothing of all this. His experiences are of a different order—viz., consciousness, thought, emotions, etc. Viewed from the outside, there is, there can be, nothing but motions; viewed from the inside, nothing but thought. From the one side, only physical phenomena; from the other side, only psychical

---

* Evolution and its Relation to Religious Thought, p. 291.

phenomena. Is it not plain that, from the very nature of the case, it must ever be so? Certain vibrations of brain molecules, certain oxidations with the formation of carbonic acid, water, and urea on the one side; and on the other there appear sensations, consciousness, thoughts, desires, volitions. There are, as it were, two sheets of blotting paper pasted together. The one is the brain, the other the mind. Certain ink scratches or blotches, utterly meaningless on the one, soak through and appear on the other as intelligible writings, but how we know not and can never hope to guess.

Granted [says Tyndall] that a definite thought and a definite molecular action in the brain occurs simultaneously, we do not possess the intellectual organ, nor apparently any rudiment of the organ, which would enable us to pass by a process of reasoning from the one to the other. They appear together, but we do not know why. Were our minds and senses so expanded, strengthened, and illuminated as to enable us to see and feel the very molecules of the brain—were we capable of following all their motions, all their groupings, all their electric discharges, if such there be; and were we intimately acquainted with the corresponding states of thought and feeling, we should be as far as ever from the solution of the problem, How are these physical processes connected with the facts of consciousness? . . . In affirming that the growth of the body is mechanical, and that thought, as exercised by us, has its correlative in the physics of the brain, I think the position of the materialist is stated, so far as that position is a tenable one. . . . I do not think he is entitled to say that his molecular motions and groupings explain everything. In reality they explain nothing. The utmost he can affirm is the association of two classes of phenomena, of whose real bond of union he is in absolute ignorance.*

Can the oscillations of a molecule [says Herbert Spen-

---

* Fragments of Science, vol. i, pp. 86, 87.

cer] be represented in consciousness side by side with a nervous shock, and the two be recognised as one? No effort enables us to assimilate them. That a unit of feeling has nothing in common with a unit of motion becomes more than ever manifest when we bring the two into juxtaposition. . . . Here, indeed, we arrive at the barrier which needs to be perpetually pointed out, alike to those who seek materialistic explanations of mental phenomena and to those who are alarmed lest such explanations may be found. The last class proves by their fear, almost as much as the first prove by their hope, that they believe mind may possibly be interpreted in terms of matter; whereas many whom they vituperate as materialists are profoundly convinced that there is not the remotest possibility of so interpreting them.*

The true theory of the universe is not that of monism, but that of dualism. Mind and matter belong to separate orders of being. The material universe is a mechanism, but it is a mechanism which is partially under the control of finite mind; while, in the uniformities both of the things in stable and of the things in unstable equilibrium, it is endowed by its Creator with an independent existence which it is not unscientific to believe is absolutely subject to the Creator's control, so far as wisdom dictates. If finite knowledge gives man power partially to control the mechanism of the universe, infinite knowledge may readily enough be supposed to give the Creator complete control. Infinite knowledge is infinite power.

The Monistic Theory inadequate.

But this view of the Creator's power over material creation is a very different thing from saying that

---

* Principles of Psychology, vol. i, sects. 62, 63, p. 158.

he will use this power to its utmost capacity. Even with men there are countless things which they might do, but which are left undone. "Can you give an address at our Fourth of July celebration?" "Yes," was the reply, "I can, but I won't." This illustrates as well as anything the fact that contingency does not always imply uncertainty. The honest man might pilfer daily from his employer's till, but the purpose of his honest heart prevents him from doing it, thus establishing a uniformity dependent upon moral choice. So the Creator might throw the universe into confusion at any moment, but his wisdom and goodness are involved in the orderly course of events established at the original creation. The laws of Nature are the realistic expression of his general wisdom and good will.

<small>Freedom compatible with certainty.</small>

This view of the relation of God to the universe both leaves room for science and revelation and sets limits to their scope. It is the duty of science to take into consideration all the facts, and to suffer its inferences to be guided by the survey. It is equally the duty of those who believe in revelation to recognise the divine ideas incorporated in the laws of the material universe. The uniformities of natural law are but expressions of divine wisdom incorporated into the constitution of the universe; but, as we have seen, they are not absolute uniformities—they are subject to limited disturbance by finite wills. From the point of view of science, therefore, there can be no insuperable objection to the belief that they are subject also to modification by the divine will, thus leaving room for

<small>Creation has not exhausted God's Power.</small>

Providence, for miracles, and for special divine revelation.

The Greatness of Man.

The basis for our readiness to believe in these three methods of divine intervention with the mechanism of the universe is found in the inadequacy (already alluded to) of a mechanical universe fully to meet the wants of such beings as we know ourselves to be.* At first thought this seems to be a limitation of the divine omnipotence; for, asks the deist, is anything too hard for an omnipotent Creator? Why is it not possible for him to construct a mechanical universe so perfect that it should anticipate all the wants of man? Our answer is, that evidently this has not been done, and we are not sure that it is within the power of Omnipotence to do it. Indeed, we recognise in man a spiritual creation so exalted in his powers, so complex in his wants, that it is by no means inconceivable that material mechanism is incapable of providing adequately for all his wants. The omnipotence of God does not require that he should be able to satisfy the wants of man wholly through mechanical contrivances. To build a house for one's family does not of itself make a home.

"Home's not merely four square walls."

The universe to be a perfect home requires the living presence of the Heavenly Father. The Christian doctrine freely admits this seeming limitation of the divine power. It is as absurd to suppose that our

---

* See Chapter I.

Heavenly Father could satisfy the wants of his children by the construction of a merely mechanical universe, however wonderful, as it would be to expect a fond earthly father to make a palace so commodious and beautiful that his children would not care for his personal presence.

It is just at this point that considerations concerning man's high mental endowments and moral aspirations have scientific value. We do not approach the doctrines of Christianity altogether devoid of presumptions; for presumptions of the highest evidential value are raised in favour of the Christian system by innumerable well-known facts in human experience. Man is not made like the beasts that perish. He has high and noble aspirations. He is by nature a religious animal. He not only longs for, but looks forward to, a future life. He is not satisfied with what he sees and hears and feels; he reasons upon these sensations, and rises to constantly higher and higher conceptions of the unseen realms which surround him. The unsatisfactory nature of his material surroundings oppresses him on every hand. In his body he is so limited by the material universe and by the shortness of his life that he can not attain to the perfection for which he is evidently designed. His connection with the world hangs upon the slenderest of threads. A breath of malaria may corrupt it; a microbe may gnaw it asunder. Reasoning, therefore, from the very greatness of his own nature, and from the inadequacy of mere material forces to meet his wants, man enters the field of Christian evidences with weighty presumptions in favour of a universe in which God is actively present supplementing and adjusting the

The Insufficiency of the World.

mechanical expressions of his will by those which are more direct and personal.

At the same time the prevalence of order in the universe and the reality of the natural laws with which he comes in conflict and by which he largely guides his course should be recognised as themselves revelations of a divine will to whose behests it is his bounden duty to conform. The discoveries of science in some respects increase this sense of dependence upon natural law, while in other respects they diminish it. If science shows that we both live and perish by natural means, it equally shows that whether we ride upon the crest of the wave or sink in its trough depends upon the directing forces which are guiding our bark. We encounter dangers enough to life and limb any day to destroy us were it not for the directing power which guides us safely past them.

Man not altogether the Architect of his own Fortune.

To a considerable extent these directing agencies which shield us from danger are embodied in our own wisdom and in that of well-meaning friends. It is the faithfulness of the officers and crew upon the ship, of the lighthouse keepers along the shore, and of the builders and inspectors of the vessel, which give us safety in an ocean voyage. It is the faithfulness and skill of the city officers and of their engineers and experts which insures the inhabitants of a city against epidemics of fever and cholera and many less obtrusive diseases. But so numerous are the hazards of life, so concealed are the germs of disease, and so unknown is our individual susceptibility to them, that no man can certainly calculate the degree of his immunity from bodily harm. Upon looking over his own life, every one can see amplest opportunity for the divine mind to determine the issues of life and death by operating through natural laws just as man himself is conscious of doing. Science can raise no objections against the doctrine of Providence but those which can be raised against the belief in human interference with the regular course of Nature.

The question of miracles is therefore only the larger question of Providence. A miracle is no more a direct interference with the laws of Nature than are the providential dispensations of life, or than are the ordinary actions of man in carrying out the behests of his free will. A miracle is simply an interference with the ordinary course of Nature by the Creator so pronounced as to command public assent and attention, and so timed as to confirm an important revelation or enforcement of truth. This definition of miracle is not merely theoretical, but, as we shall later see, is drawn from the actual facts of Scripture. The miracles of the Bible are not mere prodigies, but are interruptions of the natural order so impressive as to give authority to a revelation, and at the same time so infrequent as to indorse the wisdom embodied in the ordinary laws of Nature.

Miracles defined.

On this view of the case there is no objection to saying that a miracle is a violation of the order of Nature, for it is an interference from the outside giving new direction to the forces of Nature—a direction which they would not otherwise have had. But this is not different in kind from what is involved in the whole use of Nature by man. If we know anything, we know that man is a disturbing force in Nature; for, as we have seen, Nature is to a large extent his servant. Through his bodily organization man is able to penetrate the joints in Nature's harness, and to disturb the unstable centres of Nature's stored-up energy, and bring about combinations and effects which did not lie in the original mechanism. To some extent this is the case with all the phenomena of life. A living germ possesses a power which can not be resolved into mere physical force: it is more than matter and motion. The life force in the seed directs the physical elements which are attracted to it, and builds up a complicated structure of plant and leaf and flower in which the material particles in these movements set at naught the law of gravitation and rise in stately symmetry to look down upon the earth from which they have sprung.

When dwelling upon the mystery of life, it is not surprising that many of the profoundest naturalists are inclined to regard every portion of animate matter as in possession of an independent soul. Such at least would seem to be the ultimate though perhaps unacknowledged conclusions of most of the distinguished evolutionists whose efforts to explain the variations of plants and animals were described in the preceding chapter. Only the boldest, and we must believe the least considerate, of them could rest in a mere mechanical statement of facts, and assert that what made the difference between one microscopical cell and another was merely the mode of motion in its constituent molecules.

Philosophical Tendencies of Scientific Men.

In passing under review these various scientific theories concerning the origin of species and the secrets of Nature's organization and laws, we find ourselves, like Paul in Athens, among a people who are overreligious, erecting altars at the shrines of each individual force of

7

Nature, but sometimes failing to acknowledge the one only Unknown God whom they ignorantly worship.

It is often affirmed that the progress of science, and especially the establishment of the doctrine of the conservation of energy and its extension of the reign of law, have constantly tended to separate God from his works, and to reinstate the deistic conception of the universe as an independent, self-regulating mechanism. But, on the other hand, it may be contended with equal plausibility that as modern science is little else than the history of the triumphs of man over Nature, and as the increase of scientific knowledge has been accompanied with a corresponding increase in man's ability to direct the forces of Nature, and as man's knowledge of Nature brings him into closer contact with it, and enables him to accomplish more far-reaching results than before were possible; so, by correct analogy, we may reason that the infinite knowledge of the Creator gives to him *complete* control over *all* its forces.

Reverence of Sir Isaac Newton.

When Sir Isaac Newton had completed the long line of mathematical demonstrations in his Principia, there followed an outburst of religious adoration which is worthy of being engraved upon the memory of every student of natural science.

This most beautiful system of the sun, planets, and comets could only proceed from the counsel and dominion of an intelligent and powerful Being. And if the fixed stars are the centres of other like systems, these, being formed by the like wise counsel, must be all subject to the dominion of One, especially since the light of the fixed stars is of the same nature with the light of the sun, and from every system light passes into all the other systems: and lest the systems of the fixed stars should, by their gravity, fall on each other mutually, he hath placed those systems at immense distances one from another.

This Being governs all things, not as the soul of the world, but as Lord over all; and on account of his dominion he is wont to be called Lord God, παντοκράτωρ, or *Universal Ruler*. . . . It is the dominion of a spiritual being which constitutes a God: a true, supreme, or imaginary dominion makes a true, supreme, or imaginary God. And from his true dominion it follows that the true God is a living, intelligent, and powerful Being; and, from his other perfections, that he is supreme or most perfect. He is eternal and infinite, omnipotent and omniscient; that is, his duration reaches from eternity to eternity; his presence from infinity to infinity; he governs all things, and knows all things that are or can be done. . . . In him are all things contained and moved, yet neither affects the other. God suffers nothing from the motion of bodies; bodies find no resistance from the omnipresence of God. It is allowed by all that the Supreme God exists necessarily, and by the same necessity he exists *always* and *everywhere*. Whence also he is all similar, all eye, all ear, all brain, all arm, all power to perceive, to understand, and to act; but in a manner not at all human, in a manner not at all corporeal, in a manner utterly unknown to us. As a blind man has no ideas of colours, so have we no idea of the manner by which the all-wise God perceives and understands all things. He is utterly void of all body and bodily figure, and can therefore neither be seen, nor heard, nor touched; nor ought he to be worshipped under the representation of any corporeal thing. We have ideas of his attributes, but what the real substance of anything is we know not. In bodies we see only their figures and colours, we hear only the sounds, we touch only their outward surfaces, we smell only the smells, and taste the savours; but their inward substances are not to be known either by our senses or by any reflex act of our minds—

much less, then, have we any idea of the substance of God. We know him only by his most wise and excellent contrivances of things and final causes; we admire him for his perfections, but we reverence and adore him on account of his dominion; for we adore him as his servants, and a god without dominion, providence, and final cause is nothing else but Fate and Nature. Blind metaphysical necessity, which is certainly the same always and everywhere, could produce no variety of things. All that diversity of natural things which we find suited to different times and places could arise from nothing but the ideas and will of a Being necessarily existing. But, by way of allegory, God is said to see, to speak, to laugh, to love, to hate, to desire, to give, to receive, to rejoice, to be angry, to fight, to frame, to work, to build; for all our notions of God are taken from the ways of mankind by a certain similitude, which, though not perfect, has some likeness, however. And thus much concerning God, to discourse of whom from the appearance of things does certainly belong to natural philosophy.*

Such were the artesian waters which this prince of mathematicians found to turn the dry Sahara of his demonstrative mechanical formulas into an oasis of spiritual beauty and pleasure.

---

* Principia, p. 504 *et seq.*

CHAPTER IV.

DARWINISM AND DESIGN.

IF asked whether or not "evolution" is compatible with design in Nature, and more particularly with such specific designs as are involved in the Christian system, one may properly answer that it depends upon what kind of evolution is had in mind, for no term is more vague than "evolution" as it appears in the literature of the present day, and no word is in more need of a qualifying adjective to define its character in any particular connection. Atheistic evolution and materialistic evolution involve the denial of design at the very outset of the argument, and are, of course, incompatible with Christianity. But an evolutionary system may be thought of which is initiated by a personal Creator, and which is complete in itself, working out all the results by inherent resident forces without interruption. This would be called deism, and is closely allied to the extreme forms of Calvinism, in which everything is resolved into the direct results of the original decrees or purposes of the Creator. "Paroxysmal" evolution is a phrase of recent invention devised to make the system accord more closely with the apparent facts of Nature. But it still leaves open the

Evolution too vague a Word for Common Use.

vital question whether or not the results are all produced by inherent resident forces. This question, however, is really a part of the broader one concerning the relation of God to Nature, and its discussion may be relegated to the chapter upon that subject. In the present chapter we will limit ourselves to the narrower discussion relating to the specific scientific theory proposed and defended by Charles Darwin.

Properly speaking, Darwinism has nothing to do with ultimate causes. The theory of the origin of species through natural selection relates solely to the mode of the action and interaction of definite secondary causes.

Darwinism not a System of Philosophy.

From a philosophical point of view, the problem does not differ from that which was presented to Newton in the action of the centripetal and centrifugal forces which he harmonized in his theory of gravitation. Newton did not ask what was the cause of these tendencies; but, accepting the fact, or the hypothesis that all material objects tend toward each other with a force which is directly as the product of the combined masses and inversely as the square of the distance separating them, he proved that the motions of the heavenly bodies would be produced by the combination of this centripetal tendency with a given amount of force tending to produce motion at right angles to it. But upon this theory Newton was left as free as any one to regard the material universe as a product of design. The problem, however, was shifted from a consideration of design in each part by itself to that of design in the system as a whole. Henceforth the doctrine of design as related to the material universe became one of mechanical adjustment in a cosmos whose limits were unknown and the movement of whose parts was intricate beyond conception.

There can be no question that the larger views of the universe entertained by modern astronomers involve important modifications in the doctrine of design. A large and complicated machine can not do everything which a simple machine could readily enough perform. A railroad train is a far grander product of design than is a stagecoach or a Japanese jinrikisha; but the jinrikisha has the advantage of the train, and of the stagecoach even, in being able to pick up its passengers in the narrow alley, and not merely upon the broad street and at the grand station. Under the Copernican theory of the solar system, the sun and stars can no longer be thought to shine solely for the benefit of the inhabitants of this insignificant planet; for these centres of light fill the universe with their rays, while we on our tiny globe, presenting now one side and now another, catch but an infinitesimal portion of their life-giving power.

Designs are both general and special.

It is possible, however, to conserve the doctrine of intelligent design by enlarging our conception of man's mental and moral powers. With a mind capable of interpreting the mechanism of the universe, and a moral nature subordinated to eternal law, and needing to be impressed by the supreme value of spiritual things as compared with material, it is possible to see that after all there may be no waste in Nature's design. The very doctrine of the conservation of energy may involve the conservation of design. Especially is this conception allowable when we think of man

Possible Complexity of Designs.

with all his exalted powers of interpretation as but beginning here an immortal career of intellectual advancement. A hint of these possibilities is seen in some of the recent triumphs of science in the interpretation of the hitherto unrecognised vibrations which fill all space. The spectroscope reveals to us the constitution not only of our own sun, but to a certain extent of the most distant stars and nebulæ. The Roentgen ray penetrates bodies that had heretofore been regarded as opaque, and which are indeed opaque to light. Indeed, it is quite conceivable that all the history of the whole universe is recorded every instant in the vibrations which are passing through every point of space; so that man needs but to improve his capacity of mind and the mechanism of his perception to read the history of the past on the photographic plate of the present wherever he may be and at any time.

Darwinism, so far as it is related to the doctrine of design, is simply an application of a mechanical theory to the harmonization of biological facts. Like the Newtonian theory of gravitation, it rests upon two observed conflicting tendencies which by their interaction are thought to be competent to produce all the varied classes of facts which are unfolding before us in the animal and vegetable kingdoms. These ultimate tendencies, like the centripetal and centrifugal forces of the solar system, are unexplained and to a great extent unexplainable. They are assumed as ultimate principles to meet the emergencies of the case. Both the assumptions have to be broad enough to sustain the structure of development that is reared upon them.

Ultimate Assumptions of Darwinism.

The first class of tendencies upon which the Darwinian theory rests relates to heredity and variation. These, like the motions of the heavenly bodies, are simply facts of observation. In general, the progeny of plants and animals is like the parent. Each seed and each germ produces after its kind. But there is never exact repetition. The productive organisms of plants and animals do not turn out their products with the exactness of purely mechanical contrivances. The child is never exactly like the parent. It is the variations thus produced that serve as the basis of natural selection.

But to be available for selection the variations must be sufficient in amount, specific enough in character, and coincident in enough individuals to furnish available material for natural selection to act upon. It is easy to see, therefore, that the variations which serve as a basis for progressive development through natural selection can not be chance variations. This fact is forced upon the attention of naturalists upon every hand, and forms the burden of Weismann's most recent utterances upon the subject. How is it, he says, that we shall account for "the occurrence of the right variations at the right place?" How is it that "the useful variations were always present, or that they always existed in a sufficiently large number of individuals for the selective process?" Until these questions are answered, he says, "something is still wanting to the selection of Darwin and Wallace." * The constant refrain in the writings of the late Prof. Cope

What is the Origin of the Fittest?

---

* Monist (January, 1896), pp. 261, 263, 264.

was "the survival of the fittest does not explain the origin of species until we explain the 'origin of the fittest.'" Asa Gray also, in his correspondence with Darwin, continually insisted that variations were evidently "led along certain beneficial lines." * Here, therefore, is a wide door left open for the entrance of design into the field of natural selection.

The impossibility of obtaining advantageous variations in a highly organized being by chance is admirably shown by Mr. Spencer in the case of animals like the cat which are fitted for leaping. The difficult question for those who deny any purposive element at the bottom of organic evolution is how to secure the complicated co-ordination of results involved in the development of any decidedly advantageous anatomical variations.

The Fittest does not arise by Chance.

For example, the anatomical variations by which an animal accustomed to regular movement over smooth ground is transformed into one adapted to the work of leaping over rough surfaces is not confined to changes in a single organ, but involves co-ordinate changes in almost every part of the system. The ability to leap like a kangaroo, or even like a cat, involves a striking development not only in the length and strength of the bones in the hind limbs, but in the articulation of the joints and in the development of the muscles. A change must take place not only in one bone and one set of muscles, but in all the bones of the hinder extremities simultaneously. Not only must the long bones and their

The Limbs of the Cat.

---

* Darwiniana.

co-ordinate muscles, by which the limbs are suddenly lengthened for a leap, be properly modified, but the bones of the toes, which sustain the reaction of the leap, and their co-ordinate muscles, must be correspondingly modified. Otherwise there will be no fulcrum for the increased exertion to act upon. Thus, without counting the changes which would be required in the pelvis as well as in the nerves and blood-vessels, there are, counting bones, muscles, tendons, and ligaments, at least fifty different parts in each hind leg which have to be enlarged. Moreover, they have to be enlarged in unlike degrees. The muscles and tendons of the outer toes, for example, need not to be added to so much as those of the median toes. The chances that all these changes shall occur together spontaneously are as one in favour to many millions against. Their concurrence brings most clearly to view a divinity shaping the development of animals as well as the lives of men.

But the argument does not close even here. An animal adapted in the hinder portions of his body for leaping high in the air must also be adapted for protection against the violence of the descent which is involved in every such ascent. The fore limbs must be changed as much as the hind ones are, but in a radically different manner. To learn the different character of these changes, one has but to " contrast the markedly bent hind limbs of a cat with its almost straight fore limbs, or contrast the silence of the upward spring on to the table with the thud which the fore paws make as it jumps off the table." To make the changes in the hind limbs advantageous there must be a simultaneous change in the fore limbs. When the number of these changes is taken into account, the probabilities against their arising fortuitously and in progressive adjustment to the first runs up into the billions, so that it is outside any rational recognition. The changes involved in the transformation can not have been fortuitous, but must be attributed to some undiscovered law.

A single other illustration drawn from Weismann will suffice. The protective colouring of butterflies is one of the most striking facts in all natural history. In numberless cases it is evident that the safety of these defenceless creatures is secured by such a resemblance to objects for which predatory enemies have no desire that they are overlooked or avoided. More often they imitate so perfectly the colour of the leaves of the forest that even sharp-eyed birds do not recognise the difference, while sometimes species which are good for food and palatable take on the guise of other species which are unpalatable or poisonous. But as it is in rest that these butterflies are mostly in danger, the protective colouring usually appears only upon that side of the wing which is exposed when they are folded. In one of these instances, the *Kallima inachis* and *Parallecta,* species of Indian leaf butterflies, the leaf markings are exquisite in an extremely complicated manner.

Protective Colouring of Butterflies.

From the tail of the wing to the apex of the fore wings runs with a beautiful curvature a thick, doubly contoured dark line, accompanied by a brighter one, representing the midrib of the leaf. This line cuts the " veins " and the "cells" of the leaf in the most disregardful fashion, here in acute and here in obtuse angles, and in absolute independence of the regular system of divisions of the wing. . . . The midrib is composed of two pieces, of which the one belongs to the hind wing and the other to the fore wing, and the two fit each other exactly when the butterfly is in the attitude of repose, but not otherwise. Now these two pieces of the left rib do not begin on corresponding spots of the two wings, but on absolutely nonidentical spots. And the same is also true of the lines which represent the lateral ribs of the leaf. These lines proceed in acute angles from the rib; to the right and to the left in the same angle, those of the same side parallel with each other. Here, too, no relation is noticeable between the parts of the wings over which the line is passed. The venation of the wing is utterly ignored by the leaf markings, and its surface is treated as a *tabula rasa* upon which anything conceivable can be drawn. In other words, we are presented here with a bilaterally symmetrical figure engraved on a surface which is essentially radially symmetrical in its division.*

But Spencer and Weismann would account for these concurrent variations which lie at the basis of natural selection on very different theories.

Spencer's critique of Darwin's doctrine of natural selection is designed to prepare the way for the readier acceptance of his own theory that the effects of use upon organs are more largely inherited than is generally supposed. In this respect his theory is an approach to the Lamarckian hypothesis, which has been so much caricatured and misrepresented. According to the caricatures of this hypothesis, all that an animal would have to do to acquire the neck of a giraffe would be intensely to desire such a length of neck, and eagerly and persistently to struggle to lengthen it by stretching upward for the attainment of objects which

---

* Monist (January, 1896), pp. 259, 260.

were just beyond his reach. Within certain limits, Darwin did not deny the importance of this principle, and was ready to admit that the effects of use were, to some extent, inheritable. Spencer, while not going to the extent of Lamarck, would, however, again push the principle forward to great prominence.

On the other hand, Weismann, and those who are more or less in agreement with him, persist in affirming that the advocates of Darwinism must fall back upon some theory of variation like that maintained by Prof. Asa Gray, which asserts that the physiological causes involved are designed to produce definite tendencies of development. Referring to the remarkable facts already recounted concerning the protective colouring assumed by the Indian leaf butterflies, Weismann says:

<small>Variations caused by Physiological Forces.</small>

I lay unusual stress upon this point because it shows that we are dealing here with one of those cases which can not be explained by mechanical, that is, by natural means, unless natural selection actually exists and is actually competent to create new properties; for the Lamarckian principle is excluded here *ab initio*, seeing that we are dealing with a formation which is only passive in its effects: the leaf markings are effectual simply by their existence and not by any function which they perform; they are present in flight as well as at rest, during the absence of danger as well as during the approach of an enemy.

Nor are we helped here by the assumption of the *purely internal motive forces* which Nägeli, Askenasy, and others have put forward as supplying a *mechanical* force of evolution. It is impossible to regard the coincidence of an Indian butterfly with the leaf of a tree now growing in an Indian forest as fortuitous, as a *lusus naturæ*. Assuming this seemingly mechanical force, therefore, we should be led back inevitably to a teleological principle which produces adaptive characters and which must have deposited the directive principle in the very first germ of terrestrial organisms, so that after untold ages at a definite time and place the illusive leaf markings should be developed. The assumption of pre-established harmony between the evolution of the ancestral line of the tree with its prefigurative leaf, and that of the butterfly with its imitating wing, is absolutely necessary here.

For who or what is to be our guarantee that dark scales shall appear at the exact spots on the wing where the midrib of the leaf must grow? And that, later, dark scales shall appear at the exact spots to which the midrib must be prolonged? And that, still later, such dark scales shall appear at the places where the lateral ribs start, and that here also a definite acute angle shall be accurately preserved, and the mutual distances of the lateral ribs be alike and their courses parallel? And that the prolongation of the median rib from the hind wing to the fore wing shall be extended exactly to that spot where the fore wing is not covered by the hind wing in the attitude of repose? and so on.

If I could go on more minutely in this matter, I should attempt to prove the markings, as I have just assumed, have not risen suddenly, but were perfected very, very gradually; that in one species they began on the fore wing and in another on the hind wing; and that in many they never until recently proceeded beyond one wing, in other species they went only a little way, and in only a few did they spread over the entire surface of both wings.

That these markings advance slowly and gradually, but with marvellous accuracy, is no mere conjecture. But it follows that the right variations at the right places must never have been wanting, or, as I expressed it before, *the useful variations were always present.* But how is that possible in such long extensive lines of dissimilar variations as have gradually come to constitute markings of the complexity here presented? Suppose that the useful colours had not appeared at all, or had not appeared at the right places? It is a fact that in constant species— that is, in such as are not in process of transformation— the variations of the markings are by no means frequent or abundant. Or, suppose that they had really appeared, but occurred only in individuals or in a small percentage of individuals?*

In similar strain the late Prof. Asa Gray, in various publications from the first announcement of the Darwinian theory to the day of his death, pointed out the impossibility of anything being accomplished by natural selection without designed variations and adaptations to work upon. In his remarkable chapter upon Evolutionary Teleology, written near the close of his life, Dr. Gray compares variation to the wind, which is the propelling force of the ship, while natural selection corresponds to the rudder. Variation, he says, "is not a product of, but a response to, the action of the environment. Variations, . . . however originated, are evidently not from without, but from within—not physical, but physiological." So, in 1863, he writes to Darwin that he finds it impossible to imagine that the numerous and nice coadaptations in orchids could have been formed by any number of chance combinations. Darwin's suggestion that such might have been the case makes Dr. Gray "feel the cold chill." Again, in 1872, Gray writes to Dana, "Variation in particular directions is your idea and mine, but is very anti-Darwin." To the same effect, in his Atlantic Monthly articles in 1860, he advises Darwin "to assume a philosophy of his hy-

Asa Gray's Early Discussions.

---

* Monist (January, 1896), pp. 260–262.

pothesis that variation has been led along certain beneficial lines," and insists upon what he takes to be a well-known fact that, "as species do not now vary at all times and places and in all directions, nor produce crude, vague, imperfect, and useless forms, there is no reason for supposing that they ever did."

Indeed, the forces which are personified as natural selection present in their correlation to those of heredity evidences of design surpassing anything else which has ever entered into the mind of man. Prof. Shaler has recently stated in a most felicitous manner the striking facts concerning the narrow limits within which the development of life must go on and concerning the critical points through which it is compelled to pass.

". . . Organic life, as manifested on the earth's surface, depends," he says, " upon a coincidence in the qualities of a score or more substances within a certain range of temperature, and also on the occurrence on the earth's surface of a certain limited range of heat which must be maintained in order to make it possible for these substances, at their particular critical points, to co-operate in the production of life. The maintenance of a certain temperature on the earth's surface depends in turn upon the coincidence of a variety of physical conditions, the action of which, in order that life may be possible, must be balanced with extreme nicety. The delicacy of this adjustment may be judged when we consider the vast range in heat which exists within the limits of our solar system. The temperature of the sun is probably to be measured by the hundred thousand degrees; that of the space intervening between the solar centre and the earth is certainly hundreds of degrees below zero; that of the earth's interior is probably more than ten thousand degrees above. In this great scale of heat organic life can only occupy the narrow span of about one hundred degrees, or from about thirty-two to near one hundred and thirty-five, or perhaps the one thousandth part of the temperature variation which the solar system affords. Thus the possibility of organic life depends upon the occurrence at the earth's surface of a temperature not exceeding a range of about one hundred degrees, while the actual temperature range of the solar system exceeds one hundred thousand degrees of variation.

". . . If at any time the temperature of the earth's surface should in general fall below or rise much above the narrow limits which have been indicated, the result would, in a brief time, be the destruction of organic life." *

To maintain its existence, therefore, this principle of life has to run the gantlet of all the changes that take place in such a world as this. The power of life may be compared to a rove of cotton, and the conditions of life to the spinning jenny and the combined machinery of a cotton mill. The nature of the product depends on a vast complication of movements and adaptations, from those of the water wheel to those which secure the proper tension of the thread. All these movements are independently adjusted with reference to the nature of the cotton. Too much tension will break the thread, too little will loop it.

The Gantlet of Life.

The Darwinian supposition is that life has been so

---

* The Interpretation of Nature, pp. 66-69.

adjusted to the changing conditions of the material forces of the world that for a period of one hundred million years, more or less, it has been continuous. That surely makes a demand for a Contriver who is omniscient as well as omnipotent; for the conditions through which that plastic principle has passed have been extremely trying. Time and again land and water have shifted place, and transferred the scene for organic development from one portion of the globe to another. The alternations of climate have been extreme between distant periods of time. Now an arctic climate has crept slowly down far toward the equator, to give place in due season to ameliorating influences that should dispel even the rigour of the frigid zones. Volcanoes have at times belched forth their fires in almost every portion of the world, and earthquakes have everywhere shaken her solid foundations. Vast regions have sunk beneath the sea, while elsewhere plains as vast, and bearing mountain chains on their summits, were rising toward the sky. Amid all these changes, however rapidly they may have occurred, the equation of life has had continually to readjust itself not only to forces outside, but to its own inherent tendencies. Race has warred on race, and individual has been brought into sharp competition with his fellow. The mystery is that the higher forms of life have been preserved at all. The hand of Providence certainly is not dispensed with, but rather called for, by this theory.

Origin of Man.

The Darwinian speculations which at first sight seem most seriously to disturb the foundations of our Christian faith relate to the origin of man. At any rate the impression seems pretty generally to prevail that if there is a physical continuity between man and the lower animals there is something in the thought derogatory to man's dignity and specially subversive of the Scriptures. These impressions may best be corrected by briefly considering the parallel perplexities which attend our efforts to understand the origin of each individual soul.

One of the most hotly contested questions in theology has reference to the relation of the parents to the spiritual nature of the child. That the bodily organization of the child is directly derived from the parents is held by every one who believes in secondary causes at all. But in reference to the soul there is the greatest diversity of opinion. On the one hand, those who emphasize the solidarity of the race and minimize the freedom of the will logically enough hold that the whole nature of man is in his progenitors, and is derived from them. These are called traducianists. On the other hand, those who especially exalt the prerogatives of human free will are inclined to hold that children receive only their bodily organization from their parents, while the soul of each is a direct and fresh gift from God. These are called creationists.

Traducianism and Creationism.

Among theologians the traducianists have been well represented in every generation from Augustine to that of Profs. William G. Shedd and Augustus H. Strong. Augustine touches the point in the following pertinent words: "I have created all (or every) breath, is undeniably spoken of each individual soul. Well, but God also creates the entire body of man and, as nobody doubts, he makes the human body by a process of propagation. It is therefore, of course, still open to inquiry concerning the soul (since it is evidently God's work), whether he creates it, as he does the body, by propagation or by inbreathing, as he made the first soul. . . . All our question is as to the *mode* of the formation. Now let us take the eye of the body and ask, Who but God forms it? I suppose that he forms it not externally, but in itself, and yet most certainly by propagation. Since, then, he also forms the human spirit, or soul, in itself, the question still remains whether it be derived by a fresh insufflation in every instance or by propagation." *

Augustine's Views.

In reading the hot controversies between the traducianists and the creationists it is plain to see that theologians are as perplexed to come to any agreement about the origin of each individual soul as naturalists are upon the question of the origin of species. Indeed, the difficulties are really identical. In both cases we are led into the fruitful fields of discussion opened in trying to settle the questions between nominalism and realism. Prof. Agassiz † could

Theological and Scientific Theories analogous.

---

* De Anima, lib. i, cc. 21, 22.
† Contributions, Nat. Hist., etc. (Boston, 1857), pp. 39, 40, 165, 166.

not believe that there was any physical bond connecting together the species of a genera. To his mind the bond was wholly ideal. The Creator willed it, and his ideas became embodied directly in the origination of a new species with all its generic affiliations. So the creationists hold to what would be called "occasionalism" in philosophy respecting the origin of individual souls. The Creator wills that when the conditions arise furnishing the appropriate occasion then, and only then, he puts forth his direct power in the creation of a freshly formed soul to occupy the body which has been prepared.

In view of these analogies between Darwinism and traducianism, it does not seem that there need to be any further theological controversies over the mode of the origin of species. For until theologians can scientifically determine at just what point in the life of the fœtus the physical organism comes into union with a responsible spirit, it is with ill grace that they demand a clear statement from the men of science concerning the mode by which specific qualities are acquired by the race as such. In other words, it is as difficult to tell when or how the fœtal germ passes from a purely physical organism to become a living, immortal soul as it is to frame an hypothesis concerning the mode of the formation of a species from an incipient variety of plant or animal.

It is easy to see, therefore, that Darwinism really raises no new questions in the philosophy of Christianity. Indeed, in emphasizing as it does the complexity of the causes by which species are both propagated and varied, it makes it more conceivable that there should be interventions by the Creator anlogous to those which are effected by man. A general theory of the derivative origin of species no more shuts off miracles and supernatural intervention in cases of necessity than does any other conception of the orderly processes of Nature. Darwinism only emphasizes in his department what is emphasized still more strongly in other departments of science—that there is economy in the general processes of Nature. There is a law of parsimony according to which no unnecessary causes are introduced. In this respect Omnipotence has in the laws of Nature condescended to work according to the capacity of our minds so that we can follow out his designs and trace the continuity of his plan. We are set to study the universe as it actually exists, and not to chase a phantom created wholly by our own imaginations.

Darwinism not a General Theory of Creation.

Along the line of thought suggested by this general law of parsimony as it is emphasized in Darwinism, there are some analogies presented in the New Testament which it is worth while to keep in mind. One of the most striking features in the histories of Christ which have been left us by the four evangelists is the limitation incidentally set upon his miraculous activities. According to their representations, he had all power given him both in heaven and on earth. His miraculous power was in theory unlimited, but in practice it was most strangely limited. Jesus was most careful, according to their representations, not to waste his prerogatives, and not to cast his pearls before swine or to prostitute his power for the gratification of either idle curiosity or of the indolent propensities of men.

Darwinism and the Law of Parsimony.

This appears most impressively in the account of the miracle of the multiplication of the loaves and the fishes. After this most striking account of miraculous deeds, in which five loaves and a few small fishes were multiplied to meet the wants of thousands, how strange it sounds to hear him exhorting his disciples to save the twelve baskets of fragments which remained! Incidentally we may remark that it never could have entered the mind of a fabricator of facts or of a mythical story-teller to have added this touch of naturalness to the account. It bears, therefore, most striking testimony to the genuineness of the history.

But especially does this great law of parsimony appear in the representation which is given in the New Testament of the manner in which the supernatural Christ is introduced into the world. That he is represented as having a supernatural character, and as having existed before his incarnation, is clear to any one who even cursorily reads the account. But it is significant that, while he is not represented as being born of a human father, he did have a human mother, so that he was a real descendant of David, and truly belonged to the seed of Israel. Why was there this partial dependence on secondary causes? Why could not an angel have been fashioned in the form of a man without the intervention of secondary causes at all? It would have been as easy for Omnipotence to have performed a whole miracle as a half miracle. For the miracle which is represented as being performed in the incarnation of the supernatural nature of Christ is as real and as great as it would have been if he had been introduced purely as a supernatural being. But

Miracles and the Law of Parsimony.

it is instructive to notice that the alleged ingrafting of Christ's supernatural nature upon the human nature is closely analogous to what the theistic advocates of the derivative origin of species suppose took place in the creation of man. In his body and animal instincts he is allied to the animal creation, but in his spiritual powers he is above them.

We should not fail to notice, in conclusion, the great service which has been rendered by Darwinism in restoring what is called moral or probable evidence to its proper position of respect in scientific circles. The argument for the derivative origin of species does not claim to be demonstrative. Its convincing power depends upon an accumulation of probabilities, each one of which in turn is dependent upon a more general theory of the order of Nature. Indeed, the stock objection to Darwinism has been that it is a series of unproved "may be's," in which hypothesis crowds upon hypothesis in ever-increasing confusion; so that the principal task of the Darwinian evolutionists has been to answer objections and explain away difficulties. While apologetics has come into disfavour among a certain class of Christian writers, it has come to be the chief stock in trade with a large part of the scientific world. As already noted, Darwin admitted that he had come to be the chief of wrigglers, though contending that Herbert Spencer was much more of one than he was.*

Darwin's Method of dealing with Difficulties.

This change of attitude, brought about by the discussions concerning the origin of species, is of great

---

* Life and Letters, vol. ii, p. 239.

significance. In rescuing natural history from the depressing influence of empiricism and positivism, it has restored to the world the true doctrine of design in the universe. In the doctrine of the derivative origin of species, we have before our thoughts a comprehensive design worthy of an all-powerful and all-wise Creator. The chief difference between the creationists and the evolutionists is in the limits which they set to the Creator's power. The creationists affirm that it is not only inconceivable but impossible that living matter should have been endowed with the multifarious capacity for development and adaptation to changing conditions which we see in plants and animals.

What are the Limits of Creative Power?

The Darwinian evolutionist replies that where all is mysterious we have nothing to do with the inconceivable and the seemingly impossible. On *a priori* grounds one thing is as conceivable and as possible as another. We must follow the lead of the actual facts, and draw our conclusions on the lines which they work out. For example, we have experience in witnessing and producing varieties in domestic plants and animals. By selection we secure the beautiful varieties of flowers that crowd our greenhouses and the varieties of grains and fruits and garden vegetables which meet the wants and minister to the appetites of civilized man. It is by man's selection that all the varieties of domestic animals are preserved, if not produced. The Shetland pony and the dray horse; the pug dog, the greyhound, and the mastiff; among pigeons, the fantail, the pouter, and the tumbler, together with the varieties of numerous other species of animals subservient to the use of man, have been produced by human selection. This all admit. But man is limited in his power over species. The question between the evolutionists and the creationists is, To what extent is God also limited? If man can produce varieties by judicious selection, is it too hard to suppose that God can produce species by selection? Leaving out the spiritual nature of man, shall we limit the Creator short of the bounds of the whole realm of life? If man can direct the varieties of the common rock pigeon until he has all the fancy forms with which we are now familiar, and which are so widely separated from each other, could not the Creator have so adjusted the original forces of Nature that species and genera of plants and animals should have descended from the more generalized original forms? This certainly is not beyond belief if there is a reasonable amount of evidence pointing to that as the actual course of natural history.

The only effect which the establishment of this theory would have on the doctrine of design in Nature would be to make it more comprehensive. In the words of Whewell:

Comprehensiveness of the Creator's Designs.
The assertion appears to be quite unfounded that as science advances from point to point final causes recede before it, and disappear one after the other. The principle of design changes its mode of application, indeed, but it loses none of its force. We no longer consider particular facts as produced by special interpositions, but we consider design as exhibited in the establishment and adjustment of the laws by which particular facts are produced. We do not look upon each particular cloud as brought near us that it may drop fatness on our fields; but the general adaptation of the laws of heat and air and moisture to the promotion of vegeta-

tion does not become doubtful. We do not consider the sun as less intended to warm and vivify the tribes of plants and animals because we find that, instead of revolving round the earth as an attendant, the earth, along with other planets, revolves round him. We are rather, by the discovery of the general laws of Nature, led into a scene of wider design, of deeper contrivance, of more comprehensive adjustments. Final causes, if they appear driven further from us by such an extension of our views, embrace us only with a vaster and more majestic circuit. Instead of a few threads connecting some detached objects, they become a stupendous network which is wound round and round the universal frame of things.*

Nor if this theory is adopted should we need to change our language concerning the Creator's relation to these designs. The fact of design is not affected by the mode in which the design is made to enter. The homespun clothes of our grandparents were manufactured—i. e., made by hand, according to the literal meaning of the word. The wool was shorn from the sheep by hand; it was carded into rolls by hand; it was spun by the housewife upon the wheel in the kitchen, and woven by the same hands into a web of cloth. This was literally a manufacture. But we still retain the word to describe a web of cloth which human hands have scarcely touched. To-day the wool is shorn from the backs of sheep in Australia by a machine; it is loaded upon the steamer at Melbourne and unloaded from it at Liverpool or Boston by machinery; it is tossed by machinery into one end of a mill that

margin: Meaning of Words enlarged but not changed.

---

* Whewell, The Philosophy of the Inductive Sciences, vol. ii, pp. 88, 89, 93, 94.

has scarcely anything in it but machinery and a few overseers to watch it. After passing from one machine to another in long procession, it comes out broadcloth, and is stamped as a *manufactured* article, made by a corporation which if it has a soul certainly has no hands that have ever been hardened by toil.

Still we are not wrong in saying that this web of cloth was made by this corporation. From beginning to end there has been a continuous thread of design leading to the finished product. Indeed, the design compassing the end is much more impressive in the products of the great factory than in the products of the hand loom. Increased knowledge has given the corporation increased power in bending the forces of Nature to its will. In its enlarged use of Nature it has displayed larger intelligence and compassed broader and more numerous ends. However much the word "manufacture" may have changed its costume to suit modern conditions, it has not parted with its central and essential idea. The hands are but material objects made to do the bidding of the thought of the mind. In this sense the modern man has a thousand hands to do his bidding where his ancestors had but a single pair.

In this as in every other department of reasoning we should carefully distinguish between the fact of creation and the mode of creation. Of the fact we may be always sure. Our conception of the mode is ever subject to enlargement. We may leave it to the common sense of mankind to make the adjustments in the use of language which the nature of the case requires. When we ask a cabinetmaker to "bring" a bureau to the house, we do not need to define how he is to bring it. When the judge orders the sheriff to "bring" the prisoner to the bar, the accompaniment of handcuffs and latent display of authority is readily supplied by the imagination. But when the mother asks the son to "bring" his friend home to dinner, the word conveys no thought but that of the gentlest persuasion. The critic who should insist that the word must have the same outward meaning in all these cases would simply demonstrate his unfitness as a guide in such simple matters. It is equally so with those who become so entangled in subtleties of logic that they can see design only in handicraft, and creation only in the work of a carpenter.

CHAPTER V.

MEDIATE MIRACLES.

THREE characteristics of the miracles of the Bible are especially noteworthy: They are not incongruous; they are all for a worthy purpose; they are not superabundant.

Miracles difficult to invent.

Reasoning from what we know of human nature, the combination of such characteristics in a miraculous story furnishes the strongest possible marks of the truthfulness both of the narratives and of the general system which they are made to support; for experience abundantly teaches that the human mind is limited in its power to control the fancies which take possession of it. The actions of the man who has come to believe that he can perform miracles are sure to be grotesque. He is sure to attempt impossibilities, and thereby prove himself a fit candidate for an insane asylum. Nor is it easy for a writer to introduce a miraculous element into his plot and preserve the congruity of his story. He will be sure to be intoxicated by his own ideas, so that he will produce a monstrosity. Such are the miraculous stories in the apocryphal Gospels. Such are the mythologies of all nations.

As illustrating the economy of the miraculous element in the Bible, we may properly pause at this stage of our discussion to consider a class of occurrences which stand midway between true miracles and the ordinary occurrences of Nature, although it must be confessed that there is no exact hard-and-fast line of demarcation possible.

Difficulty of Exact Definition.

This, however, need no more interfere with our attempted classification than would the corresponding difficulty of distinguishing exactly the border line between day and night interfere with our use of the distinction designated by those words. It is sufficient to note that specific differences between Nature, providence, special providence, and miracles are as readily recognised as are those at the basis of the scientific nomenclature relating to the animal and vegetable kingdoms. In denominating a certain class of occurrences, ordinarily regarded as miraculous,- "mediate" miracles, there is, however, no denial of the strictly miraculous character of certain other events, nor is there any denial of the immediate exercise of supernatural agency in effecting the total result in this class of occurrences.

The economy of the strictly miraculous element in the Bible can never cease to be a surprise to the scientific student of human history. That Israel should have been delivered from Egypt by such signs and wonders as are recorded in the Old Testament, and then should have been left by the same Almighty Protector to the vicissitudes of the nation's subsequent career, does not have the air of a myth or bear the marks of fiction. The congruity of the story is maintained by such a limitation of the miraculous elements and by the subordination of it to so lofty and pure a moral purpose that it can not reasonably be looked upon as a product of the

Economy of Biblical Miracles.

human fancy, much less of human cunning and deceit. It is neither a myth nor a story of fiction.

That Jesus, endowed as he was, in the conception of the writer of the fourth Gospel, with unlimited power over Nature, should be represented as sitting at the well of Sychar hungry and thirsty because there was no food at hand and no bucket with which to draw water from Jacob's well,* can not be a myth. That, again, after he is said to have multiplied the bread to feed the hungry thousands on the shores of Galilee,† he should be represented as exhorting his disciples to gather up the fragments that nothing be lost, is not a fictitious product of the human brain. Such conceptions must be parts of some grand system of truth.

Evidently there is in the Christian system an "economy of grace" in which miracles are as conspicuous for their absence in certain connections as for their presence in others. In view of this principle it is both proper and important to scan the records with the view of pruning them of such excrescences of interpretation as may belong not to the original accounts, but to the hasty generalizations of the reader. It will not be strange if such critical examination shows that we are sometimes in danger of gratuitously attributing miraculous elements to Scripture narratives which do not really contain them. It will therefore be a real advantage gained if we succeed in more clearly drawing the line between what is indubitably designed to be represented as miraculous and what seems to be miraculous only by reason of a false interpretation.

---

* John iv, 5–29.   † John vi, 5–13.

EVENTS DOUBTFULLY CLASSED AS MIRACLES.

Among the narratives of this class specially liable to misinterpretation may be mentioned the escape of Jesus from his fellow townsmen at Nazareth when they had led him out to cast him down headlong from the brow of the hill. The narrative simply reads, "But he, passing through the midst of them, went his way,"* without any intimation of a miracle properly so called. Ordinarily one would simply suppose that his enemies were overawed by the manifest majesty of his person, and that their courage failed them. Nothing more than this can with certainty be drawn out of the narrative.

Escape at Nazareth.

Another example of the tendency to read into the narrative more of the miraculous than is expressly stated is found in the account of the two instances of Christ's driving the money changers from the temple.† By many this transaction doubtless is regarded as miraculous. But there is no intimation of the miraculous in the narrative itself. The scourge of small cords with which Jesus symbolized the intensity of his indignation was a most effective use of natural means. The ease with which Jesus accomplished his purpose was probably due to the combined influence of his own majestic bearing and of the guilty fears of those who were trespassing upon the sacred precincts of the temple. Both the law, and the sentiment of the masses came to the support of the bold measure entered upon

Driving out of the Money Changers.

---

* Luke v, 30.   † John ii, 15; Matt. xxi, 12.

MEDIATE MIRACLES.   119

by Jesus at this time. The transaction was one which would seem to be wholly within the range of natural means.

Other instances in which the miraculous element is probably introduced into the Bible without due warrant occur in the accounts of Christ's vanishing out of the sight of the two disciples at Emmaus, and of his unexpected appearance to the disciples "when the doors were shut where the disciples were assembled for fear of the Jews." * In the first of these instances a natural explanation is offered in the narrative itself, for we are told that the two disciples had not recognised their Master at all until "their eyes were opened." Apparently they were so dazed by the whole transaction that they could not make note of everything which occurred. When they were in such a state of mind it required no miracle for Jesus to slip away from their sight unobserved; while in the second case there is no direct intimation that Jesus entered the room by any other than natural means. The doors were shut for fear of the Jews. They would not be closed against one of their own number.

Marginal note: Mysterious Appearances.

SPECIAL PROVIDENCES.

While the foregoing instances would not necessarily be classed in any sense among miracles, there are other events, standing midway between them and such unequivocal miracles as the resurrection of Christ and the descent of fire upon Elijah's altar upon Mount Carmel, which are appropriately termed by some "mediate

---

* Luke xxiv, 31; John xx, 19.

miracles." Such miracles consist in a miraculous *adaptation* of the laws of Nature rather than a direct *suspension* of them. In the words of the late Dr. Edward Robinson, they are events "wrought by natural means supernaturally applied." In the ultimate analysis this class of events is perhaps resolved into miracles of foreknowledge, and is closely akin to what we often call special providences. Determining epochs in history may be brought about either by directing the course of the great operations of Nature so as to cross the course of human history at a particular stage of its development or by directing the development of history so that at some critical point it shall encounter an extraordinary event in the course of Nature. It makes no difference whether we regard the Midianite merchants on their way to Egypt as divinely directed past the pit into which Joseph had been thrown, or whether Providence had so overruled the wickedness of his brethren that they had undesignedly left him in a pit which lay in the pathway in which it was foreordained that these merchants should pass on that particular day. The event is too momentous in its consequences, and too complicated in its relations both to cause and effect, to be thought of as accidental. It is one of those cases in which we see most clearly that in events both great and small

> There's a divinity that shapes our ends,
> Rough hew them how we will.

Among the events which may be classed as mediate miracles is the darkness which enveloped Jerusalem at the time of the crucifixion. According to the narrative, there was at the same time an earthquake, and we are not compelled to go any further than the natural accompaniments of such a convulsion to find a cause for the darkness. In this case the providential element consists simply in that exercise of divine foresight by which it came about that the events of the crucifixion were so timed as to coincide with the occurrence of the earthquake; or, we might put it the other way and say that in the creative plan of God the earthquake was provided for to meet this particular juncture of human history. Such grand combinations of human and natural events are as clearly indicative of a divine ordering as were the military combinations on the fields of Europe, in the early part of this century, of the active agency of the genius of Napoleon. The striking character of the combinations and their obvious relation to the great plan of divine redemption lift the events above the category of ordinary special providences and make them in a very true sense miraculous.

Darkness of the Crucifixion.

PASSAGE OF THE RED SEA.

A clearer case of the mediate miracle is probably that connected with the passage of the Israelites through the Red Sea. At Suez there is a remarkable sand bar extending from one shore to another which is occasionally almost laid bare by a favourable conjunction of low tide and strong east wind, so that it is quite possible still at times to ford the sea by means of it. It is related that in 1799 Napoleon attempted to cross by means of the ford, but failed to accomplish his purpose because of the darkness of the hour and because of the unexpected rise of the tide which brought his life into imminent danger. But, according to all authorities, the passage of this ford is no infrequent occurrence. The variation of water level at this point is stated by the French engineers who accompanied Napoleon to be about seven feet.*

Major-General Tulloch,† of the British army, when assigned to duty on the Isthmus of Suez, two or three years ago, was led to place the crossing of the Israelites at the north end of the Bitter Lakes, where he supposes, with others, the sea extended at that time. This would make the passage about twenty miles from Pithom or Succoth. While on duty at this point, he himself witnessed the driving off of the water by the wind from the east end of Lake Menzelah. By this means it was lowered six feet. The wind described in the Bible as opening the way before the children of Israel would need to be no stronger than this to produce the required result. To a military man the movements of Pharaoh's army were all quite natural. Not suspecting the course actually to be pursued by Moses, Pharaoh was disposing his forces across the isthmus to prevent the Israelites from following the only road ordinarily open. On perceiving what they were actually doing, he followed after just in time for his advance guard to meet the returning tide and be destroyed.

Recent Observations.

The reference of the narrative in Exodus to the employment of the natural means which would open this road to the children of Israel across the Suez arm of the Red Sea is precise and emphatic. It is said that "the

---

* Robinson's Biblical Researches in Palestine, vol. i, p. 49.
† Proceedings of the Victoria Institute, vol. xxviii, pp. 267-280.

Lord caused the sea to go back by a strong east wind all the night, and made the sea dry land, and the waters were divided. And the children of Israel went into the midst of the sea upon dry ground; and the waters were a wall unto them on their right hand and on their left." The mention of the east wind is significant, for it is a wind from that direction which would naturally produce the phenomena here spoken of.

Natural Agencies mentioned.

The power of the wind to affect the level of long, narrow bodies of water is much greater than is ordinarily supposed. It is, for example, well known that the level of Lake Erie at Buffalo is often affected to the extent of several feet by strong westerly or easterly winds. So powerful is this influence that on certain occasions the Niagara River has been left for several hours almost dry when a strong wind was blowing from the east. At such times the water is raised correspondingly at the west end of the lake. According to the report for 1894 of the chief engineer of the United States army, a westerly gale on Lake Erie, October 14, 1893, depressed the water at Toledo, near the western end of the lake, 6.8 feet, while at Buffalo, at the eastern end, it was raised 5.3 feet, making a total difference of 12.1 feet in the water levels at opposite ends of the lake. In 1848 an easterly wind at Buffalo depressed the water fifteen and a half feet below the level produced by a westerly gale in 1849.* To similar effect it is recorded that at two different times (January 9, 1495, and January 19, 1645)

Effect of Winds on Water Levels.

---

* Mr. William T. Blunt, United States assistant engineer, gives many additional instances and details in the Report of the United States Deep Waterways Commission, 1896, pp. 155-168.

Lake Geneva, in Switzerland, has been so blown back by strong winds as to lay bare the bed of the Rhone where it passes through the city.*

The lowering of the water through such agencies, while laying bare the bar at Suez and other shallow places, would still leave the deeper pools of water on either side to serve as a wall of defence and protection against any flank attacks.

On this view of the case the divine agency in the production of a notable miracle is no less real than on any other view. The simple difference is that, according to this explanation, the purposes of the miracle are accomplished by means which are more in harmony with the ordinary course of Providence. To bring Israel to this point at this particular crisis in their relation to the army of Pharaoh, when there should occur this particular juncture of wind and tide, as clearly and strikingly reveals the designing hand of God as a greater absolute miracle would have done. Such a combination of natural and historical forces can not be thought to have occurred either through human calculation or by mere chance. As a combination secured by divine forethought it is sufficiently striking and impressive to insure its influence upon all the subsequent development of human history.

Direct Divine Agency not excluded.

DESTRUCTION OF SODOM AND GOMORRAH.

The description of the destruction of Sodom and Gomorrah, though brief, is sufficiently vivid and pre-

---

* Proceedings of the Victoria Institute, vol. xxvi, pp. 12-33.

MEDIATE MIRACLES.

cise to indicate the natural character of the catastrophe which overwhelmed those cities. We are told that the "Lord rained upon Sodom and upon Gomorrah brimstone and fire from the Lord out of heaven," * and that when Abraham, who was living near Hebron, upon the highlands twenty-five or thirty miles away, arose in the morning and looked toward Sodom and Gomorrah he "beheld, and, lo, the smoke of the land went up as the smoke of a furnace." † Recent studies in the physical geography and geology of this region, when coupled with the knowledge which has lately been so rapidly acquired concerning the extent of the oil and gas accumulations in various parts of the world, bring clearly to view the natural causes which there and then seem to have come into operation.

The depression of land in which the Dead Sea occurs, and on whose shores stood the ancient cities of Sodom and Gomorrah, is justly regarded as one of the most remarkable geological phenomena in the world. The surface of the Dead Sea is twelve hundred and ninety-two feet below that of the Mediterranean, which is but forty or fifty miles distant, while the summit of the tableland constituting the main part of Palestine between the two seas is not far from three thousand feet above the general sea level. The depth of the Dead Sea is also in some places twelve hundred feet. This depression of more than five thousand feet, in which lie the Dead Sea and the valley of the Jordan, is part of a great geological fault extending from Antioch, in Syria, southward between the Lebanon Mountains

The Crevasse of the Jordan Valley.

---

* Gen. xix, 24.   † Gen. xix, 28.

and the range of which Mount Hermon is the summit, and onward through the Jordan Valley and its continuation to the Gulf of Akaba and the Red Sea. The frequent earthquakes which from early times have been reported as occurring in the region of the Dead Sea are but the last shivering movements of the earth's crust which have been in progress here since the middle of the Tertiary period, and which in their total result have produced the depression. It is as if a vast block of solid rock fifty or sixty miles wide and hundreds of miles long had broken off from the main mass extending eastward, and thus had created the gaping crevasse which separates Palestine from the plains of Moab. And such is indeed the case, only that, in addition, a vast block underlying the Dead Sea seems to have settled down far below the rest to produce the depth of twelve hundred feet already referred to.

The geological history of this crevasse since its original formation is most interesting of all. Its fossiliferous and gypsum-bearing beds have been the sources of the vast quantities of bitumen and sulphur, which from the earliest times have been exuding from the precipitous sides of the valley. Changes in the earth's climate, associated probably with the Glacial period, have occasioned also great variations from time to time in the water level. For a while the precipitation within the drainage basin so exceeded the evaporation that the water rose almost high enough to run south into the Red Sea, though never quite sufficiently for that result, so that the Dead Sea has never been actually turned into a fresh-water lake. According to recent investigations of

Its Geological History.

Blankenkorn,* this earliest pluvial period was followed by one which was arid until the sea shrank to within three hundred feet of its present level, when vast deposits of rock salt accumulated all along its southern end.

Again, amid those mysterious climatic changes which have been specially characteristic of recent geological time, the rainfall of the region came to exceed the evaporation until the sea increased to nearly its former dimensions. During this stage the vast salt beds were covered with sand and gravel washed down from the sides of the valley, and these were cemented together by the bitumen, which is slowly accumulating from the gas and oil springs which characterize the region. The conglomerates thus formed, capping the earlier salt deposits along the eastern wall of Jebel Usdum for seven miles, are three or four hundred feet thick.

The second drying up of the waters of the lake brought things nearly to their present condition, but the process was completed by a recent subsidence of a portion of the bed and surrounding plain, thus exposing the strata of salt and conglomerate deposits which are so prominent all around the southern margin.

From this description it will readily be seen that here is a condition of things inviting such a catastrophe as that which is said to have overwhelmed Sodom and Gomorrah. Indeed, the whole region about the Dead Sea has every appearance of being an exhausted "oil district," in which the reservoirs of gas and oil were

---

* Prof. B. K. Emerson has given a clear statement of the geological facts in his presidential address to the Geological Section of the American Association for the Advancement of Science at Buffalo in 1896 (Proceedings, vol. xlv).

long ago tapped by natural agencies. To understand the significance of this statement we need briefly to review the facts which have recently come to light concerning these remarkable accumulations of stored-up energy.

The wide distribution of oil and gas reservoirs is a new revelation to geologists. These highly inflammable accumulations take place in geological formations of greatest diversity both of character and of age. On the western flanks of the Alleghanies they occur in the Devonian strata immediately underlying rocks of Carboniferous age, and are probably due to the decomposition of vegetable matter; while in western Ohio and in Indiana the vast stores of oil and gas are found in the Lower Silurian rocks, where they have doubtless been derived from the decay of animal organisms. In the region of the Caspian Sea and about the Dead Sea the oil is from rocks of later formations.

<small>Reservoirs of Gas and Oil.</small>

The pressure in some of the gas wells is almost beyond comprehension, being sometimes seven or eight hundred pounds to the square inch—a pressure five times as great as that in the cylinder of a locomotive engine when doing its best work. A jet of mingled gas and oil from such a well when ignited presents a wonderful appearance. Its roar can be heard for many miles, and its smoke rises like that of a volcano. At times the burning liquid falls down in destructive showers over a wide area. In the oil regions near the south end of the Caspian Sea the pressure is so enormous that it is impossible to tube the wells after they are drilled. When, therefore, the workmen perceive that they have struck a vein, they instinctively run for their lives, for the jet of gas frequently comes up with such violence as to throw out vast quantities of sand, gravel, and stones, breaking the derrick to pieces over the well, and eventually heaping up a great cone of *débris* about its mouth. The only way in which the first flows of the oil can be secured is to surround the well with a trench at a safe distance, and thus conduct the stream into a basin in the earth prepared for it.

These facts concerning the phenomena which follow insignificant artificial openings of natural reservoirs of gas and oil dimly illustrate what might happen in such a region as the Dead Sea, where earthquake movements were liable to open and at the same time ignite them upon a larger scale. The description given in Genesis is so simple, straightforward, lifelike, and accurate that it can be regarded as scarcely anything else than the report of an eye-witness who beheld the scene from the heights of Hebron, fifteen or twenty miles distant. The raining of brimstone (or pitch) upon the plain from heaven, and the picture of the smoke coming up from the deep depression of the Dead Sea as " the smoke of a furnace " is something unique in literature. It is not that of an ordinary volcano or earthquake, but most forcibly suggests the accompanying phenomena of the bursting and burning of such pent-up reservoirs of gas and petroleum as we have abundant scientific reason for believing existed in the rock cavities of the region. The brevity with which the narrative is given, and the entire subordination of facts to the moral purposes of the history, mark the description as belonging to the realm of truth and not of fancy; while the " slime pits " mentioned as characterizing the valley, and the

Vividness of the Description.

recently discovered evidence of the use of bitumen in the construction of ancient Jericho, give fresh reality to the whole description of the sacred writer.

As thus viewed, however, while the mediate character of the miracle is manifest, the transaction is not removed from the realm of the truly supernatural. Though wrought by natural means, to accomplish all the purposes these had to be supernaturally applied in order to emphasize both then and forever a great moral principle. By natural means all the main elements of the plot had been prepared. During long geological ages the Cretaceous limestones with their included carbonaceous matter had been accumulating upon the floor of a widespreading sea. Subjected to heat and pressure during later ages, the tremendous reservoir of force represented in the accumulations of gas and oil under high pressure had been formed by slow distillation. In the plan of the universe the forces had been so balanced and set at work that in the shrinkage of the earth's crust the great geological fault of the Dead Sea should be slowly formed. By an equally comprehensive and still more mysterious parallel plan the course of human history had been such that the development of wickedness in Sodom and Gomorrah had reached its height, so that Abraham, in obedience to an impulse from heaven, was sojourning amid the hills of Palestine and was exercising special solicitude for the welfare of his relatives in Sodom when the earthquake and the lightning from heaven became God's ministers to unlock the forces of Nature and unfold before the world a spectacular moral lesson which mankind has always needed and can never forget.

God's Presence in the Event.

MEDIATE MIRACLES. 131

Thus it is that the hand of God is frequently revealed in history through the combination of the innumerable forces of Nature which bear upon the development of mankind. The close student of history can but be more and more impressed with the extent of the providential factors which determine its development. It is still as true as ever that the race is not always to the swift or the battle to the strong. The keys which unlock the great events of the future are in the hands of the Almighty. It is as easy for him to direct the forces of the universe as it is for us to direct the forces stored up in our bodily organization.

A startling illustration of how other events like that which destroyed the cities of the plain may be included in the constitution of the world and in the parallel development of human history, has recently been brought to light in the investigations of Mr. G. K. Gilbert,* of the United States Geological Survey, with reference to the hazards of Salt Lake City. Like Sodom and Gomorrah, this great centre of Mormonism is built on the line of an extensive geological fault, along which for ages there have been intense periodic movements of the earth's crust. It is only a few years since there was a vertical displacement of ten or twelve feet along the line of faulting on the opposite side of the basin facing the Sierra Nevada Mountains, which almost totally destroyed the small villages contiguous to it, and which would have been sufficient to have demolished in a moment any city which should have been built upon

The Analogy of Salt Lake City.

---

* See Monograph of the United States Geological Survey on Lake Bonneville, pp. 360–362.

it. Doubtless the contingency of a destructive earthquake along the line of fault skirting the face of the Wahsatch Mountains and passing through Salt Lake City is slight at any particular time. The contingency is perhaps too remote for human calculation, and would probably offer a profitable business for any association that should insure against earthquakes. But it is certain that this is a line along which the strata have been for a long time subjected to special stress, producing extensive upward movements along one side of it within recent geological times.

The Noachian Deluge.

The Noachian deluge is another of those great historic events embedded in the Mosaic account whose claim to a miraculous character chiefly rests upon its relation to human history. The flood is said to have been brought upon the earth for the punishment of man, who had so deeply corrupted his ways that there was only a single family left which was worthy of preservation—an application of the law of natural selection which very readily falls in with the underlying principles of the Darwinian hypothesis.

The question of the credibility of the Mosaic account of the flood calls for attention both to the proper interpretation of the account itself and to the scientific aspects of the physical forces which were involved in the catastrophe. Careful study of the account itself and a reasonable interpretation of it will prepare the way both for confidence in its general representations and for a plausible theory of its adjustment to the startling facts of recent geological history.

A comparison of the biblical account of the deluge with that which is found on the cuneiform tablets from the ruined cities of Babylonia clearly shows that they both relate to the same event, and that both had assumed their present form at a very early date, while at the same time it is equally apparent that they had independent literary origin, and that the biblical account is upon its face much more conformable to a probable development of the natural forces involved than the Babylonian account is. Indeed, while the Babylonian account transcends all bounds of reasonable probability, the biblical account can not be shown to transcend it in any particular, except it should be thought by some that a prophetic announcement of it to Noah is incredible.

The Biblical and Cuneiform Accounts compared.

Going through them, item by item, we find that the cuneiform inscription is parallel throughout with the account as it stands in Genesis.*

1. Noah and Xisuthrus are each the tenth generation in Chaldea, though in the case of Noah the locality is an inference, since there is no account of any migration from the valley of the Euphrates in Gen. ii, 14, but the use of pitch in large quantities in building the ark incidentally indicates the same region in Babylonia.

2. Both accounts describe the vessel and its construction, but they do not agree in the dimensions. The translation of the cuneiform tablet is not certain, but is generally supposed to make the length 600 cubits (1,000 feet), and the width and height 140 cubits (240

---

* In preparation of this parallel I am much indebted to Prof. John D. Davis's valuable volume on Genesis and Semitic Tradition.

feet); while the Hebrew makes the length 300 cubits (500 feet), the width 50 cubits (80 feet), and the height 30 cubits (50 feet), which is not far from the dimensions of some of our modern transatlantic steamers. (The Kaiser Wilhelm du Grosse, built in 1897 for the North German Lloyd line, is 648 feet long, 65 feet broad, and 43 feet deep.) The proportions are mechanically reasonable, while those of the cuneiform tablets are unreasonable. No such craft as that described in the Babylonian tablets could hold together. It violates all mechanical laws. Berosus was still more unreasonable in this respect, since he made the ark 3,000 feet long and 1,200 feet broad!

3. According to both accounts, the ship was built by "divine direction, and was divided, according to divinely furnished plans, into compartments provided with a door and window, pitched within and without with bitumen, and roofed over to protect it from the sea." But the cuneiform tablet represents the ark as a ship demanding a pilot, while the Bible represents it as drifting on the water.

4. According to both accounts, the hero and his family, with animals needing preservation, were told to enter the ark; but Xisuthrus takes with him "his wife, his menservants and maidservants, the artisans, and a pilot," while Noah takes only his wife and his three sons and their wives.

5. According to both accounts, the heroes obeyed the divine command and entered the vessel. Whereupon "the storm burst, and the flood prevailed, and mankind was destroyed." The Bible account refers both to rain and to the breaking up of the fountains of the great deep as causing the flood. The cuneiform also

speaks not only of the rain but of the deluge "which had destroyed like an earthquake." *

6. Both accounts agree that the ship finally stranded on a mountain. The Bible says on the mountains of Ararat, a very general term anciently designating the plain of the Araxes in Armenia, while the cuneiform tablet gives the name of the mountain as Nitsir, about three hundred miles south of Ararat proper, near the little Zab River, east of Mesopotamia. It is significant that both of these places are up stream from the starting place.

7. Both of the accounts mention the sending out of birds to determine the condition of the country; but, in addition to the dove and the raven, the cuneiform tablets mention a swallow instead of the second dove in Genesis.

8. Both accounts mention the promise that the earth shall not again be destroyed by flood. In the cuneiform this is represented as being the result of the god Hea's intercession. Instead of with a flood, he asks that men should be destroyed hereafter by lions, leopards, famines, and pestilence, singling out individual sinners.

9. Both accounts represent the hero as building an altar and offering sacrifices upon leaving the ark, the savour of which was sweet to the Deity.

It is proper to observe also that the cuneiform tablets combine in one account, and in substantially the same order with that of Genesis, both the so-called Elohistic and the Jehovistic documents, supposed by many critics to have been united into one only after the exile. In this comparison, therefore, we have well-nigh scientific

---

* Davis, Semitic Tradition, pp. 117, 118.

demonstration that these critics are wrong in their inferences from literary analysis. The elements of the story had certainly been put together in Babylonia long before the migration of Abraham, more than a thousand years before the exile.

Furthermore, the variations between the accounts show that Genesis was not derived directly from the Babylonian document, but either from an independent or from an older common tradition: 1. The cuneiform tradition is polytheistic; the Hebrew, monotheistic. 2. They differ in details concerning (a) the birds; (b) the chronology; (c) the character of the ship; (d) its size; (e) the number of persons that were saved; (f) and the mountain upon which the ark rested.

Variations in the Two Accounts.

Again, there is abundant evidence that the tradition of the flood was current among the Hebrews before the time of the exile. The critics admit that the Jehovistic account preceded the exile. This includes chaps. vii, 1–5, 7–10, 12; the latter part of 17, 22, 23, except the middle part of 23; viii, the latter part of 2 and first part of 3, 6–12, and the latter part of 13, 20–22.

But the abruptness with which this begins in vii, where Noah is told to come into the ark, implies the preceding Elohistic account of the preparation of the ark. If this Elohistic portion is really from a different document, it must have covered about the same ground which was covered by the confessedly older Jehovistic document.

Again, there is to some extent the same combination of rhetorical and prosaic styles in both the accounts. For example, in describing the storm, the Babylonian writer says:

"As soon as the dawn appeared, a dark cloud ascended on the horizon. In the midst of it the storm god rolled the thunder. The gods Nebo and Marduk marched on before and went as guides over hill and dale; the mighty pest god tore loose the ship; the god Ninib caused the streams to overflow their banks; the Anunnaki lifted torches and made the land to flicker; the storm god raised billows which reached to heaven. All light was turned to darkness; man saw not his fellow, human beings were not discerned by those in heaven." This is the language of enthusiasm and poetry. But when the narrator comes to state how long the storm lasted, he adopts a very different style of speech, saying: "Six days and six nights wind, storm, and rain prevailed; on the seventh day the rain abated, the storm, which had struggled like a woman in travail, rested, the sea withdrew to its bed, the violent wind and the flood storm ceased."*

Unity of the Account in Genesis. The attempt to make out that there are two combined accounts in Genesis containing irreconcilable chronologies is little more than a gratuitous supposition, for they can readily enough be arranged in one continuous chronological scheme.†

vii, 4 and 10.	COMMAND TO BEGIN EMBARKING THE ANIMALS,	2d mo., 10th day.
vii, 11.	ENTRANCE OF NOAH INTO THE ARK, and, later in the day, bursting of the storm,	2d mo., 17th day.
vii, 12.	Rain was upon the earth forty days and forty nights, so that the RAIN CEASED toward evening,	3d mo., 27th day.
vii, 24. viii, 3b.	The waters prevailed on the earth one hundred and fifty days, so that the	
viii, 4.	ARK STRANDED,	7th mo., 17th day.

---

* Davis, Genesis and Semitic Tradition, p. 127. † Ibid., p. 132.

	The waters decreased continually until the	
viii, 5.	TOPS OF THE MOUNTAINS WERE SEEN,	10th mo., 1st day.
viii, 6.	After seeing the mountain tops, Noah waited forty days, expecting that, as the rain had fallen forty days, the waters would perhaps abate from the ground in forty days; and then (or on the following day) the	
	RAVEN RELEASED, which returned not,	11th mo., 11th (or 12th) day.
	After seven days ("Yet other," v. 10), a	
viii, 8.	DOVE RELEASED, which returned,	11th mo., 18th (or 19th) day.
viii, 10.	After yet other seven days, the DOVE RELEASED, which returned with an olive leaf. So Noah knew that the waters were abated from off the earth.	11th mo., 25th (or 26th) day.
	And yet other seven days, a third time the	
viii, 12.	DOVE RELEASED, which did not return, since by this time food and shelter were to be found outside of the ark,	12th mo., 2d (or 3d) day.
	Notwithstanding these favourable indications, Noah did not leave the ark, but waited for God's command. After nearly a month's waiting, on New Year's day,	
viii, 13b. viii, 13b.	NOAH REMOVED THE COVERING OF THE ARK, and saw that the waters were dried up and the face of the ground was dried,	1st mo., 1st day.
	But Noah still awaited God's bidding, and eight weeks later, the earth being dry, God gave the	
viii, 14, 15.	COMMAND TO GO FORTH FROM THE ARK,	2d mo., 27th day.

If it should be said that it is exceedingly improbable that in that early age of the world a ship of the dimensions mentioned in Genesis should have been built, we reply that we are in danger of underestimating the mechanical capacity of the civilized races of those times. If it were not for the facts themselves which greet our eyes in Egypt and amid the deserts of Syria, it would be thought incredible that the vast stones which are built into the pyramids or set up as monoliths could have been carved out of the granite mountains and transported and elevated to their present position. But, as it is, the facts speak for themselves, and indicate a development of mechanical capacity thousands of years before the Christian era which is scarcely exceeded by that of the present day. Many of these blocks are of such size that modern engineers would hesitate to attempt their removal. In view of such facts, the cautious historian will be slow to discredit the ability of the early Babylonian people to build a vessel of the dimensions given for the ark in the book of Genesis. Especially is this the case since the whole tendency of recent discoveries is to remove to earlier and earlier dates the rise of civilization in the valley of the Euphrates.

Improbability exaggerated.

It is important to notice also that the Bible account of the deluge describes the flood as due not only to the rain from heaven, but to the breaking up of the fountains of the great deep, thus naturally describing the incoming of water in connection with a subsidence of land.

Natural Agencies invoked.

Special notice is due also to the fact that both accounts represent the ark as moving up stream and landing far to the northward of the place where it was built. This is not the description of an ordinary river flood which would have swept the vessel out to the sea, and it can scarcely be imagined that such a description of its course can be anything but a real photograph of the event. No *a priori* ideas or natural tendencies of thought would have led to that kind of embellishment of the story, for it is contrary to all the natural suggestions which would be stimulated by ordinary experience.

So far the facts look toward a flood caused by a local subsidence of greater or less extent which should admit the waters of the ocean into the area of the Euphrates Valley where the civilization described in the early part of the book of Genesis had arisen. From a naturalistic point of view, it is instructive to notice that the miraculous element in this account is not excessive, but is introduced with due regard to the scientific law of parsimony. It is not represented that there was a total destruction of the human race or of the animal creation, but these are preserved by natural means for the repeopling of the earth. A reasonable interpretation of the account also, which is in accordance with our known knowledge of the frequent use of language in literature, brings the events of the narrative easily within the limits of possibility.

Interpretation of the Biblical Account.

Long before the rise of geology and of the doubts which it has raised concerning the contemporaneous universality of the flood, it was noted by various learned commentators that the biblical account of the deluge bore evidence that it was written by an eyewitness, and hence should be interpreted according to the natural limitations of such writing. In documents thus prepared metonymy has a pre-eminent place. The language describes what appears to the senses, and does not go beyond the phenomena which are visible. It does not try to settle minute extraneous questions. Nothing is more common than this figure of speech, where the part is put for the whole, and the horizon which limits our vision is spoken of as the horizon of the whole world. It falls to the lot of scientific methods of interpretation to determine the extent to which this figure of speech legitimately modifies the literal interpretation of the text.

For example, we are told in Deut. ii, 25 that the dread and fear of Israel should that day be put "upon the nations that are under the whole heaven." But the interpreter who should insist upon the absolute literality of such a phrase would prove not the point which he intended to prove, but rather the narrowness of his own range of familiarity with literature. So when, in Gen. xli, 54 and 57, it is said that there was a famine "in all lands," or "over all the face of the earth," and that "all countries" came to Egypt to buy corn, it would be only an interpreter of a very narrow acquaintance with literature who should insist that the language was literal, and that the irrigated plains of Babylonia were as dependent upon Egypt as were the hills of Judea. So when the writer of the book of Kings says that Solomon exceeded all the kings of the earth for riches, and that all the earth sought to hear his wisdom,* and when the Saviour says that the Queen of Sheba came "from the uttermost parts of the earth," † he would be a very narrow and ill-informed interpreter

---

* 1 Kings x, 23, 24.   † Matt. xii, 42.

who should insist upon the strict literality of the words. In Acts ii, 25 we are told that there were present in Jerusalem on the day of Pentecost people " out of every nation under heaven," but when the enumeration is made it includes only the region extending from Italy to the Persian Gulf, over which the Jews are known to have spread.

Thus it will readily appear that such general expressions are ordinarily limited in their significance by the circumstances connected with their utterance. When Cæsar is said to have taxed " all the world," and we say that it means all the Roman Empire, we should not be construed to assert that the writer supposed there were no outlying provinces yet unsubdued by the Roman power. And so, when Paul (in 58 A. D) asserts that the faith of the Church at Rome was already " spoken of throughout the whole cosmos," it would be supremely puerile to insist upon the bare literal interpretation of the words.

In accordance with this principle of interpretation, we are permitted to regard the universal statements concerning the flood as being the language of appearances such as would present themselves to eye-witnesses of the catastrophe, and limited in its general results to the main purpose for which it came. As Sir William Dawson has well expressed it, the story of the flood in Genesis reads like a log book in which many things are set down as they actually appeared, and without attempts to reconcile apparent discrepancies.

It is therefore doing no violence to the spirit or letter of this ancient document to give to it an interpretation which limits the phenomena to a comparatively small area in which the civilization of the world was then centred. It is not necessary to suppose that any species of animals were thought to have been taken into the ark for preservation except those which belonged to the limited area concerned.

When now we come to consider the scientific evidence bearing upon the credibility of the Mosaic narrative, we shall naturally expect it to be circumstantial and indirect. The most which science can be asked to do is to determine whether the geological conditions which have prevailed since man came into the world have been such that a catastrophe like that of the flood is within the range of credibility. Is violence done to our knowledge of meteorological and geological forces if we suppose a temporary subsidence of land in the valley of the Euphrates sufficient to destroy the races which inhabited the region? We answer that, instead of such a catastrophe being scientifically impossible of belief, it is rendered peculiarly credible by several lines of recent investigation.

The Scientific Evidence Indirect.

Lessons from the Glacial Period.

It is with constantly growing wonder that the scientific world is looking upon the rapid accumulation of facts relating to the Glacial period and the instability of the earth's crust illustrated by them; while the widespread effects which the conditions of this period produced in the destruction and redistribution of the species of animal and plant life upon the globe are more and more impressive as we follow them out in detail. Evidence has also accumulated till it is practically beyond controversy that the human race has a greater antiquity than was formerly supposed, and has shared the vicissitudes of at least the later portion of the Glacial period. A brief enumeration of the facts will be sufficient for our present purpose.

During the Glacial period an area of about four million square miles in North America and of two million in Europe was covered with ice to an average depth of three quarters of a mile or more, while all the high mountain ranges of Europe and Asia bore on their flanks local glaciers of great size. Probably there was not less than six million cubic miles of water locked up in these great glacial accumulations. This water had been evaporated from the surface of the ocean, thereby lowering its level the world over to the extent of nearly two hundred feet. It requires but a moment's calculation to see that this transfer of water from the ocean to definite land areas was an event of great significance among the physical causes which are modifying the surface of the earth. The pressure of its immense weight was removed from the ocean beds and was added to that of the land masses of the northern hemisphere. If, therefore, there is even any moderate degree of instability in the earth's crust, this transfer of force from the ocean to the land would naturally disturb the equilibrium and lead to a variety of important but not easily calculated results. Certainly the northern lands were greatly depressed during this period, whether by reason of this great weight of ice or from other causes which acted concurrently with it is immaterial to our present purpose.

The complexity of the cause was increased by the subsequent melting of the ice and the consequent relief of pressure from the glaciated region and restoration of the former amount of pressure to the ocean bed. As this melting evidently took place before the return of the land to its present altitude, the increased volume of the waters of the ocean must have added to the height of the flood which submerged much of the northern hemisphere. From the direct evidences of old shore lines and terraces we know that at the close of the Glacial period the coast of Maine was submerged to a depth of 230 feet, the central portions of the St. Lawrence Valley to a depth of 500 feet, the northern part of Labrador to a depth of a 1,000 feet, and of Grinnell Land 2,000 feet, while in Scotland and Scandinavia the depression was somewhere between 500 and 1,000 feet.

While it is not probable that the account of the Noachian flood takes direct cognizance of this whole post-glacial submergence, we shall see a little later that there are many reasons for believing that it may refer to a submergence which was much more extensive than the Euphrates Valley. It will be important also to notice the bearing of these general facts concerning the Glacial period upon the distribution and destruction of the plants and animals which were in existence previous to the advent of the period.

The indirect influence of this advancing ice sheet of the Glacial period probably exceeded the direct influence in its effects upon the plants and animals which fled before it. All the species which had before spread over British America and the northern part of the United States were gradually crowded down into the restricted areas between the Atlantic coast and the Mississippi basin in the southeastern part of the

Indirect Effects of the Glacial Period on Life.

United States and of Mexico. It is a matter of pure speculation to determine what would be the effect of such a struggle for existence between competing species, for it would be a question whether the original occupants of this restricted area would be better able to endure the changed climate produced by the advance of the northern ice or whether the migrating species would be better able to adjust themselves to the conditions of a more southern climate.

In addition to this changing climate and restricted area, there were, during the closing stages of the Glacial period, floods of enormous extent coursing at intervals down the Delaware, the Susquehanna, and the Mississippi Rivers, the marks of which are seen in high-level gravels from one hundred to two hundred feet above the present streams.

As a result of these or other contemporaneous causes, there is known to have been a great destruction of the species at one time associated with man throughout North America. Among these are the mammoth, the mastodon, the rhinoceros, the horse, the grizzly bear, the walrus, the Greenland reindeer, the bison, the moose, and the musk ox, all of whose remains are found in the eastern part of the United States south of the glaciated area, but which had become extinct there before its discovery by Europeans.

Mr. Darwin early called attention to still more general evidence of a destruction of life during the Quaternary period in the southern hemisphere. During his voyage around the world in the Beagle, in 1833,* he

---

* Naturalist's Voyage around the World (New York, 1880), pp. 80, 130, 174.

encountered in Buenos Ayres the clear evidence which that region furnishes of the sweeping changes in forms of animal life which have taken place everywhere in recent geological times. At the time of the discovery of America by Columbus, the horse was entirely absent from the continent; but in those South American plains, where now immense herds of this animal run wild, and where it is no figure of speech to say that beggars ride horseback, there is abundant evidence that the horse, with a large number of immense quadrupeds associated with him, lived and flourished up to recent geological time, and then mysteriously disappeared. Among these companions of the horse in South America were the mastodon, the megatherium, the megalonyx, a species of camel, the toxodon, and a hollow-horned ruminant closely allied to the European cattle. By comparison it will be seen that these are substantially the same species of animals which characterized North America at this same period; and whose bones are found in the recent geological deposits of California, of the Rocky Mountain plains, and in eastern United States.

It is impossible—Darwin remarks—to reflect on the changed state of the American continent without the deepest astonishment. Formerly it must have swarmed with great monsters—now we find mere pigmies compared with the antecedent allied races. . . . The greater number, if not all, of these extinct quadrupeds lived at a late period, and were the contemporaries of most of the existing sea shells. Since they lived no very great change in the form of the land can have taken place. What, then, has exterminated so many species and whole genera? The mind at first is irresistibly hurried into the belief of some great catastrophe; but thus to destroy animals, both large and small, in southern Patagonia, in Brazil, on the Cordillera of Peru, in North America up to Behring's Straits, we must shake the entire framework of the globe. An examination, moreover, of the geology of La Plata and Patagonia, leads to the belief that all the features of the land result from slow and gradual changes. It appears from the character of the fossils in Europe, Asia, Australia, and in North and South America, that those conditions which favour the life of the *larger* quadrupeds were lately coextensive with the world; what those conditions were no one has yet even conjectured.

Nevertheless, if we consider the subject under another point of view, it will appear less perplexing. We do not steadily bear in mind how profoundly ignorant we are of the conditions of existence of every animal, nor do we always remember that some check is constantly preventing the too rapid increase of every organized being left in a state of Nature. . . . If asked how this is, one immediately replies that it is determined by some slight difference in climate, food, or the number of enemies, yet how rarely, if ever, we can point out the precise cause and manner of action of the check! We are therefore driven to the conclusion that causes generally quite inappreciable by us determine whether a given species shall be abundant or scanty in numbers.*

To what extent glacial man was exterminated by these forces that were so clearly operative with other species can not be definitely determined; it is, however, the more prevalent opinion of archæologists that he did not survive the changes, but became extinct both in North America and in Europe, and that these regions were repeopled by subsequent immigrants. Certain it is that there is a notable gap between the remains of

Man and the Glacial Period.

---

* Naturalist's Voyage around the World, pp. 173-175.

paleolithic man found in the glacial gravels and in the lowermost beds of the cave deposits (in connection with the remains of many extinct animals) and the remains of neolithic man which are associated only with existing species. This wholesale destruction of animal life in connection with the changes of the Glacial period may with great plausibility be regarded as giving special significance to the culminating event of the series which is recorded in the literature of the Semitic nations. It is even not wholly beyond the limit of reasonable possibility to suppose that the last remnants of the human race, long depleted by the successive inroads made by these changes upon their vitality, may have been cooped up at that time in western Asia and the regions adjoining.

Prestwich on the Recent Submergence of Western Europe.

It remains to recount some of the direct evidence of an extensive but short submergence extending to a depth of twelve or fifteen hundred feet, which seems to have taken place in western Europe and about the shores of the Mediterranean since the advent of man to that region. The evidence has been collected with scrupulous care and discussed with great acumen by the late Sir Joseph Prestwich,* whose authority, it is

---

* The Raised Beaches, and "Head" or Rubble Drift, of the South of England: their relation to the Valley Drifts and to the Glacial Period; and on a Late Post-glacial Submergence. From the Quarterly Journal of the Geological Society, vol. xlviii, pp. 263–343. London, 1892.

The Evidences of a Submergence of Western Europe, and of the Mediterranean Coasts, at the Close of the Glacial or So-called Post-glacial Period, and immediately preceding the Neolithic or

needless to say, is second to that of no other geologist of his generation.

One class of facts described by the distinguished author relates to numerous deposits of "head," or rubble drift in southern England and northern France containing paleolithic implements and the bones of extinct animals. These accumulations are so distributed as to preclude their explanation by the ordinary agency of ice or running water. The deposits are distributed upon all sides of central areas of higher land in a manner which would indicate that they were carried to their places by the waves produced by numerous short and sharp successive shocks of elevation. The number and variety of animal bones found in this rubble drift would indicate, according to Prof. Prestwich, that the animals had been driven in motley array to the summit of the elevations and

Rubble Drift or "Head."

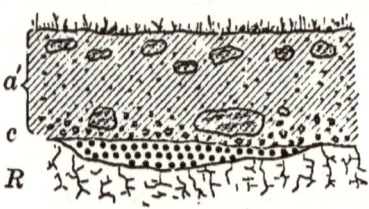

Fig. 1.—Section of the raised beach and head on the north side of Port Ann Bay. *a'*, "head," largely composed of loam roughly bedded with fragments, and a few angular blocks of the rocks above the hills, 12 feet; *c*, raised beach, chiefly of diorite pebbles, 2 feet; *R*, diorite rock.

Recent Period. [From the] Philosophical Transactions of the Royal Society of London, vol. clxxxiv (1893) A, pp. 903-984. (Plate 33.) London: Kegan Paul, Trench, Trübner & Co., 1893.

A Possible Cause for the Origin of the Tradition of the Flood. Author's copy. Pp. 38.

The argument is further summarized in the last production from the lamented author's pen, On Certain Phenomena belonging to the Close of the Last Geological Period and of their Bearing upon the Tradition of the Flood. Pp. 87. Macmillan & Co., 1895.

there had perished together beneath the slowly rising tide.

Another class of deposits of even more striking character occur in the ossiferous fissures, some of which were originally described by Dr. Buckland in his Reliquiæ Diluvianæ. These are not caverns in the ordinary sense of the word, but simply fissures, open at the top and extending down perpendicularly or at a slight inclination sometimes one hundred and forty feet. They are filled with angular rock fragments, broken and splintered bones whose fractured edges are unworn and sharp, all cemented together in a matrix of sand, earth, and clay through which lime has filtered, making what is called a breccia. The bones represent the horse, ox, deer, wolf, hyena, tiger, hare, water rat, weasel, boar, and some other animals; but in no case is there a whole skeleton found, nor had any of the bones been worn by running water or been gnawed by the teeth of other animals.

Ossiferous Fissures.

One of the most remarkable of these ossiferous fissures occurs at Santenay, near Chalons, in central France. This is situated upon an isolated hill one thousand feet above the valley of the Saone and sixteen hundred feet above the sea. Near the summit of this hill the fissure under consideration occurs, containing the same promiscuous variety of bones that has been before mentioned. None had been gnawed, and the fractures are not such as would have been made by men or animals for the purpose of extracting the marrow. M. Gaudry, of the French Academy, justly asks, "Why should so many wolves, bears, horses, and oxen

At Santenay.

have ascended a hill isolated on all sides?" Prof. Prestwich, after a careful discussion of all the facts, agrees with the French geologists who visited the place together, that there is no adequate explanation except that of a gradual submergence of the land driving the animals in the plains to seek refuge on the higher hills. Flying in terror and cowed by the common danger, the carnivora and herbivora alike sought refuge in the same spot, and alike suffered the same fate wherever the hill

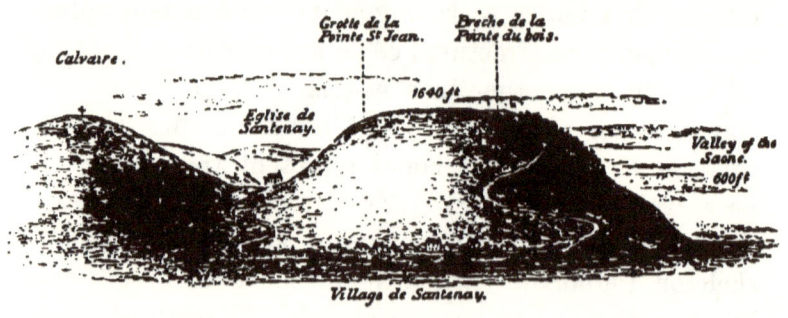

Fig. 2.

was isolated and not of a height sufficient for them to escape the advancing flood. "We may suppose the subsidence to have been so slow that there was no sudden rush of waters to carry the bodies far away, so that as they decayed the limbs fell and were scattered and dispersed irregularly on the submarine surface. When that surface was again upheaved, the bones and detached limbs, together with the detritus on that surface, were carried down by divergent currents to lower levels, or they fell into fissures of the rock over which the detrital matter passed."

Similar facts from the rock of Gibraltar are even more impressive. There we have fissures of the same character filled with a breccia containing the same motley intermingling of bones of herbivorous and carnivorous animals. These animals could not at any time have lived together upon the rock. The deer and other ruminants whose remains abound must have "frequented the surrounding plains

At Gibraltar.

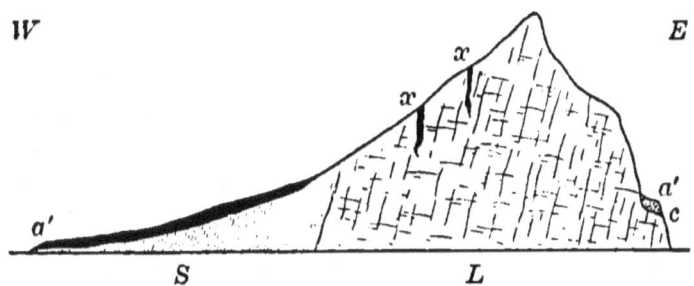

Fig. 3.—Section across Sugar Loaf Hill, Gibraltar, 1,370 feet high.

and forests, where they could have found food, shelter, and water, rather than the scrags—dry and in great part barren. . . . It could only have been a great and com-

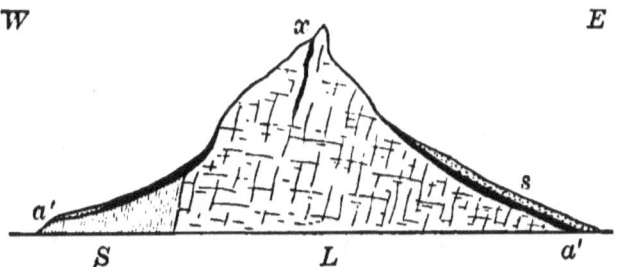

Fig. 4.—Section across Middle Hill, Gibraltar, 1,138 feet high. a', limestone breccia or rubble drift; L, limestone; S, shale; x, ossiferous fissures; c, raised beach (Fig. 3); s, sands.

mon danger, such as that of the gradual encroachment of the sea on the land, that could have so paralyzed their natural instincts as to have driven those various animals to flock together in search of a common place of refuge from a catastrophe which threatened all alike. Under such circumstances the ruminants would naturally flee from the plains to the higher hills, and when these were isolated, as in this and other cases I have named, whenever the waters rose above those hills, they were drowned, and their limbs dispersed in the manner I have before described." *

Another striking deposit of similar significance occurs near Palermo, upon the island of Sicily, where there is an ossiferous breccia of a very remarkable and unique character, containing an enormous number of hippopotamus bones, which are so fresh that they are cut into ornaments and polished, and when burnt give out ammoniacal vapour. More than twenty tons of bones were shipped from this one place for commercial purposes in the first six months after their discovery. The bones were mostly those of hippopotami, with a few only of deer, ox, and elephant. They belonged to animals of all ages down to the fœtus. The bones of the various animals were mixed together without order, and were broken, scattered, and dispersed in fragments, and none of them bore marks of gnawing. The collection is at San Ciro, about two miles from Palermo, and is at the base of the remarkable amphitheatre of hills surrounding the plain on all sides, except toward the sea. The hills are from two thousand to four thousand feet in height. The amphitheatre is from two to four miles in diameter, and the elevation of the rock shelter is about two hundred feet above the sea.

At Palermo.

---

* The Evidences of a Submergence of Western Europe, etc., pp. 944, 945.

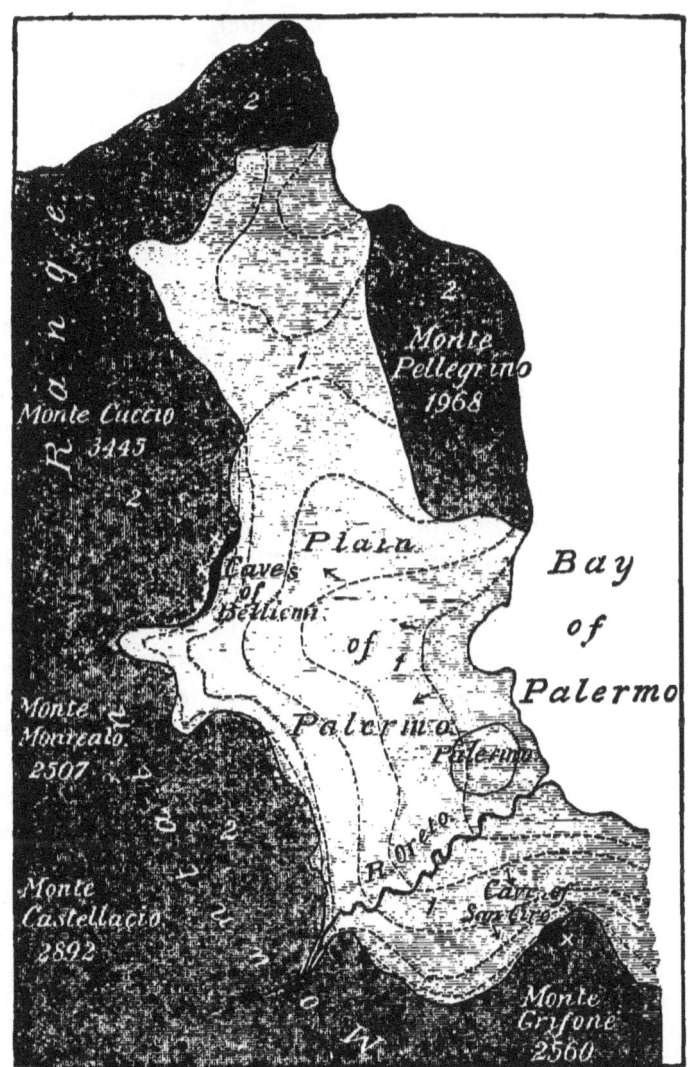

Fig. 5.—x, caves—ossiferous breccia; 1. Pliocene strata; 2, Cretaceous and Jurassic strata. The boundary line between 1 and 2 is from 150 to 200 feet above tide. The slope thence to the sea is very gradual. The limestone rocks above this rise abruptly, forming steep cliffs and mural precipices, with breaks in the direction of Monrealo and the head of the River Oreto. The dotted lines represent the portions of the plain gradually occupied by the advance of the sea.

The circumstances, therefore, which led to these remarkable accumulations of the remains of the hippopotami must have been *extraordinary*, and I see no hypothesis which meets the case so well—remarks Prof. Prestwich—as the one that I have suggested to account for the bones of mammalia in the rubble drift and in the ossiferous fissures, though the local conditions in this case are peculiar.

On the submergence of the Sicilian area, the wild animals of the plains would, as in the case of Santenay, Cette, and Gibraltar, be driven to seek refuge on the nearest adjacent high ground and hills. In the instance before us, the animals must have fled to the amphitheatre of hills which encircle the plain of Palermo on all sides except the sea, and on the slopes of which the Cave of San Ciro and the others are located. As the waters rose, the area of this plain became more and more circumscribed, and retreat more and more impossible, except through a few rare passes in the range of hills, until, at last, the animals were driven together at the base of the hills, where they were stopped by mural precipices impassable to the larger and heavier animals, though some of the more active and agile ruminants and carnivores may have, and, judging by the rarity of their remains, probably did escape to the mountains behind. Retreat entirely cut off by projecting promontories on either side, the only paths yet open to the imprisoned herds were those that led to the caves, which were a little above the general level of the plain. Hither the animals must have thronged in vast multitudes, crushing into the caves and swarming over the ground at their entrance, where they were eventually overtaken by the waters and destroyed, and, as their bodies decayed, a confused mass of their remains were left and scattered on or near the spot where they had finally congregated.

For reasons before given, the land could not have remained long submerged. As it rose intermittently from beneath the waters, our supposition is that the rocky *débris* on the sides of the hills was hurled down by the effluent waters on to the piles of bones below, breaking them into fragments, and forming, together with them, the heterogeneous mass of bones and rubble constituting the breccia. The last more rapid uplift, the effects of which are so frequently seen in many sections of the *head*, brought down the larger blocks of rock that now lie on the top of the whole. Scinà, an independent witness, inferred from the character of the rock fragments, and from the red clay in which they are embedded—and which comes from decomposed rock surfaces on the hills above—that, in the case of the Belliemi breccia, both the detritus and the bones had been washed down from Monte Belliemi. All this must have been effected in a space of time comparatively so short, that, though the bodies of the animals decayed, the bones underwent but little change, nor, encased as they became in an almost impermeable breccia, has the change they have since undergone been great.

Thus there is, in all the essential conditions, a close agreement between this Sicilian breccia and the rubble drift of the south of England, as likewise with the rubble on the slopes of the rock of Gibraltar, and of other places mentioned in the preceding pages. In all, the *débris* consists strictly of local materials; the fragments are angular and sharp; the bones are mostly in fragments, and are neither gnawed nor worn; and the faunal remains are those alone of a land surface, and of species such as then were to be found in the district. This rubble, also, forms in all these cases the last of the drift beds. The only apparent difference arises from the circumstance that, in the Sicilian area, the geographical configuration was that of a landlocked bay with many minor bays or embrasures in the front of the hill range, so that, as the waters rose, the animals of the plain were driven together, as in a seine, into those bays where, as a last resource, they sought shelter under the mural precipices and in the more accessible caves. As these precipices were nearly vertical, they formed, as the land rose again, a partial protection from the effluent currents, which otherwise might have carried the *débris* to a greater distance outward. Under no other circumstance that I can conceive could the animal remains have been massed as they are at the foot of the escarpments encircling the plain of Palermo.

It may be asked how could large herds of hippopotami have existed in so limited a plain as that of Palermo. It needed then to have had much greater extent and larger rivers. I have shown that the present height of the raised beaches on the English coast does not give the initial upheaval, but is the sum of the differences of several earth movements—that the primary upheaval of the beaches was not less than a hundred to a hundred and fifty feet greater than the altitude at which they now stand, and that this led to the conversion of a considerable extent of the area of the Bristol and English Channels into dry land. What little evidence we have on the coast of Malta, and of Greece, points to similar elevations of the coasts of the Mediterranean, so that large tracts of dry land may then have existed between the Sicilian and Italian shores, and formed suitable pasture grounds for the hippopotami. With the increase of the land area, so would the rivers also have had increased size, and though they may not have been very large, yet as Sir S. Baker has shown, perennial waters are not indispensable to the hippopotamus, for in the Settite and other rivers of the Soudan, these huge animals tide over the dry season by resorting to the few pools left in the dried-up channels of the rivers.*

Not to pause too long upon the numerous other facts collected by Prof. Prestwich bearing upon this point, we turn finally to select one from his many illustrations drawn from the "loess deposits of Europe." It is well, however, to call the attention of the reader to the fact that the origin of the loess is one of the most

<small>Deposits of Loess.</small>

---

* Evidences of a Submergence of Western Europe, etc., pp. 959–962.

difficult problems which geologists have to consider, and that here, as in the other evidence, it is the wide experience and great skill of Prof. Prestwich which have enabled him clearly to see the bearing of the facts presented. For evidently the loess has been distributed by a variety of agencies. It is only in special conditions that its occurrence can have the significance which Prof. Prestwich assigns to it in the instances adduced by him.

Loess is a very fine loam without any intermixture of sand or gravel, or indeed of any grit, and without any remains of marine or fluviatile shells, which in various regions occurs upon the surface of the country. Along the Missouri River from Kansas City far up into Dakota, loess forms the lining bluffs of the valley, having a depth of more than a hundred feet. Large areas in China are covered with it to even greater depths, while its occurrence along the valley of the Rhine accounts for the German name by which it is ordinarily designated. The anomalous facts connected with its distribution have greatly puzzled geologists. The material is so fine that it is readily blown about hither and thither by the wind, so that Baron Richthofen and others maintain that the loess of China is but the accumulated dust which the westerly winds have brought over from the parched and elevated plains of Mongolia and Thibet. The definite relation, however, of the areas of loess to water levels in the valleys of the Mississippi and the Rhine make it certain that in these cases, at any rate, it is a water deposit. Still, the facts are so complicated that Geikie and others think it necessary in central Europe to bring in both wind and water to account for its distribution. In the glaciated regions both of Europe and America many anomalous local deposits of loess can be readily accounted for by the action of water held in place by ice during the retreat of the continental glaciers. No doubt the greater part of the arguments for the flood drawn from the loess by Mr. Howorth and others are explained by fuller knowledge of the irregularities produced by the slowly melting ice sheet which covered the northern parts of the continents of Europe and America. But the facts adduced by Prof. Prestwich have been carefully selected with reference to this danger of error, and strongly confirm the other evidence pointing so clearly to the occurrence of a recent catastrophe in western Europe closely analogous to that described in the biblical account of Noah's flood. A single one of the facts under this head must suffice.

The Channel Islands of Guernsey and Jersey are surrounded by a raised beach which is overlaid by rubble drift such as was described under that title. The greater part of the island, however, consists of a plateau

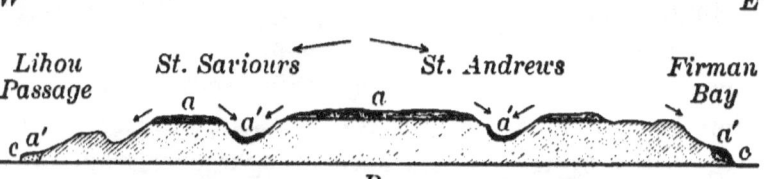

Fig. 6.—Diagram section across the island of Guernsey. *a*, brick earth or loess; *c*, raised beaches; *a'*, rubble drift or head; *R*, slates and granitic rock. The arrows represent the direction of the effluent currents as the land emerged from beneath the waters, leaving portions of the fine sediment on the plateau, but sweeping it off the slopes and down the valleys.

of granitic rocks from three hundred to three hundred and fifty feet above sea level, but without any commanding heights. This plateau is covered very generally by a deposit of loess or brick earth from five to ten feet thick, extending over the highest points of the surface. In character this is identical with that on the mainland.

It is not possible to account for this deposit of loess on any of the theories which are limited to river floods, glacial inundations, or rain wash as the distributing agencies; for—

there are no rivers in either island, and the water courses are mere small brooks that could scarcely flood the lowest ground, and certainly could never, in present nor past times, have reached the plateau on which the loess occurs. Nor are there any hills rising above the general level of the plateaus, the wash from which could have been spread over those plateaus. Nor can it be admitted that it was formed when the island was connected with the mainland, and that the loess is due to the extension of the land flood waters, over what was then part of the continental area; for, unless the loess were older than the raised beaches, it is obvious, as those beaches extended all round the islands, that at the time of the deposition of the loess, the islands were then, as now, detached from the mainland.*

The loess, in fact, is closely connected with the "head" and not infrequently associated with it. A thin layer of an angular rubble similar to that which forms the "head" is also often to be found at the base of the loess, and as the rubble is newer than the beaches, so must the loess likewise be newer, and subsequent therefore to the severance of the islands from the mainland.

. . . That a uniform sediment of that character should be formed during such a submergence as we have described is, owing to the waste of the softer surface beds and decomposed rocks by the advancing waters, what we

---

* Evidences of a Submergence of Western Europe, etc., pp. 913, 914.

might expect. This waste was general over all the area submerged, and the waters must have been rendered turbid to a considerable distance from the coast,* so that not only the mainland but the adjacent islands also were covered with a mantle of sedimentary matter deposited during

Fig. 7.—Sections from La Motte Islet to Mont Ubé, Jersey. *a'*, rubble drift, composed of granitic and diorite *débris* from Mont Ubé, in a brick earth or loess, covered by a sandy earth and soil; *c*, raised beach—only portions of this remain. The elevation of Mont Ubé is 150 feet. La Motte Islet is 1,000 feet from the shore, and is of only a few acres in extent and accessible at low water. It consists of a base of diorite, capped by the remains of an old beach, overlaid by a mass of rubble drift or *head*, the section of which is very similar to that shown in Fig. 1, page 150. The distance to which this rubble drift is here spread out over a gentle slope from its source is too great to have been produced by snow slides.

those periods of comparative quiet or lulls, which are shown to have occurred in the formation of the head.

If we suppose that the loess in these islands was deposited during and after submergence, it follows that as the land rose it would be removed where it was in the way of the effluent currents, and carried with the angular rubble down to lower levels, or to a distance. That this was the case is shown by the fact that the "head" which covers the beaches consists of angular local rubble, with loess or brick earth (derived from the plateaus) as a matrix and forming occasional seams and overlying beds.†

A large number of other confirmatory observations are adduced by Prof. Prestwich in proof of a general

---

* On the coast of China the sea is coloured yellow to a distance of a hundred miles from land by the fine loess mud carried down by the rivers.

† Evidences of a Submergence of Western Europe, p. 914.

submergence of western Europe and the Mediterranean basin which occurred, as he thinks, not more than ten or twelve thousand years ago. How far the evidence of this submergence east of the Mediterranean extends is not known. That region remains still to be investigated.

It is important to observe, however, that reference to these conclusions of Prof. Prestwich is not adduced here so much for the purpose of presenting positive confirmatory evidence of the biblical account as for the sake of illustrating the difficulty of disproving the occurrence of the Noachian deluge. The geological forces which are known to have been in operation since the advent of man upon the earth are so extraordinary and so complicated in their interactions, and the changes which are known to have taken place are so stupendous and have been so rapid, that the Noachian deluge is no extraordinary tax upon our credulity. A faith far less robust than that which Huxley reposed in the capacity of the original atoms will have no difficulty in believing in the occurrence of the Noachian deluge.

Tentative Conclusions.

Accepting the story when properly interpreted as a credible account of actual events, it takes its place among those special providences which are by no means infrequent in the world, and which become significant in proportion to the intimacy of their connection with the main line of divine revelation. In this case the history of the whole human race was intersected by extraordinary physical phenomena of most impressive significance, the story of which has become more firmly embedded in the world's traditions than that of any other event.

We may conclude, therefore, (1) that the biblical story of the flood in substantially its present form was current in Babylonia before the time of Moses; (2) that the biblical form is independent of the Babylonian form; (3) that the traditions imply as a basis of fact the occurrence of a deluge of far greater proportions than the mere overflowing of a river's bank; (4) that there was probably a subsidence in the valley of the Euphrates and of the table-land of Armenia so as to allow the water of the Indian Ocean temporarily to extend far up into Armenia, carrying the ark up stream; (5) that it is not necessary to suppose a destruction of animals except in that single zoological province; (6) that the number of animals known to Noah and to be saved in the ark may have been very limited; (7) so many destructive agencies had been at work in other parts of the world that it is by no means unreasonable to suppose that outside of this region man had perished in company with a large number of other animal species which we know became extinct amid the catastrophes accompanying the Glacial period; (8) while we need not maintain that science demonstrates the truth of the biblical account, we can say that it presents no insuperable objection to the account when properly interpreted, while it does add plausibility to the story by bringing clearly before our minds a period of geological history, since man came into the world, during which there was great instability of the continents and a succession of catastrophes startling in their magnitude and short in their duration which may well have culminated in the Noachian deluge. It certainly would seem important to look more carefully in western Asia for such elevated beaches, shore lines, and other recent deposits as Prof. Prestwich has so fully reported in western Europe.

Bearing of the Discussion upon the Credibility of the New Testament.

It is not necessary in this connection to make an exhaustive study of the miracles of the Old Testament. It is sufficient for our present purpose merely to call attention to their general historical reasonableness. Thus viewed, however, some important objections to the New Testament record are removed, for it can not be denied that the New Testament writers appear to regard the entire record of the Old Testament as authentic. Indeed, Christ himself knew no other literature, and in the most diverse and emphatic manner expressed his confidence in it.

While it is not necessary to impugn the candour or ability of those who attempt to explain away Christ's indorsement of the Old Testament by resorting to theories of accommodation and of self-imposed limitations upon his knowledge in certain directions, the conviction seems inevitable that such theories are so forced and unnatural that their acceptance will endanger our whole confidence in the revelation which Christ and the apostles purported to make. That Jesus was limited in his knowledge is readily granted, since it is involved both in the statements which are made concerning his natural and gradual development in childhood and in his own assertion that he was ignorant of the time of the end of the world.* But that he did

---

* Matt. xxiv, 36.

not fully understand the things which he definitely undertook to state and explain is more than can easily be granted.

Neither is the doctrine of "accommodation" applicable in this case without being stretched beyond "reasonable" bounds. At any rate it is most certain that Jesus did not attempt to "accommodate" himself in general to the erroneous views of the scribes and Pharisees. On the contrary, he did not hesitate to contradict in most emphatic manner many of their false interpretations of the Old Testament.* These well-known denunciations of the scribes and Pharisees by the Saviour make it extremely difficult to believe that he would have hesitated to expose their grand illusion respecting the historical basis of the Old Testament if he had known it to be such. Such evidence, therefore, as we are able to adduce to strengthen the historical basis of the Old Testament is, so far as it goes, a distinct support of the credibility of the New Testament writers who have so emphatically indorsed it.

It should, however, be added that we are at liberty to disclaim the indorsement by the New Testament writers of the unreasonable and incorrect interpretations of the Old Testament which many, especially the enemies of Christianity, impose upon it. The general indorsement of the Old Testament by the New extends only to a fair interpretation of it, and is tempered by the consideration that the text of the Old Testament is enveloped in some such degree of uncertainty as has all along pertained to that of the New. We do not know

Reasonable Interpretation.

---

* See especially the Sermon on the Mount.

that any scholars would now deny that in minor particulars there have been changes and additions to the original text, and that therefore some of the infelicitous and incongruous statements in the Old Testament may be due to this textual corruption.

For example, in certain cases the names applied to places in Palestine are known not to have come into use until after the time of Moses. One clear instance occurs in Gen. xiv, 14, where we are told that Abram pursued Lot's captors unto Dan; but we are elsewhere distinctly told that the original name of this city was Laish (see Josh. xix, 47; Judges xviii, 27–29). Even the most conservative expositors would maintain that the original name was Laish, and would find no difficulty in admitting that the well-known later name had been substituted for the earlier under the easily recognisable influences that bring about minor changes of text in the process of transmission. The substitution of the modern for the ancient name is so natural that it creates no general distrust of the work of the copyist.

Uncertainties of the Text.

Similarly in Gen. xxiii, 2, where Kirjath-Arba is mentioned, an explanation is inserted stating that this is the same as Hebron; while in Gen. xiii, 18 the place is referred to simply as Hebron. Now, since in Josh. xiv, 15 and Judges i, 10 we are expressly told that Kirjath-Arba is the earlier name, the most conservative commentators have had little difficulty in supposing that the explanation in Gen. xxiii, 2 is an addition of a later scribe, and that in Gen. xiii, 18 there was a substitution of the later for the earlier name, such as we supposed had occurred in the case of Dan. Numerous other examples analogous to those which are discussed in connection with the textual criticism of the New Testament (where we have abundant witnesses demonstrating both the existence of such textual corruptions and their limited extent) might be given, to which nearly all conservative scholars would give their assent. We simply allude to them here to illustrate how readily many of the difficulties alleged respecting the Old Testament might be removed if we had the same opportunities for correcting its text which we possess in the case of the New Testament. But in suggesting this mode of relief from minor difficulties we are far from intimating any wholesale distrust of the text of the Old Testament, since the principles of textual criticism so well established in the New Testament do not warrant any such conclusion. In the main we believe it to be established that the sacred literature both of the Old and of the New Testament has been preserved from any serious corruption.

There is, however, one passage in which the incorporation of a marginal note may so easily have produced a difficulty respecting one of the miracles already discussed that we can not refrain from considering it. We refer to the statement in Gen. xix, 26, that Lot's wife "became a pillar of salt." The temptation to the insertion of this clause is so similar to that relating to the descent of an angel to trouble the water in the pool of Bethesda,* which is now generally believed to be an interpolation, that it need occasion no general distrust of the context to suppose that this, like that, is an interpolation which crept in from the margin.†

Lot's Wife.

---

* John v, 4. † See the principle discussed in Chapter VIII.

MEDIATE MIRACLES. 169

Although it would not indeed do any particular violence to the rules of interpretation to say, with Murphy, that this phrase indicates no more than that "the dashing spray of the salt sulphurous rain seems to have suffocated her [Lot's wife] and then to have encrusted her whole body," * still, from what has been said concerning the extent of the salt deposits at the south end of the Dead Sea, it will seem to many more likely that the account has been so modified in transmission as to furnish a reference to some of the prominent pedestals of salt which characterize the region. The introduction of such a reference would rather confirm than invalidate the general correctness of the story, since, while it of itself has an air of incongruity, it coincides with the general representation of a scene the description of which could have come only from eye-witnesses. The entire story could not have been made out of whole cloth. The patchwork, if manifest, is insignificant.

One other alleged miracle which is a special object of the shafts of ridicule is that of the sun's standing still at Joshua's command.† But proper attention to the details of the passage would seem to remove it entirely from the list of miracles in the sphere of Nature. The prose account of the victory of Joshua over the men of Gibeon is found in the tenth and eleventh verses, while the following three verses consist of a poetical account of the same event parenthetically introduced from the book of Jasher which describes the event in the familiar forms of strong figurative lan-

The Sun's standing still.

---

* Commentary of Genesis, *in loco.*   † Josh. x, 12–14.

guage, such as is found in the Eighteenth Psalm, where it is said that the Lord "bowed the heavens also and came down." It is specially to be noticed that the quotation from the book of Jasher throws emphasis upon the object to be accomplished, asserting that the "sun stood still.... until" the nation had avenged themselves of their enemies. The rhetorical nature of the language clearly appears in the variations which characterize the repetition of the same idea; for there we are told not simply that the sun "stood still," but that it "hasted not to go down," which is a very different thing. With our attention properly directed, therefore, to the form of these poetical statements and to the emphasis which is thrown upon the purpose of the prayer, there is no necessity of drawing any further literal meaning out of it than is found in the prose narrative of verses 10 and 11. The day did not close until the victory was complete. In the judicious words of Keil, "The only difference is in the form in which those events are described, for in reality it is the same thing whether the omnipotence of God extends one day to the length of two, or causes as much to be accomplished in *one* day as, without the help of the Almighty, would inevitably require *two*." *

Conclusion.

But it is unnecessary for present purposes to illustrate this subject further here, and it would be impracticable to consider in detail all the opportunities for cavil which spring from possible misinterpretations of the Old Testament literature. It is important, however, that the unsophisticated student be warned against the cool confidence

---

* Commentary *in loco*.

with which many critics assume that the absurdities and incongruities which they impose upon the Old Testament are necessarily drawn from it by fair modes of interpretation. If, on the other hand, we limit ourselves to what is necessarily implied in a fair interpretation of the Old Testament, it will not be difficult to show that its miracles, like those of the New Testament, are neither excessive in amount nor incongruous in character, but are scrupulously confined to the accomplishment of the high moral purposes of the whole revelation. Even the miracle of Jonah's remaining three days and three nights in the whale's belly does not involve so much of an interruption of the ordinary course of Nature as is implied in the account of Christ's death and resurrection. Indeed, on surveying the Old Testament in its entirety, one can not avoid a feeling of surprise and admiration at the success with which the miraculous accounts are limited to the critical points in the history of the race when new revelations of world-wide importance were to be made. In the Old Testament no more than in the New is there anything approaching that indiscriminate opening of the floodgates of the supernatural which has so uniformly overwhelmed those who have without authority assumed to draw down fire from heaven.

CHAPTER VI.

BEYOND REASONABLE DOUBT.

THE subjective law of obligation is unvarying and absolute. Its best popular statement is that given in the New Testament, "Thou shalt love the Lord thy God with all thy heart, and with all thy soul, and with all thy strength, and thy neighbour as thyself." Stated in the language of abstract philosophy, this would be, Thou shalt choose the highest good of sentient being. Obligation begins and ends in good will. So far ethical science deals with an absolute certainty. There is no question that the attitude of one's will should always be that of benevolence. Every one should stand ready always and everywhere to do what will promote the highest good of sentient being.

Benevolence an Absolute Duty.

But what specific actions will promote the good of being? That is the perplexing question. So complex are the conditions of life, and so limited is the horizon of our sight, that we are but imperfect judges of what will be the outcome of our daily activities. We are like children casting pebbles upon the surface of an ocean whose nearer shores are but dimly surveyed, while the more distant are completely out

Subordinate Choices beset with Uncertainty.

of sight. What the disturbances may be which are occasioned by our actions is beyond human calculation. Even if the limit of human life were indefinitely extended so that we should rival the reputed age of the antediluvians, our individual experience would furnish but an infinitesimal base line from which to calculate the distant future. When we endeavour to substitute for our individual experience the experience of others and of previous generations, we are at once launched upon the uncertainties of human testimony and of historical evidence. So manifold and great are these uncertainties that in the matters which most concern mankind later ages do not seem to have much advantage over the earlier. It is, for instance, doubtful if much has been learned in the art of government since the founding of the Roman republic, or, indeed, since the reign of the Pharaohs, while in social life it is doubtful if there is any real improvement over that which prevailed in Judea during the palmy days of Israel's development.

Even in the narrower range of such experiences as are more largely dependent on physical science, the uncertainties of life have been but slightly diminished. The hazards of travel are indeed different from those which formerly beset us, but they still lurk in numberless unexplored recesses both of natural law and of human capacity. The inopportune loosing of a stone by an unwonted shower may hurl the railroad train to destruction at the foot of a precipice. Temporary forgetfulness or mental confusion may lead the long-trusted telegraph operator or switchman to open the way for an accident rather than to close the

Science does not remove Uncertainty.

door against it as he is set to do. In business the most carefully laid plans are only partially adapted to the exigencies of future demand and supply. Even so good a thing as wheat may be produced in larger quantities than is called for by the annual demand, and so the market over a large area be depressed below the margin of profitable production.

In our individual plans the uncertainty of life, as well as its inevitable brevity, interferes with all our activities. No reasonable man can hope for one hundred years of continued activity in the accomplishment of his deepest laid plans; while nothing is more certain than that this activity may be interrupted at any time without a moment's warning. In literal truth, no man knows what a day may bring forth. With all our modern improvements, medicine is still pre-eminently an inexact science, so that it is not strange that many a sensitive student has drawn back from its practice because he dared not take the risk of interfering, except in the plainest of cases, with the operation of the unknown combination of forces ever presenting itself in the disordered mechanism of the human body.

With this degree of uncertainty respecting that which is present and near at hand, we need not be surprised that with respect to things which are far distant from us, both in time and space, the density of the darkness increases to that of almost absolute night. This, however, may not be because there is lack of intelligible marks of design in any portion of the universe, but because of our present inability to interpret the marks.

In presence of what Asa Gray called "the general awe and sense of total insufficiency with which a mortal man contemplates the mysteries which shut him in on every side,"* one naturally and properly turns for guidance to a wisdom that is higher than his own. The real justification of man's dependence upon instinct and authority for the regulation of his conduct lies in his well-grounded belief that it is easier for the Creator to afford us satisfactory grounds for trusting the testimony of well-informed witnesses than it is directly to reveal to us the truths themselves.

While we can not fully fathom the designs of Providence in the limitations which he has imposed upon our faculties, it is not difficult to see that many very valuable advantages come to us from this actual situation. A certain amount of limitation to our knowledge is by no means an unmixed evil; but, when considered with relation to our moral development, and to our social and religious nature, the dependence which is created by our natural limitations is seen to be a positive good, and is clearly indicative of the wisdom and benevolence of the Creator who, at the same time that he has imposed the limitation upon us, has provided the means by which we can gradually escape from its barriers. As it is, no small part of the joy of life consists in the efforts which we put forth to escape from our limitations and solve the mysterious problems of experience.

Uncertainty the Spice of Life.

Indeed, what would life be worth if there was nothing in it but the dull routine of machinery and organized labour? As it is, every day opens to us a new page in the twofold mystery of the relations of human freedom to divine omniscience. The theme is constant, but the variations are endless. Curiosity is both one of the

---

* Asa Gray, Natural Science and Religion, p. 64.

most active and one of the most beneficent impulses of the human mind. If its perversion may be ignoble in the extreme, its proper exercise leads to the noblest results. To have mysteries to inquire into is most essential to man's well-being. Science with her unceasing activities is continually extending the range of human knowledge; but if she were ever to compass the whole sphere of surrounding mysteries, the announcement would be regarded as that of the direst calamity. Henceforth the charm of life would be gone, and the pall of stagnation and death would quench all ambition and stifle all activity.

In all departments of life these limitations to our knowledge drive us to a rational exercise of *faith*—that is, of trust in the wisdom and goodness of superior intelligences and of obedience to the laws of conduct which they reveal to us. It is not difficult to show that ultimately the whole confidence in the order of Nature, by which we guide our investigations in science and direct our several courses in the future, rests upon a latent recognition of all the fundamental attributes of the divine nature. If the Creator reveals himself to man only in part, it is because man is incapable at the time of receiving a larger revelation. The rapidity with which water can be poured into a vessel is determined by the capacity of the orifice as well as by the supply of the liquid. To discharge an ocean upon a narrow-necked bottle would result chiefly in a waste of water.

Faith Inspires all Rational Activity.

The conclusion from all this is that in every branch of human activity man is compelled to accept probability as the guide of life. The ignorance of man relieves him from responsibility as to the outcome of his benevolent choice of specific lines of conduct. He can rest assured that the Creator, who has imposed these limitations of knowledge upon his creatures, has taken upon himself the responsibility of the results. The dictates of conscience, therefore, are absolute in their requirements. Man is made for action. The dimmest light which God has given, if it be all we have, is an infallible basis for right action. Our willingness to act upon the best evidence we have, even though it be imperfect, is the surest touchstone of our character. Neutrality with reference to evidence is impossible. We act if we decide not to act. The hazard of standing still may be greater than that of motion. The military commander never knows exactly what to do. But he does know that he must take the responsibility of doing something. A beleaguered army must choose between the risk of slow starvation and the hazard of battle. The ten lepers outside the walls of Samaria do not know what the result will be if they enter the enemy's camp, but they know that they must do something or die. They do not escape responsibility by sitting still.

<small>Probability the Guide of Life.</small>

Touching matters of mere knowledge, we may be comparatively indifferent. The machinery of the heavens is relatively of little concern to us. God makes the heavens go. It is indeed an ennobling pursuit to find out how he makes them go. But it is an infinitely more important inquiry to ask how we shall make the best of our own opportunities, and make our own lives go well. We shall always find it more important to seek the road that leads to heaven than to seek the paths in which the planets move.

A drowning man is not to be blamed for catching at a straw. Indeed, he is under obligations to catch at a straw if that is the best thing which presents itself. In moral matters doubt is no excuse for inactivity. We are under as complete and imperative obligation to use to the best of our ability the little light we have as we should be to use a good deal more light if we had it. A little knowledge lays on us the responsibility of *beginning* to move.

Respecting the standard of evidence which it is proper to adopt for guidance in practical affairs we may learn much from the rules of procedure in our courts of law. It is more important to give attention to these rules from the fact that they have arisen to meet the exigencies of common life—the very realm in which religious faith is most needed and most effective.

Lesson from the Law.

It must be admitted, however, that legal rules have grown up to meet special conditions, and hence do not apply in full force to the whole range of evidence on which we are compelled to base the daily activities of life. For in Anglo-Saxon countries the jury, to whose decision both civil and criminal cases are submitted, is supposed to be made up of citizens possessing no more than the average amount of experience and intelligence. Such a jury is not expected to be familiar with all the subtleties attending the discussion of many of the obscurer lines of evidence, and which have weight with those who have been amply trained in logic. Indeed, the admission of evidence has to be regulated by the supposed intelligence of the lower half of the jury, so that special pains is taken to admit before them only the main points of evidence, and to shield them from the liability of having their minds diverted by extraneous considerations. On the Continent of Europe, however, trials occur for the most part before trained judges, and a much wider range of evidence is permitted with safety because of their ability to sift the testimony more closely than could be done by inexperienced and uneducated men.

A prime advantage in maintaining trial by jury consists in its adaptation to the prevailing necessities of mankind. The vast majority of men are comparatively uneducated, undisciplined, and inexperienced. But it is upon such a class of minds that we must depend for the support of all the most necessary institutions of society. Their beliefs constitute the most important working force in the progress of civilization. It is the highest duty as well as the highest privilege of statesmen, scholars, and religious leaders to present so clearly the broader views which they have obtained that these shall command the assent of the masses of the people. Unless scholars are thus able to command the assent of the unprejudiced minds of ordinary persons, there is usually good reason to doubt the correctness of their conclusions. It is therefore, we are persuaded, of more account than is sometimes supposed, for the students and investigators in all departments of knowledge to give close attention to the reasons underlying the rules of investigation employed in our courts of justice. The average audience addressed by the preacher is, in its limitation of knowledge and experience, very much like the average jury which is addressed by opposing counsel and instructed by an impartial judge. The preacher is therefore in honour bound to combine in his own address the good qualities supposed to be present both in judge and counsel.

Two Legal Phrases. The limitations of human knowledge and the necessity of deciding upon some line of action in the midst of imperfect knowledge and in the absence of demonstrative proof is very prominently brought to light in two stereotyped phrases which occur in almost every charge given by a judge to the jury. In criminal cases the jury is told to insist that the guilt of the prisoner must be proved beyond a "reasonable doubt," but that they should not insist upon absolute demonstration. In civil cases, however, the injunction upon the jury is that they should give a verdict on the side to which in their opinion there belongs a mere "preponderance of evidence." When inquiry is directed to ascertain just what these phrases mean, it is found that they are incapable of exact definition, and that no hard-and-fast line can be drawn between that which is proved beyond a reasonable doubt and that which is proved by mere preponderance of evidence. Any attempt to give a more specific meaning to "reasonable doubt" is usually set aside, on appeal to the higher courts, as a refinement tending " to confuse the jury, and to render uncertain an expression which, standing alone, is certain and intelligible."

To illustrate the subject, we select extracts from a recent charge given to a jury upon this point.*

As this subject of reasonable doubt [says an Ohio judge] is not always accurately understood, I will explain more

---

* Charge of Judge Nye, State of Ohio *vs.* Berk; approved and adopted by the Supreme Court of the State.

fully what is meant by a reasonable doubt as defined by law.

If, when the jury have considered all the evidence in the case, the guilt of the defendant is not fully proved, then that reasonable doubt exists which should acquit, for the legal presumption of innocence would in such case demand an acquittal.

A Typical Charge to the Jury.

In civil cases it is said the jury weigh the evidence, and when it is sufficient decide according to the preponderance, though a reasonable doubt may exist of the correctness of the decision; but in a criminal case there is neither a preponderance, nor any weight of preponderance which is sufficient, unless it produce in the mind full belief beyond a reasonable doubt.

A reasonable doubt is one which exists in the mind of a reasonable man, after giving due weight to all the evidence, and such as leaves the mind in a condition in which it is not honestly satisfied and not convinced to a moral certainty of the guilt of the accused.

A reasonable doubt is an honest uncertainty existing in the mind of an honest, impartial, reasonable man, after a full and careful consideration of all the evidence, with a desire to ascertain truth regardless of consequences.

But a reasonable doubt is to be distinguished from a mere captious doubt, a mere possible doubt, a mere arbitrary and speculative doubt. If a jury should be fully and clearly convinced of the guilt of the defendant in a case where the evidence established it, and, because of an aversion to punishment, should for that reason create a doubt in the mind that would not otherwise exist, that would not be a reasonable doubt.

The jury have nothing to do with the consequences of their verdict aside from the duty imposed to ascertain truth according to law. A mere speculative doubt, excited in the mind against evidence from any cause to furnish a pretext for acquittal, is not a reasonable doubt. A mere possible doubt, or an idea that there is a very remote possibility that the accused may not be guilty, is not a reasonable doubt.

The defendant is entitled to the benefit of every reasonable doubt; but this does not mean that a jury shall acquit in any case, if the defendant is fully, clearly, and legally proved guilty, for that would not only be unreasonable but unlawful.

The law does not require that the proof shall satisfy the mind of the jury beyond all possible doubt, but only beyond all reasonable doubt; and while it is true that the law deems it better that many guilty persons should go unpunished for want of adequate proof of guilt rather than that an innocent person should be convicted upon insufficient evidence, yet absolute, unequivocal, positive certainty is not required in any case.

In order to find the defendant guilty, it is not necessary that the mind of the jury should be convinced so as to feel satisfied that their verdict is absolutely, unequivocally, positively, certainly correct. Possible and contingent doubt hangs over almost all human affairs. Absolute, unqualified certainty is rarely attainable; and this is a degree of perfection not required by the law of the jury.

The doubt which acquits must be real, not imaginary and without foundation.

The evidence in order to convict the defendant must be such as not only to prove the guilt of the defendant, but such as, to a moral certainty beyond a reasonable doubt, to exclude or disprove every hypothesis but that of the guilt of the defendant.

I admonish you, then, to give to the defendant the benefit of every reasonable doubt as I have thus defined it, for that is his right.

If the jury should entertain this reasonable doubt, it is your duty to withhold your assent to the rendition of a verdict of guilty.

But if you are fully and clearly satisfied, beyond a reasonable doubt as I have thus defined it, of the guilt of the defendant, you should say so by your verdict.

It must be confessed that this does not seem to be a very precise definition. But in the nature of the case a more precise definition is impossible. There are no absolute rules for the persuasion of men. We present our arguments to our fellows on the assumption that they have had the ordinary experiences of mankind, and have unconsciously adopted the practical standards of reasoning by which men generally form their opinions. And this is the correct scientific test of that truth which is to be the guide of life. It is instructive to note that Jesus committed the fortunes of his cause to the agency of preaching addressed to the common people. He assumed that the evidence of his divine commission was such as would command the assent of the masses of mankind who are shaping their conduct on the evidence presented in the ordinary experiences of life.

Returning to the legal aspects of the case, it is important to note the reasons for insisting upon a higher degree of proof in criminal cases than in civil cases. This is demanded from the simple fact that an adverse decision in a criminal case is fraught with much more serious consequences than those which are involved in matters of mere pecuniary interest. Common prudence requires greater caution in the formation of a final judgment where serious consequences are involved than where the consequences are comparatively insignificant. It is instructive also to observe that the superior amount of evidence required for conviction in a criminal case stands over against a less amount which will be sufficient for acquittal. But either of these verdicts on the part of a jury is a posi-

The Seriousness of the Result can not be ignored.

tive decision supposed to be reached by a preponderance of evidence. In criminal cases, however, the interests involved are such that conviction is to be rendered only on a very strong preponderance of evidence. It is a more serious thing to hang a man than it is to deprive him of his property rights.

It is interesting to notice the recognition of this principle by Mr. Huxley, the leading agnostic of this generation, and that, too, in a case where the reason for the recognition is comparatively insignificant. In discussing the question of animal automatism, he arrives at a point of suspended judgment where he is in absolute doubt as to whether or not animals have consciousness and suffer pain. But from his contemplation of the severe struggle for existence that goes on in the animal world, and on account of the frightful amount of pain with which it must be accompanied, he says he would be glad if the probabilities were in favour of Descartes's hypothesis that animals have no feeling, but that their cries are merely automatic. But, he goes on to say, "considering the terrible practical consequences to domestic animals [connected with vivisection] which might ensue from any error on our part, it is as well to err on the right side if we err at all, and deal with them as weaker brethren who are bound, like the rest of us, to pay their toll for living and suffer what is needful for the general good." *

Even Mr. Huxley admits it.

Still, as already intimated, juries are always cautioned not to set up an impracticable standard of evi-

---

* Science and Culture and Other Essays, pp. 240, 241.

dence, and that is what is indicated in the stereotyped phrase by the word "reasonable." It is unreasonable to set up such a standard of proof as will prevent the formation of practical judgments and paralyze human activities. What the necessities of the case are is learned from the average experience of human life, and is supposed to be known by the juror.

Excessive Caution Unreasonable and Suicidal.

If the execution of justice awaited our proving a crime beyond all possible doubt, the wheels of government would be at a standstill. We do not hang a man because he has killed another, but because there are so many signs of his being a murderer that we must presume him to be one. If a man is a victim of circumstances to such an extent that a certain number of signs create an irresistible belief that he is one, he, as a benevolent man, should not count it a hardship that he is executed as a murderer. Human institutions are all imperfect. If a human ruler resolves to execute justice with the impartiality of the judgment day, he will commit the worst of all mistakes—viz., not try to execute it at all, for he will never have the perfect knowledge of the judgment day.

The necessity of forming practical decisions which lead to positive action is sometimes so urgent that even a very slight degree of evidence is required to place us under obligation to act with promptness and vigour. As Bishop Butler has truly said, " Our nature and condition necessarily require us, in the daily course of life, to act upon evidence much lower than what is commonly called probable; to guard not only against what we fully believe will, but also guard against what we think it supposable may happen; and to engage in pursuits when the probability is greatly against success, if it be credible that possibly we may succeed in them." *

This principle comes out clearly in the whole range of obligations connected with insurance and kindred acts which we are called to put forth for protection against danger. In fire insurance, for example, the probabilities are a hundred times as great that one's house will not burn as that it will burn. Still, for this one hundredth of a probability, which scarcely amounts to more than a possibility, one is under very strong obligation to make provision. In this case it may be said it is true that there is a certainty that some houses will burn, and that the common principles of benevolence would urge us to share the losses with the unknown persons who are sure to suffer. But this does not express the whole extent of the obligation. In matters where the liabilities are wholly personal, there is often the same urgency of action in view of a mere possibility. It is recognised as an obligation urged by ordinary prudence to carry an umbrella in fair weather, because we do not know but that it may rain, and to take extra clothing in mild weather in view of the possibility that the weather may change. A government does not delay the erection of a lighthouse until it becomes highly probable that every vessel passing that way will be wrecked upon a reef, but a warning signal is set up in view of a low degree of probable danger affecting each case.

The Reason for Insurance.

Likewise the laws insist that outgoing vessels shall

---

* Butler's Analogy (London, 1835), p. 203.

be provided with boats and life-preservers, not on the ground that in each case they will *probably* be needed, but that *possibly* they may be required. The familiar provision of axe and bar and saw for use in effecting deliverance in the case of the wreck of a railroad train is, fortunately, not required because there is probability that any particular train will be wrecked. Thousands and tens of thousands of trains will run in safety, and the vast majority of cars provided with these suggestive appliances will never have occasion for their use. Still, on account of the possibility, the obligation to provide them is generally recognised. In all these cases the smallness of the amount of the evidence required for positive action stands over against the greatness of the evil which is to be feared.

It is equally true that when a valuable prize is offered the bare possibility of obtaining it may be an imperative incentive to action. Those who would obtain great things must be willing to risk much. Low aspirations among a people are not merely *indicative* of a low civilization, but they are a procuring cause of it. Within "reasonable" limits the gospel of discontent must be preached before a people can rise in the scale of civilization. If the people limit their action too exclusively to the attainment of ends which are clearly within their reach, they will fail to win the highest prizes of life. In enterprising and progressive communities there must be capitalists who will venture upon schemes that involve much risk of loss. No merchant can be sure that his ships will safely ride the seas which they encounter. No husbandman can be sure that the seed he sows will yield him many fold or will even return to

<small>Civilization involves Hazard.</small>

him measure for measure. If we insist on riding so slow that we avoid all danger of accident, the aggregate loss from delay will be greater than that from an occasional calamity.

In weighing the evidences which we permit to control our religious faith, the principles just illustrated are of prime importance. The beliefs which shape our religious conduct relate to the most important interests both of the race as a whole and of each individual. So momentous are the consequences of an eternal life that preparation for it is inconceivably urgent. So great is the prize of blessed immortality that even if the evidence of immortality were extremely slight we should be under obligation to give it a prominent place among the regulative ideas of conduct. So that, as Bishop Butler has properly contended,* the mere possibility that man is immortal, and that his life beyond the grave is determined by his conduct here, furnishes ample ground to justify both the fact and the character of the divine revelation which the Bible purports to contain. In the presence of such a possibility the burden of proof comes upon those who deny the truth of a religious system which has such *prima facie* evidence supporting it as Christianity possesses.

Blessed Immortality a Prize.

There is an erroneous view much too prevalent that we are to approach Christian evidences without any presumptions respecting their truth and force. Whereas, this is a natural impossibility, since, in fact, no small part of the evidence lies in the ante-

The Presumptions in the Case Favour Christianity.

---

* See various passages in Chapter I of his Analogy, pp. 1, 18.

cedent presumptions with which we approach the specific allegations of facts.

In ordinary cases the presumption against the occurrence of a miracle is so great that it would be extremely difficult to accumulate sufficient proof to make it credible. The course of Nature is so well known in certain respects and so fixed that only the most important reasons could suffice for a miraculous interference with it. But to the student of Christian evidences such a reason is clearly present in the field. Man is great. His wants are profound. The remedial agencies of the Gospel are of such transcendent value and their adaptation to human necessities so perfect that they clearly constitute a sufficient reason for such an inauguration as shall make them effective. So complete is this adaptation that the antecedent presumptions against its miraculous inauguration is more than overcome in the minds of those who most fully understand the condition of things. The presumption is not that the Gospel is "too beautiful to be true," but that it is "too beautiful not to be true."

Under ordinary circumstances the presumption may be great that an express train will not stop at an obscure road crossing. But if it be known that a high officer of the road is there in distress, the presumption is reversed. It is more than likely that the schedule will be varied, and that the stop in this particular instance will be made. It is thus that the profound student of human history is prepared to believe in great interventions by the Creator in man's behalf. While this presumption is not sufficiently definite to enable us to foresee the proper time and place

The End justifies the Means.

for miraculous interposition in which the course of Nature shall be arrested or made to bend in man's behalf, it is sufficiently clear to render belief in miracles easy upon the production of a "reasonable amount" of evidence; while the same profound study of the habits, capacities, and wants of human nature renders it easy to believe that such interventions should be few and far between. The manifest advantage to mankind of being compelled to make the most of secondary causes, and especially of historical forces, is so great that the limitation of miracle to a few strategic points in history can by no means be made to appear unreasonable. Christ makes a more comprehensive impression upon the world through the historical evidences that perpetuate his name than could well be made if he had localized himself in a permanent bodily residence here.

Having admitted the central miracle of the Bible—namely, the resurrection of Christ—the presumptions become altogether in favour of other miracles connected with the system. There is no incongruity in representing that a person who has triumphed over death as Jesus did in his resurrection, performed other miracles during his life. Nor is there any incongruity in the introduction into the system, at an earlier stage, of miracles preparatory to the consummation of the system. The one who accepts the consummation of Christianity in the resurrection, and the supernatural doctrines connected with it (such as the abiding presence of the Spirit and the forgiveness of sins through the death of Christ), may reasonably presume that the miraculous manifestations were not limited to that one supreme moment. He is prepared, therefore, to accept

The Resurrection of Christ the central Miracle.

a preliminary miraculous history which has a "reasonable" amount of direct evidence supporting it, and which is not manifestly incongruous with the system. As already remarked, the general congruity of the Christian system and the remarkable restraint under which the miraculous narratives have been written form a large part of the evidence compelling us to accept the Bible as true history.

In recent years much misapprehension of the truth has arisen through the tendency to confound scientific proof with demonstrative proof. The mistake has frequently been made of assuming that nothing was to be believed that could not be demonstrated mathematically or by experiment and direct observation. This has been the great mistake of the so-called positive philosophy. The truth, however, is that the larger part not only of the beliefs which are properly permitted to regulate our daily life, but the larger part of the beliefs of the inductive sciences, rest upon probable or, as it is often called, moral evidence. For us to expect or to demand any other kind of evidence is as unreasonable as for us to expect or demand a new heavens and a new earth before the providential time for the arrival of the millennium. Nothing is clearer than that man is so placed in the world that for the larger part of his practical knowledge he is dependent upon his fellowmen and upon the experience which has been embodied in the habits and institutions of society. Life is too short, and his unaided powers are too feeble, to permit any man to verify directly, even in the simplest matters, everything which he accepts as true; while in regard to historical matters and the far-reaching lines both of

Scientific Proof not demonstrative.

individual and social movements which are determined by the past, there is no possibility of direct verification.

How little we pause to verify the great mass of the most important events of life, and how serious would

<small>Lack of Demonstrative Proof in Ordinary Affairs.</small>

be the results of our attempting to do so, will appear by reflecting a moment upon the simplest actions even of our daily life. The breakfast of which we partake in the morning is eaten in reliance upon the most intangible kind of evidence. An expert chemist might possibly by direct analysis determine that the food was proper and free from poison. But to do so by what would be called even a chemical demonstration would absorb so much time that he could do nothing else, while he would probably perish from hunger before the demonstration was complete. But as it is, we receive our flour from the miller, our meat from the butcher, our sugar from the refiner, our coffee and condiments from the grocer, our milk from the milkman, and the various other things which are upon the table and allow them to pass through the hands of the cook and to be served to us by the waiter without question. Were we to pause and challenge the evidence and demand demonstration at every step of the preparation for our morning meal, the presumption of our insanity would be well-nigh overwhelming. At any rate, the burden of proving that we were not insane would imperatively rest upon us.

A similar result is reached when we consider the confidence with which we commit ourselves to the ordinary means of travel. It is entirely beyond the capacity of the traveller to inspect the engine and cars and track of the railroad upon which he rides, or to satisfy himself directly of the competence and good will of the employees who set in motion and control these tremendous agencies of modern commerce. Nevertheless, except under peculiar circumstances, we raise in a civilized country no question concerning any of these points, and this notwithstanding the fact that we hear the greed of the corporations and the carelessness of the management liberally advertised in every paper of the land.

These illustrations bring clearly to light the fact of the very widest significance that, when there are not present special motives to induce fraud and dishonesty and dereliction of duty, human nature is in general to be trusted. The very existence of society, and in still greater degree the existence of a high civilization, imply that the motives to honesty and to the faithful performance of duties are in the main overwhelming. In face of these general presumptions, the burden of proof is thrown upon him who doubts. Doubt is properly called upon to give a reason for itself. Before it can claim attention it must show by special and conclusive evidence that it is a reasonable doubt.

Men naturally love to tell the Truth.

The unreasonableness of calling for demonstrative evidence in proof of the historical facts that are most properly and certainly believed may be illustrated in demanding that it should be proved beyond all possible doubt that Abraham Lincoln really composed and delivered what passes as his famous Gettysburg address. I have been unable to find any one who heard the address, much less any one who took notes at the time,

Possibility of Cavil concerning the Authorship of Lincoln's Gettysburg Address.

or who, if he did take notes, would be able to prove that he could record the speech exactly as it was given. And even if one had heard it himself, it would be difficult for him to be perfectly confident that after thirty years his memory retained all the facts. And when it comes to the documentary evidence, it is far too slight to remove every shadow of doubt.

It is true that a purported facsimile of this address in Lincoln's own handwriting has been published, but a suspicious thing about this is that it is admitted that it was written out by its distinguished author some months after its purported delivery. Besides, about all the evidence we have of this facsimile is that it was published in a popular magazine by one of Lincoln's own satellites who was not entirely above the charge of being a hero worshipper and unduly subservient to his master's influence. Such is the indefinite evidence upon which we are compelled to repose at the present time. How much worse will it be after the lapse of one or two centuries; for, examination of the various publications which contain this document and the reports of it reveals the alarming fact that the paper upon which they are published is extremely perishable. It is mostly made of wood pulp, and so imperfectly cleansed of its destructive chemical ingredients that in many cases it has already fallen to pieces by reason of age after a lapse of only thirty years. Indeed, a distinguished authority has personally assured us that so poor is the quality of paper in use at the present time that not a single book published in the last quarter of this century will be legible after the lapse of another hundred years. From the perishable nature of the writing material now in use, it is thus evident that after the lapse of one or two centuries we shall probably find it more difficult to furnish convincing evidence of the deliverance of Lincoln's Gettysburg speech than we now find it to establish the genuineness of Sargon's inscriptions recounting his expedition to the Mediterranean 3800 B. C.; while the general readiness of the present time to rest content with the indefinite reports of newspapers and magazines will render it far less capable of proof in the near future than will be the general facts concerning Christ's life eighteen hundred years earlier.

Confidence in the telegraphic reports which appear simultaneously in all the papers of the country on such occasions is sadly shaken by the experience of General Grant in Des Moines, Iowa, on September 29, 1875, when a notable speech of his was so garbled in reaching the public through newspapers, magazines, and bound volumes that it conveyed a meaning exactly opposite to that which he intended, making him speak in direct antagonism to the maintenance of State universities, and thus to take sides in an excited State issue in which he did not mean to meddle. The historian who consults the newspapers, magazines, and annuals of 1875 will find a thousand witnesses affirming that his speech contained a sentence of considerable length in opposition to the support of the higher institutions of learning by the State, while the correction of the error will be found only in a single volume which is little read, and in an obscure place in an educational report published twenty years later.*

*Higher Education in Iowa, by Leonard F. Parker, p. 105, in United States Bureau of Education, Circular of Information No. 6, 1893.

Additional doubt also is thrown over the Gettysburg speech by certain manifest incongruities in the situation. Abraham Lincoln had a great reputation as a platform orator. It was largely through the success of his public discussions with Stephen A. Douglas and his more formal address in New York city that the eyes of the nation were so fixed upon him that he became the natural candidate to the highest office which the people had to bestow. And after his election his inaugural addresses and his various messages to Congress amply sustained his general reputation for ability to prepare extended orations. In view of these well-known facts, it seems highly improbable that after his own part in the trying experiences and the stirring events which led up to the great victory at Gettysburg, he should have been assigned a secondary place in the proceedings, and that from the fulness of his great heart he should have been content, in writing an address for the occasion, to limit himself to the few sentences which have come down to us in this reported speech.

Moreover, the evidence of those who were with him at the time is most conflicting concerning many of the circumstances. One eye-witness says that Lincoln wrote the speech while riding on the train from Washington to the celebration. Another says that he was with him all of the way, and that Lincoln did no writing on the train. One eye-witness, who sat on the platform, says that Lincoln when he rose to speak " adjusted his spectacles " and read the address from a sheet of foolscap paper. Another who had equal advantages for observation affirms that he did not read at all, but spoke freely without consulting his manuscript. Another still, says

Discrepancies in the Evidence.

that Lincoln held in his hand and occasionally consulted during the delivery of the speech a piece of pasteboard with something written upon it. On consulting the reports of the speech, also, we find many discrepancies. Those sent to Boston differ in various particulars from those sent to New York, while that sent to the Cincinnati Gazette differed widely from all others. Most of the papers say that the speech was given after that of Mr. Everett, but, according to the New York Tribune, it was given immediately after the "eloquent prayer" of the Rev. Mr. Stockton, and before Mr. Everett's oration. A specially suspicious circumstance is that the authorized autographic copy given in the standard Life of Lincoln was, as already remarked, written out a year after date, and differs from all other copies.*

Much more might be said in this line, and we venture to add that if after the lapse of two thousand years any important belief for the regulation of human conduct should be dependent upon connecting this speech with the martyred President, it would be far more difficult to produce satisfactory direct evidence of its authenticity and to free it from all possible doubt arising from internal criticism than it is now to prove the genuineness of the sayings and the truth of the record of facts which are contained in the four Gospels. And yet there is no reasonable doubt, and there never will be any *reasonable* doubt, that the record of the Gettysburg speech is correct in every essential detail.

---

* Morse's Life of Lincoln, vol. ii, p. 214; Arnold's Life of Lincoln, p. 328; Scribner's Magazine, vol. xiv, p. 26; Century Magazine, vol. xxv, pp. 596, 636; the Nation for August 26, 1875, September 9, 1875; also vol. xlvii, p. 27.

But, it is not in history alone that we are dependent upon evidence of this vague sort for our beliefs respecting things which are of the highest personal and public concern. The chemist even can perform but a small part of the experiments upon which his knowledge of the elements depends, and he is narrowly limited in the degrees of heat and pressure to which he can subject his material; while in the use of the spectroscope the chemist deals with facts which are entirely beyond the reach of experience. Chemical science is by no means, therefore, a purely experimental science. The chemist must early train himself to see with the mind's eye; for in his simplest interpretation of facts he plunges into the open sea of probable evidence and endless speculation. The chemistry of the past, the chemistry of the future, and the chemistry of the distant spaces of the universe are only surmised on evidence which rests on far-reaching philosophical assumptions; while if the experimental or "chemical" method of arriving at conclusions in the narrower sphere of its operations is adopted in astronomy, geology, history, political economy, or any other of the practical sciences, the intellectual paralysis is still more complete, and all progress ceases.

Limitations of the Experimental Method of Proof.

Without question the devotees of physical science in its narrower lines do, to a considerable extent, disqualify themselves for forming practical judgments concerning the higher matters relating to human conduct and welfare. This Darwin was frank enough to acknowledge, saying that in the course of his scientific investigations he had lost his relish for poetry,

Darwin's acknowledged Defects.

painting, and music, and that his "mind seemed to have become a kind of machine for grinding general laws out of large collections of facts; but why this should have caused the atrophy of that part of the brain alone on which the higher tastes depend "he could not conceive." "If I had to live my life again," he continues, "I would make a rule to read some poetry and listen to some music at least once a week, for perhaps the parts of my brain now atrophied would thus have been kept active through use. The loss of these tastes is a loss of happiness, and may possibly be injurious to the intellect, and more probably to the moral character, by enfeebling the emotional part of our nature." *

To similar effect Gladstone has recently remarked that in his experience " persons who are engaged in political employment, or who are in any way habitually conversant with human nature, conduct, and concerns, are much less borne down with scepticism than specialists of various kinds and those whose pursuits have associated them with the study, history, and framework of inanimate Nature." In truth, the sceptical habit induced by the excessive application of the " chemical " or experimental method of proof induces a state of mind closely bordering upon a common form of insanity, in which the subject becomes unduly suspicious of all ordinary evidence. While in this state he imagines that all his food is poisoned, that all men are liars, that all friends are unfaithful, that every public conveyance is defective and likely to break down. No

Agnosticism a form of Insanity.

---

* Life and Letters of Charles Darwin, vol. i, p. 81.

reasonable amount of evidence will satisfy him. The loss of his faith is really the loss of his reason. In theological literature this state of mind is euphemistically called "invincible ignorance," and its subjects are sorrowfully relegated to the compassionate consideration of Him who "knoweth our feeble frame and remembereth that we are dust." Great as is the danger in encouraging superstition among the ignorant, the danger of promoting unreasonable scepticism through unduly magnifying the realm of experimental science is equally great and equally to be deplored.

CHAPTER VII.

NEWLY DISCOVERED EXTERNAL EVIDENCES OF CHRISTIANITY.

THE latter half of the nineteenth century is as remarkable for its historical discoveries as for its progress in physical science. It is during this period that the monuments of Egypt and Babylonia have begun to yield their secrets to scientific methods of investigation, while it is only during the last quarter of a century that the earliest monuments of Grecian history have been scientifically explored, and that the earliest indications of the history of the human race have been connected with a definite geological era. In the brilliant glamour of these more general historical discoveries the popular attention has been too little directed to the significance of the important revelations which have a more immediate bearing upon the genuineness of the books of the New Testament. The story of the methods by which these evidences have been preserved and the means through which they have been brought to the light is more entrancing than a novel, and is in the highest degree calculated to give the student confidence in the favourable outcome of the system of events in which divine providence is so manifestly making the weak things of the world confound the mighty.

202 CHRISTIAN EVIDENCES.

A brief summary of the argument in favour of the authenticity and sufficiency of the literary documents upon which the faith of Christianity has all along purported to rest will be an essential preliminary to a proper understanding of the lines of evidence which have recently come to light.

The Evidence as it stood in 1875.

By all who have given a reasonable amount of attention to the subject, it has been acknowledged that in the last quarter of the second century of our era the four Gospels were universally accepted by Christians as the authoritative biographies of the Founder of their faith. A few representative defenders and interpreters of the Christian faith appear conspicuously above the horizon in widely scattered centres of Christian activity at that time.

IRENÆUS OF LYONS.

The first in order whom it is important for us to notice is Irenæus, a missionary bishop in southern France. Born in Asia Minor in the early part of the second century, he had been a pupil of Polycarp, who had himself been an associate and pupil of the Apostle John, and who became bishop in Smyrna, in Asia Minor, and finally suffered martyrdom at Rome about the year 155. From this very region, where two such distinguished apostles as Paul and John had lived and laboured, Irenæus went to the western bounds of the Roman Empire as missionaries now go from the centres of Christian civilization to the ends of the earth for the propagation and defence of the Gospel. Both the labours and the writings of this great missionary bishop were abundant, even when reckoned by modern standards. His principal literary production (written about A. D. 180), directed against the heretical Gnostics of his day, makes a volume of several hundred octavo pages. Defending as he did the Christian faith on the borders of Christendom, and reflecting as he did the influences upon his youth proceeding from the very centres from which the Gospel was originally propagated, there can be no doubt that upon fundamental questions of belief he was representative of the great body of Christians scattered throughout the Roman Empire.

To one of these points of belief his writings bear unequivocal testimony—namely, that the history of Christ is authoritatively embodied in the four Gospels which are now in our possession. These were accepted not only by the orthodox Christians, but generally by the heretics with whom Irenæus was contending at that period. So general, indeed, was the acceptance of this fourfold Gospel that Irenæus proceeds to show why there should have been just four, and no more. The reasons he gives are certainly fanciful and of little weight, but they none the less bear witness to the general acceptance of the fact which he endeavoured to explain—namely, that the record of Christ's history to which the world was then resorting as authoritative and final was both fourfold and substantially identical with that which has come down to us. After mentioning what he conceives to be the main peculiarities and excellences of the Gospels according to Matthew, Mark, Luke, and John respectively, he goes on to say that "it is not possible that the Gospels can be either more or fewer in number than they are. For, since there are four zones of the world in which we live, and four principal winds, while the Church is scattered throughout all the world, and the 'pillar and ground' of the Church is the Gospel and the spirit of life, it is fitting that she should have four pillars breathing out immortality on every side and vivifying men afresh." *

In what follows Irenæus presents other reasons which are equally fanciful. The fancifulness of his reasoning, however, enhances rather than diminishes the value of his testimony to the main point, and gives additional emphasis to the value of his belief in the genuineness and authority of the New Testament Scriptures. For Irenæus was merely a commentator; he was an expounder of sacred documents, and not in any sense an original mouthpiece of revelation, and he had all the faults and foibles of the class to which he belonged; while he illustrates in the contrast between the wildness of his own flights of fancy and the sobriety of the New Testament writings the transcendent excellence of our four Gospels.

Theophilus of Antioch.

At the same time that Irenæus (about 180 A. D.) was expounding and defending Christianity on the banks of the Rhone in France and appealing to the four Gospels as the sole source of information concerning the life and teachings of Jesus, Theophilus, Bishop of Antioch, in Syria, was writing An Apology for Christianity in that important centre of Roman power and Greek civilization in the East. The work was designed for the conviction of a heathen friend, and hence is not likely to be so marked by quotations from Scripture as would

---

* Ante-Nicene Fathers, vol. i, p. 428, Irenæus against Heresies.

naturally be the case in writings intended for persons who were familiar with the Scriptures, and who already looked to them for instruction and edification. At the same time, the Apology is not a long one. Nevertheless Matthew, Luke, and the fourth Gospel are distinctly quoted, the last named being classed among "the holy writings" which contain the teachings of "the inspired men, one of whom," he says, "was John, who said, In the beginning was the Word, and the Word was with God," with some further comments upon the proem to the fourth Gospel.

CLEMENT OF ALEXANDRIA.

Passing from these distant foci of Christian activity at the close of the second century to Alexandria in Egypt, we find in that great commercial and literary centre a flourishing catechetical school or theological seminary with a learned and eminent classical scholar at its head. Clement of Alexandria died as early as 220 A. D., and hence is an important witness to the prevalent beliefs of the Christians the latter part of the second century. Greek was his native language, and Greek philosophy was familiar to him and an object of great admiration. In a single work of his no less than fifty-two clear quotations from the four Gospels may be counted on fifty consecutive pages.* One of the most frequently quoted books is the fourth Gospel, from which considerably more than one hundred extracts are taken. In one instance, after quoting a saying which had been ascribed to Christ, he says,

---

* Barnes, Canonical and Uncanonical Gospels, p. 25.

"This saying, however, we do not have in the four Gospels handed down to us, but in that which is according to the Egyptians," * thus placing it beyond doubt that the four Gospels contained the history of the origin of Christianity accepted by the churches which looked to Alexandria for the training of their teachers. It was the four Gospels which had been *handed down* to them from the earliest generations of believers.

Tertullian of Carthage.

Passing westward a thousand miles along the northern coast of Africa, we come to Carthage, the centre of the commercial, social, and religious life of that portion of northern Africa which lies opposite to Rome, and which was the storehouse from which the Mistress of the World then drew a large part of the grain which fed its multitude of idlers. Carthage was the residence of Tertullian, one of the most remarkable men not only of the early Church but of the world. Tertullian was born not later than 160 A. D. In his abundant controversial writings his quotations from the New Testament are so numerous and full that when collected together, as has been done by a recent German scholar (Rönsch), they make a goodly sized volume in themselves. Tertullian wrote in Latin and for a Latin constituency, thus bearing evidence that even at that time the sacred literature of the Christians had been translated into the language of the governing race of the world. In conducting his argument against a leading heretic named Marcion, he constantly appeals to the

---

* Stromata, iii, 13; Westcott, Introduction, p. 448.

public fame of the Christian records upon which the churches of his time confidently reposed, and, speaking of the third Gospel, declares with utmost confidence that in the form in which it was then well known it had been received "from its first publication."

THE MURATORIAN CANON.

An additional witness to this same fact of the general acceptance of the four Gospels near the close of the second century was discovered one hundred and fifty years ago (published 1740) in the Ambrosian Library of Milan by Muratori, an eminent Italian scholar, and in his earlier days conservator of the above-mentioned library. This witness is the so-called Muratorian Canon, which is simply a fragment of a catalogue of the books of the New Testament, with brief remarks upon their character and the occasion of their composition. The catalogue is mutilated both at the beginning and at the end, but its first complete sentence introduces the third Gospel as the work of Luke the physician, and companion of Paul, while the fourth Gospel is said to be the work of John, a disciple of the Lord. This fragment purports to have been written soon after "Pius was sitting in the Church of Rome," which would place its date early in the last quarter of the second century.

All these witnesses indubitably belong to the last quarter of the second century, and leave no reasonable doubt that the four Gospels were universally accepted as the authoritative record of what the Christians believed at that time concerning the life and work and words of Jesus Christ while on earth. To this testimony that of Origen, the renowned pupil of Clement of Alexandria, might well have been added, since the early part of his life also falls in the period under discussion; so that his voluminous writings and extensive commentaries upon the Scriptures, with their innumerable quotations from the four Gospels, are confirmatory at first hand of the regard in which the Christians of that period held the New Testament.

It should be distinctly noted that we are not now speaking of Church councils and of the formal authority with which they are supposed to have invested the books of the New Testament, but are considering the phenomenon from a purely historical and scientific point of view. The phenomenon is in every respect a most impressive one. This unity of belief concerning the authenticity of the books of the New Testament and of their sufficiency for the interpretation of the faith to which the early Christians had committed their fortunes and their lives is a most marvellous and significant fact. According to a very moderate calculation of the late Prof. Andrews Norton,* there were at the close of the second century as many as three million Christian believers and sixty thousand extant copies of the Gospels. But these were scattered over the length and breadth of the Roman Empire, extending from the Straits of Gibraltar to the borders of India, a distance of more than three thousand miles, and this during a period of the world's history when communication was difficult and the barriers of race and language were

---

* Evidences of the Genuineness of the Gospels (1846), vol. i, pp. 45–55; compare Gibbon's Decline and Fall of the Roman Empire, chap. xv.

most insuperable. To meet the wants of believers, the Christian documents were already current in three or four distinct languages.

LIMITS OF TRUSTWORTHY TRADITION.

Before passing, however, to the evidence which relates directly to the period preceding that now under consideration, we may profitably pause to notice how short the interval is which is to be bridged over. Accepting the evidence as sufficiently establishing the authority of the Gospels everywhere among believers as early as the year 180 A. D., let us apply the historic imagination to see what natural means were in existence for the correction, criticism, and judgment of such literary documents. Whence could such documents have come? How could they have secured such universal approval, and what means and motives were in operation to prevent fraud and delusion from corrupting the original sources, so that at this time they should be beyond the reach of scientific criticism?

The crucifixion occurred in the year 30.* Thirty subtracted from one hundred and eighty leaves one hundred and fifty. On this basis, therefore, the Christian literature sprang up and spread with the advancing waves of Christian influence to the borders of the Roman Empire within one hundred and fifty years.

But the principal actors in establishing Christianity

---

* It is important to bear in mind that the chronology of the Christian era established by Dionysius Exiguus in the sixth century was based on calculations which led to an error of about four years; so that the real *Anno Domini* is four years earlier than that which is current in our present usage.

lived on long after the death of their Master. It is natural to suppose that a majority of the original disciples retained their active powers for a quarter of a century, and some of them for a half century or more, after the enactment of the scenes which through their instrumentality have so profoundly affected the history of the world. No one doubts that Paul was actively propagating his belief in the Gospel thirty-three years after the death of Christ, which would bring us to about the year 63. The Epistles to the Romans, Corinthians, and Galatians had been written a few years before this, probably about the year 58. Sixty from one hundred and eighty leaves but one hundred and twenty years to be covered by direct testimony—that is, from the time when Paul publicly declared * that the larger part of five hundred witnesses to the ascension of Christ were still living to the time when every one acknowledges that the historical books of the New Testament were universally accepted by Christian believers, there is a space of only one hundred and twenty years.

The doubts which have gathered about the genuineness and purity of the historical books of the New Testament have largely arisen because of the deficiency of positive confirmatory literary evidence during this period. A scientific examination of the subject will compel us to account for this lack of evidence. We shall show presently that the discoveries which are going on at the present time are rapidly and satisfactorily supplying this supposed lack. But we need to observe that from our knowledge of human nature and of the conditions of the times, we should naturally sup-

---

* 1 Cor. xv, 6.

pose there would be a deficiency of the kind of evidence which many demand. On the other hand, a study of the known conditions of the period will show that the evidence we have all along had is ample and even superabundant.

In the first place, we need to observe how short a period one hundred and twenty years is when reckoned in terms of human life. The Atlantic Monthly for August, 1896, contains an interesting letter from a lady less than sixty years of age giving reminiscences of her acquaintance with the widow of Alexander Hamilton. Her associations with this eminent woman occurred more than forty years before, about the year 1853, when she was a miss of twelve or thirteen; while Madam Hamilton, with powers unimpaired, and memory of early events even quickened by age, was ninety-five years old. Madam Hamilton was the daughter of General Philip Schuyler, of Saratoga, so prominent in planning the campaign which led to the defeat of Burgoyne.

Now there can be no question that Madam Hamilton in her old age retained in her memory with great accuracy a large circle of most important facts which occurred in her father's household more than eighty years before. Many of these she retailed to this writer in 1853, at a time when the memory of her admiring listener was most receptive. Thus numerous striking and significant events recorded in this letter were orally transmitted through two witnesses over a period of one hundred and twenty-five years. But the writer of this letter was forty years younger at the time of writing than was Madam Hamilton when they met, and it is not at all unlikely that she will retain her vigour of mind and clearness of memory concerning that period of life till she herself is ninety-five years old; in which case these two witnesses would transmit a certain class of historical facts through a period of one hundred and sixty years.

The oral transmission of historical facts through two witnesses for one hundred and forty years is by no means uncommon. Instances of it probably lie within reach of every one's experience. I may mention in my own case that when a lad of ten or twelve years old I was much with my aged grandmother, who was then eighty-five years of age, and I have a very vivid remembrance of many anecdotes she told me concerning her own experience in western Massachusetts and eastern New York during and immediately following the Revolutionary War. Of the general condition of things, and of many specific facts which occurred sixty-five years before her death, I received a very clear and, I have no doubt, a correct idea. Those came to me at an impressible age, when they are most likely to be retained in memory. Indeed, I can not forget them if I would. If I should retain my powers as long as Mr. Gladstone has retained his, I could easily correct serious misstatements which might be made concerning many common facts which occurred one hundred and forty years before.

Our scientific historians thus find it not difficult to believe that one hundred and thirty years is not too long a period for a large class of facts to be preserved by tradition in uncorrupted form.*

---

* See Sir G. C. Lewis, On Credibility of Early Roman History, vol. i, pp. 98–101.

For example, the three lives of Benjamin Franklin, Thomas Jefferson, and George Bancroft cover a period of one hundred and eighty-nine years. Thomas Jefferson was forty-seven years a contemporary of Franklin, while Bancroft was twenty-six years a contemporary of Jefferson, and continued with us in full vigour to the time of his death in 1891; thus our great historian could through Jefferson and his associate Franklin easily reach back to establish by the best of testimony certain classes of facts which occurred one hundred and fifty years before his own powers began to fail in the least.

Thus, then, by legitimate use of the historic imagination, we see that the time separating the most active period in the lives of all who witnessed the ministry of Jesus on earth from that when the Gospel narratives are admitted by all to have been generally accepted is less than that which can be easily bridged over by trustworthy traditional evidence. From the active period of Paul's life, about 60 A. D. to 180 A. D., the period of the unquestioned acceptance of the Gospel history, is only one hundred and twenty years. We will now consider not only what we can reasonably infer to have happened, but what we know to have happened during that period.

Shortness of even the Old Interval to be spanned.

We may reasonably infer that the contemporaries of the apostles during their most active period of life would carry down toward the close of the first century not only a distinct remembrance of the main points of the preaching to which they had listened, but a very positive knowledge of the historical writings which corresponded with their teaching, and hence were worthy of their approval. It requires no vigorous action of the historical imagination to see that no such extended biographies of Jesus as we have in our four Gospels could have become current during the first century except they correctly represented the preaching of the apostles, and except they had come with their direct or indirect indorsement. Indeed, there is no question that the Apostle John continued in active work until the last decade of the first century, while at this time there must have been still living and in full possession of their mental powers tens of thousands of Christians who had in their early life heard the Gospel story from the other apostles; for the Christians of the last decade of the first century were not so far separated from the active era of apostolic preaching as we, in the last decade of the nineteenth century, are from the palmy period of the eloquence of Henry Clay and Daniel Webster.*

Going to the other end of the period, and turning upon it the scientific light of the historic imagination, we see at a glance that the remarkable unanimity with which the four Gospels were received in 180 could not have sprung up in a night. Such a phenomenon must have been the product of causes running back a considerable distance into the past. The three million Christians of that time were very widely dispersed throughout the Roman Empire, congregating in special numbers at the four or five great centres of which we have already spoken, and two or three others—namely, Edessa, in the valley of the Euphrates, Antioch in Syria, Smyrna in Asia Minor, Alexander in Egypt,

---

* Both of these died in 1852.

NEWLY DISCOVERED EXTERNAL EVIDENCES. 215

Corinth in Greece, Rome in Italy, and Lyons in France. In all these places in the year 180 it was the same Gospels which were read in the churches, which were expounded by the bishops and teachers, and which were used both by the heretics and the orthodox to establish their various opinions. At a considerable time before this these Gospels had been translated from Greek into Syriac and Latin, and had come into general circulation, so that they were practically without rivals.

Even if we had no direct literary evidence of the existence of our Gospels before 180, the manner in which they were received at that time would be incapable of explanation except on the theory that they had come down essentially unimpaired with the indorsement of the apostles from the apostolic age. This we should naturally infer from the known elements of human nature involved in the case, taken in connection with the character of the literature constituting the Gospels.

Human nature is exceedingly tenacious of its sacred literature, and resists with great vigour even minor changes in it. Of this we have ample evidence in the difficulty we are now experiencing in securing the circulation of the Revised Version of the English Bible, and this notwithstanding the indorsement of all the leading scholars of the world and the remarkable facilities which now exist for the reproduction and distribution of books. A Bible agent recently told me that during the last year and a half he had visited ten thousand families to ascertain if they were supplied with Bibles, and to supply them if necessary. Of all these ten thousand families only one asked him for a new version.

Tenacity of Religious Convictions.

That human nature was the same in the second century that it is in the nineteenth has numerous illustrations from the Church history of that period. The great reverence which the early Christians had for the central facts of their faith led them to be also very tenacious of many subsidiary points about which there was room for controversy. Among the earnestly disputed questions of the period was that concerning the day which should be celebrated to commemorate their Lord's death. The churches in Asia Minor being largely of Jewish extraction, insisted that, as the death of Christ occurred on the day of the Jewish Passover, its celebration should continue to be observed on that exact day—namely, the fourteenth of the month—no matter what time of the week it occurred. On the other hand, the Western churches maintained that it was not fitting to celebrate such a feast upon any other day of the week than that on which the Saviour rose from the dead. Hence their Feast of the Passover came on the Sunday after the fourteenth of the month Nisan, constituting the basis of the present observance of Easter.

Human Nature unchanged.

During the last half of the second century the controversies over this subject spread from one end of Christendom to the other. The intensity of feeling upon the subject is painful to contemplate. The aged Polycarp, in the year 160, travelled from Smyrna to Rome, a distance of a thousand miles, to confer concerning the matter with Anicetus, Bishop of Rome. The Roman bishop exerted himself to the utmost to convince Polycarp of his error in continuing to observe the festival on the exact day of the month without regard to the day of the week. Polycarp, however, was incor-

NEWLY DISCOVERED EXTERNAL EVIDENCES. 217

rigible, and returned to his flock unconvinced and unchanged in his practice.

Thirty years later, Victor, Bishop of Rome, endeavoured to force upon the whole Church the Western practice, and went so far as to excommunicate the Eastern churches because they would not conform.

We have said that the lapse of time between the apostolic period and the last quarter of the second century, when the four Gospels were universally accepted as authoritative, is so brief that if the interval were an entire literary blank, we could not reasonably resist the conclusion that these books must have come down from the apostolic age essentially unchanged. This conclusion follows from the wide distribution of the documents, from their essential agreement with each other, as shown by the translations, the quotations of commentators, and the use made of the Scriptures in doctrinal controversies and in controversies with heretics. Such unity concerning such extensive and peculiar literature could not have arisen in so short a time except there had all along been sufficient ground for believing that these documents represented properly the opinions of the founders of Christianity.

INTERMEDIATE TESTIMONY OF JUSTIN MARTYR.

But we have never been without much confirmatory evidence of this proposition. Most prominent among the direct witnesses to the existence of the four Gospels in the early part of the second century stands Justin Martyr, whose death occurred shortly after the middle of the century, and whose writings were doubtless composed as early as the year 150. Justin was of Greek birth, and his early years were spent in the study of Greek philosophy. Upon his conversion to Christianity, he turned all his great abilities to the service of the new cause which he had espoused. His most important and best authenticated writings are two Apologies— one addressed to the Emperor Antoninus Pius, and the other, taking the form of a dialogue, to a Jew named Trypho. From the fact that they are addressed not to believers, but to unbelievers, we should not expect so many and such precise quotations from the four Gospels as would naturally occur in writings made for the edification of believers. Nevertheless about one hundred and twenty distinct allusions to the Gospel history are made by Justin, nearly all of which coincide in substance with the statements of either Matthew or Luke, while a fair proportion of them are exact quotations or nearly so.

But Justin's quotations, usually supposed to be from the fourth Gospel, are so inexact that there has been a strong effort made to prove that he was quoting from some other book or writing or from a primitive form of this book which had subsequently been indefinitely amended. This, coupled with the fact that Justin does not mention the four Gospels, nor distinctly name the evangelists, but simply refers to the "memoirs of the apostles," has led a certain class of critics to deny that Justin had the four Gospels before him when he wrote about the middle of the second century. In maintenance, however, of the belief that Justin did really have the fourth Gospel in his possession and quote from it, the late Prof. Ezra Abbot went into a most extended and convincing argument in which some curious facts are brought out illustrating the looseness of Scripture quotations in general even when it is known that the writer is in possession of particular copies. It is a case where the importance of the legal phrase "beyond a reasonable doubt" comes into prominence. The fact that there are slight variations in the quotations from the original is of far less weight than a certain class of critics would lead us to suppose. Very few clergymen or popular writers quote Scripture with absolute correctness; but the errors introduced are of such character that they can be scientifically accounted for—that is, the known weaknesses of the memory, especially when called upon in the midst of a heated line of argument, lead us to expect a certain class of variations which do not affect the main point of the quotation.

For example, Dr. Abbot * takes from Jeremy Taylor nine quotations of a most prominent passage from the fourth Gospel, supposed to have been quoted from the same source by Justin Martyr—namely, John iii, 3–5, beginning, "Except a man be born of water and of the Spirit, he can not enter into the kingdom of God." Now there is no question that Jeremy Taylor aimed to follow the common English version of the Bible. Nevertheless in his nine quotations of this passage, noted by Dr. Abbot, every one of them differs from it, and in only two quotations does he agree with himself. He uniformly substitutes *unless* for except. In six places he substitutes "kingdom of heaven" for "kingdom of God," and in four places says "shall not" for "can not." From one of the clauses he omits the preposition "of" in six quotations, and inserts the word

---

* Critical Essays, p. 41, *seq.*

"Holy" before "Spirit" twice where it does not belong. In short, a stronger argument could be made out to prove that Jeremy Taylor used an incomplete or mutilated Gospel than can be made out for Justin Martyr, but in neither case is there any reasonable doubt that these two writers made use of the fourth Gospel as we now have it. Justin's quotations, therefore, were properly considered by almost all Christian apologists as proving the existence of the fourth Gospel and its recognition as sacred literature in the early part of the second century, within twenty-five or thirty years of the time usually assigned to the death of the Apostle John.

Newly Discovered Evidence.

But, as we have to deal with unreasonable as well as with reasonable doubts, Providence has reserved for these later days a most important body of specific confirmatory evidence to sweep away the last strongholds of critical unbelief. The discovery of this evidence reads like a romance, and is the result of increasing knowledge concerning the treasures which are buried not beneath the dust of crumbling temples of brick and stone in Egypt or Babylonia, but in the long unused and unexplored libraries of the East.

It is now about fifty years since Tischendorf accidentally discovered the invaluable Sinaitic manuscript of the New Testament which had been for centuries neglected, and by the very neglect preserved, in the recesses of the Convent of St. Catharine on Mount Sinai. But it was only in 1889 that Prof. Rendel Harris in the same convent discovered a long-neglected Syriac manuscript containing the Apology of Aristides.* The search for this, and several other literary documents of which we shall speak, is closely analogous to that of astronomers for unseen planets whose existence is only dimly indicated by the perturbations of the other bodies of the solar system. For in the case of the documents to which attention is now to be called, while their existence was indicated by the testimony of various Christian writers who had been influenced by them, for many centuries they had disappeared from view and had been so completely lost that their very existence was doubted by many.

1. Apology of Aristides.

This Apology of Aristides was referred to by Eusebius † in the early part of the fourth century as the work of "a man faithfully devoted to the religion we profess," and who, he says, had "left to posterity a defence of the faith addressed to Adrian." Eusebius simply adds that this " work is also preserved by a great number even to the present day," but gives no further information concerning it. At a later period Jerome refers to the work as that of Aristides, an Athenian philosopher, saying that Justin Martyr in his Apology had imitated Aristides, and that the work was still extant in Jerome's day.

It was therefore a matter of extreme interest when the work was discovered by Prof. Harris, for this discovery afforded one of the best possible opportunities of verifying the hypotheses which had been formed

---

* A translation of the work, with full introductory matter, may be found in vol. ix of the American edition of the Ante-Nicene Fathers (New York, 1897).

† H. E., iv, 3.

concerning the conditions under which Christianity was developing during the early part of the second century. We have already noted that Justin Martyr's Apology was written about the year 150, being addressed to the Emperor Antoninus Pius. The Apology of Aristides was presented to the Emperor Hadrian at Athens in the year 125. As in Justin Martyr's case, so here, the object of the Apology was to convince one of the most philosophical of the Roman Emperors, we should not expect to find the same fulness and accuracy of quotation from the Scriptures as would occur in a commentary written for believers. What we do find, however, corresponds so closely with the teachings preserved in the New Testament that it furnishes strong direct proof that they were already firmly established with the churches in a form which has not subsequently changed in any essential particular. This will be evident upon reading his brief outline of Christian doctrine.

The Christians reckon the beginning of their religion from Jesus Christ, who is named the Son of God Most High; and it is said that God came down from heaven, and from a Hebrew virgin took and clad himself with flesh, and in a daughter of man there dwelt the Son of God. This is taught from that Gospel which a little while ago was spoken among them as being preached; wherein, if ye also will read, ye will comprehend the power that is upon it. This Jesus then was born of the tribe of the Hebrews, and he had twelve disciples in order that a certain dispensation of his might be fulfilled. He was pierced by the Jews, and he died and was buried; and they say that after three days he rose and ascended to heaven; and then these twelve disciples went forth into the known parts of the world and taught concerning his greatness with all humility and sobriety. And on this account those also who to-day believe in this preaching are called Christians, who are well known.*

The circumstances under which this Apology of Aristides was prepared are similar in many respects to those under which Paul defended his faith on Mars Hill seventy-five years before. Both were presented in Athens and both were designed to convince audiences which prided themselves on their knowledge of philosophy. But, as Prof. Stokes has well shown,† each apology bears special impress of the age in which it was prepared, thus showing incidentally but conclusively that Paul's speech on Mars Hill has come down to us in its authentic form, unaffected by the later influences surrounding the Christian Church. Aristides devotes a large part of his Apology to the illustration of the necessary and practical immorality of the Greek mythology. He has no difficulty in showing that paganism not only gave no support to high morality, but was itself a positive force to aid the general deteriorating agencies of the times. This is in great contrast with the course of the Apostle Paul, "who enters into no details, but merely seizes upon one or two broad general features of idolatry which naturally struck a devout Jew." Clearly the book of Acts was written in the atmosphere of Christian development which pervaded the middle of the first century, instead of that characterizing the first half of the second century, and the actual Apology of Aristides when it comes to light

---

* Contemporary Review, vol. lx, p. 109, The Apology of Aristides, by George T. Stokes.

† Contemporary Review, vol. lx, p. 113.

closely corresponds to the character which had been given to it by Jerome.

But, now that the discovery has been made, it appears that we have had the Apology of Aristides all the while and did not know it. In the Mechitarite Convent * of St. Lazarus at Venice, as long ago as 1879, there was discovered and published a portion of an old Armenian translation of this Apology of Aristides; but, on account of the interpolation of occasional theological terms in it which clearly belonged to a later date, Renan pronounced it all a forgery. Mr. Harris's discovery shows that while the Armenian translators took the liberty of introducing much theological phraseology of their own times, they had not otherwise departed from a faithful representation of the original.

Still more surprising, however, is the fact that the Apology of Aristides had been unwittingly preserved in a well-known religious romance written in Syriac by a monk in the fifth or sixth century. In the Tale of Baarlam and Josaphat, commented upon by Prof. Max Müller, who endeavours to show the indebtedness of the author to certain Buddhistic literature, it appears that the Syrian romancer had introduced the Apology of Aristides in its entirety.

From three diverse sources, therefore, scholars have been able to establish during the last decade the character of this famous apology, and to show its conformity to the descriptions given of it by the early Church writers, and thus to establish the general correctness of such incidental references in the patristic literature.

---

* See below, p. 226.

A still more important modern discovery is that of Tatian's Diatessaron. This long-lost book was, as the name indicates, a harmony of the four Gospels, Diatessaron meaning "The book of the four." It was referred to by Eusebius * in the early part of the fourth century as "a certain combination and collection of the Gospels, called the Diatessaron," which Tatian had somehow put together and which was still current in some quarters.

<small>2. Tatian's Diatessaron.</small>

Again, Theodoret, an eminent bishop in Syria about the year 430, writes: † "Tatian also composed a gospel called the Diatessaron, removing the genealogies and all the other passages which show that Christ was born of David according to the flesh. This was used not only by the members of his party, but even by those who followed the apostolic doctrine, as they did not perceive the evil design of the composition, but used the book in their simplicity for its conciseness." Furthermore, Theodoret says, "I myself found more than two hundred such books held in respect in the churches of our parts." These Theodoret proceeded to remove, substituting for them the four Gospels.

Another reference was made to Tatian's work in the early part of the thirteenth century by Dionysius Bar-Salibi, Bishop of Amida in Mesopotamia, who wrote in the preface to his Gospel of Mark, "Tatian, a disciple of Justin the Philosopher and Martyr, selected from the four Gospels and wove together and compiled a Gospel, which he called Diatessaron—that is, Miscellany. This writing Mar Ephraem interpreted:

---

* H. E., iv, 29.   † Fabulæ Hæreticæ, i, 20.

its commencement was, In the beginning was the Word." *

It has long been evident that if this work of Tatian was what it was reported to be, it was a most important witness to the existence of all four of the Gospels very early in the second century, for Tatian was a pupil and disciple of Justin Martyr; so that there can be no question that the Memoirs of the Apostles to which Justin refers, and which he quotes, are the same documents from which Tatian made his Diatessaron, or Harmony of the Gospels. If Bar-Salibi's statement, that Tatian's Diatessaron began with the passage "In the beginning was the Word," proves to be correct, we have the most positive and unequivocal testimony to the existence of John's Gospel in the early part of the second century. It is therefore a most significant fact that, upon the discovery of the Diatessaron, it is found that the document fully confirms the descriptions which had been given of it by later apologists and commentators.

Through the influence of Mechitar, a distinguished Armenian convert to the Roman Catholic Church, a flourishing Armenian monastery and church has been maintained at Venice since the early part of the eighteenth century. The congregation has been characterized by the presence of eminent Armenian scholars engaged in the twofold work of translating European books into Armenian and publishing them for the benefit of their countrymen, and, what has proved to be the still more important work, of making the treasures of Armenian literature accessible to European scholars. Among the most important of these latter contributions

---

* Ephraem's Gospel Commentary, by J. H. Hill, p. 6.

is that entitled Exposition of the Concordant Gospel made by S. Ephraem, a Syrian teacher, which proves to be based upon the famous Diatessaron of Tatian. This commentary of Ephraem Syrus was translated into Latin by Prof. Moesinger, of Salzburg, and published in 1876. In the commentary, the passages of Tatian are taken up one by one and commented upon by Ephraem, so that from it we are able, by selecting and putting together these extracts, to reconstruct a large part of the Diatessaron. Though we can not be sure that Ephraem has taken up every sentence of Tatian, what he has quoted is sufficient to establish the fact that Tatian's gospels were essentially the same as the four we now have.

The first passage commented upon corresponds exactly to the first six verses of our fourth Gospel, beginning just as Bar-Salibi said it did. After that the passage from Matthew telling of the birth of John the Baptist is given, and then the announcement to Mary is taken up, when the narrative passes to Luke and to his account of the birth of Christ. And so on through the entire harmony, ending with the great commission found at the close of Matthew's Gospel. Of course these quotations taken from Ephraem's commentary do not make a complete and continuous story, for it is only the more striking sentences upon which the commentator makes notes; but the extracts correspond to our Gospels so closely that there can be no doubt of the source from which they are drawn. Among these quotations, those from the fourth Gospel are very numerous.

As also in the case of the Apology of Aristides, so in this one, the discovery was speedily followed by others enabling us to correct and confirm the opinions formed from the Syrian commentary. In 1881 Father Ciasca at Rome discovered an Arabic manuscript which had long lain unnoticed in the Vatican Library, and which purported to be a copy of the Diatessaron. This discovery led to another of a corresponding Arabic manuscript of the same work in Egypt. From these two manuscripts a text was made for an edition of Tatian's Diatessaron which was published in 1888. A comparison of this with the extracts preserved in Ephraem's commentary on Tatian's work shows that the order of the two is the same in so many peculiar respects that no doubt is left that these Arabic harmonies are translations of Tatian's original work written in the early part of the second century. Thus we have had brought to light almost within the last decade incontrovertible evidence that John's Gospel was received equally with the other three by the generation which immediately followed the death of that great apostle.*

3. Newly discovered Syriac Version.

A third recent discovery of special evidential importance is that of a palimpsest found in 1892 by two English ladies, Mrs. Lewis and her sister, Mrs. Gibson, in the Convent of St. Catharine on Mount Sinai, the same receptacle in which had been preserved Tischendorf's famous Sinaitic manuscript of the New Testament and the Apology of Aristides, to which reference has already been made as discovered by Prof. J. Rendel Harris. Mrs. Lewis, being an accomplished Syriac scholar, was able to recognise to some extent

---

* See The Earliest Life of Christ ever compiled from the Four Gospels, being the Diatessaron of Tatian, lately found, by the Rev. J. Hamlyn Hill (Edinburgh, 1894); also Ante-Nicene Fathers, vol. ix.

NEWLY DISCOVERED EXTERNAL EVIDENCES. 229

the importance of the original writing upon one of the palimpsests which was shown to her at the convent, and by permission of the authorities took photographs of the entire work, consisting of three hundred and fifty-eight pages. Upon showing these, after her return, to Prof. Bensly and Mr. Burkitt, of the British Museum, great excitement was created, since it was found that they had before them a very early Syriac translation of the four Gospels. The later writing imposed upon the sheets contained a history of female saints, probably written about the eighth century, but the original writing was in red ink, which still retained its colour. From the photographs, imperfect as they were, enough could be made out to show that the textual variations corresponded to those of the so-called Curetonian Syriac version, discovered by Canon Cureton in 1847 among the manuscripts brought in 1833 from some of the monasteries in the Nitrian Desert in Lower Egypt.* From a variety of incontestable marks this Curetonian version is shown to be a translation preceding the Peshito version, which came into general use among the Syrian churches in the second and third centuries. One proof of this is that the textual variations of the Curetonian Syriac have a striking correspondence to those found in Tatian's Diatessaron, which, as already shown, was prepared in the early part of the second century.

The importance of Mrs. Lewis's discovery was so evident that plans were made for an immediate return to Mount Sinai more carefully to study the documents.

---

* For further evidence of the early date of the Curetonian, see Chapter VIII.

Accordingly, Prof. and Mrs. Bensly, Mr. and Mrs. Burkitt, and Prof. Rendel Harris accompanied Mrs. Lewis and Mrs. Gibson back to the scene of the discovery, and with every available appliance of modern science and scholarship set themselves to the task of copying the manuscript, using acids to restore the faded colour of the original in many places. The result completely justified the anticipations with which they set out, securing the restoration to the world of one of the earliest translations of the Gospels which was ever made. In general, it may be said that the text of this translation agrees with that of the manuscripts which demonstrably represent the oldest and best text.*

But while there is this indubitable evidence that the version represents the current text of the early part of the second century, it is equally plain that in some places it had been intentionally corrupted in the interests of a well-known heretical sect.

The most conspicuous instance of this relates to the miraculous conception of Christ, which we know to have been denied by Cerinthus at the close of the first century. According to Irenæus,† Cerinthus represented "Jesus as having not been born of a virgin, but as being the son of Joseph and Mary according to the ordinary course of human generation, while he nevertheless was more righteous, prudent, and wise than other men. Moreover, after his baptism Christ descended upon him in the form of a dove from the Supreme Ruler, and that then he proclaimed the unknown Father, and performed miracles." With these views of

---

* The argument upon this point is reserved for Chapter VIII.
† Irenæus, Against Heresies, bk. i, chap. xxvi.

NEWLY DISCOVERED EXTERNAL EVIDENCES. 231

Cerinthus concerning the person of Christ the sect called Ebionites are said to have agreed.

This new copy of the Syriac Gospels evidently aims to support the view of Cerinthus concerning the natural birth of Jesus, but it does this in such a bungling and hesitating way as to demonstrate that the ordinary account involving the miraculous conception is the original account, and must have been the one in circulation in the latter part of the first century. To exhibit the force of the argument, it will be necessary to go somewhat into details, and to present in parallel columns successive variations of texts relating to this most important matter. We will give first a translation of the revised text of 1881; secondly, a translation of the parallel verses of the new Syriac text; and then proceed to show by comparison that the new Syriac is a depraved form of the orthodox text, while the Curetonian Syriac is a purified and corrected form of the new Syriac, thus placing the new Syriac text before the Curetonian, and the text of the latest English revision first of all, and making it presumably a correct representative of the autographs of the Gospels.

MATT. I, 15-25.

Revised Text.	New Syriac Version.
15. Eliud begat Eleazar; and Eleazar begat Matthan; and Matthan begat Jacob;	15. Eliud begat Eleazar: Eleazar begat Matthan: Matthan begat Jacob:
16. And Jacob begat Joseph the husband of Mary, of whom was born Jesus, who is called Christ.	16. Jacob begat Joseph: *Joseph* (to whom was espoused the Virgin Mary) *begat Jesus*, who is called Christ.

17. So all the generations from Abraham unto David are fourteen generations; and from David unto the carrying away to Babylon fourteen generations; and from the carrying away to Babylon unto the Christ fourteen generations.

18. Now the birth of Jesus Christ was on this wise: When his mother Mary had been betrothed to Joseph, before they came together she was found with child of the Holy Ghost.

19. And Joseph her husband, being a righteous man, and not willing to make her a public example, was minded to put her away privily.

20. But when he thought on these things, behold, an angel of the Lord appeared unto him in a dream, saying, Joseph, thou son of David, fear not to take unto thee Mary thy wife: for that which is conceived (Greek, begotten) in her is of the Holy Ghost.

21. And she shall bring forth a son; and thou shalt call his name Jesus; for it is he that shall save his people from their sins.

17. All these generations from Abraham to David are fourteen generations: and from David to the Babylonian exile fourteen generations: and from the Babylonian exile to the Christ fourteen generations.

18. Now the birth of the Christ was on this wise: When his mother Mary was espoused to Joseph, when they had not come together, she was found with child from the Holy Ghost.

19. But Joseph her husband, because he was just, was unwilling to expose Mary: and he was minded that he would quietly divorce her.

20. But while he was meditating on these things there appeared to him an angel of the Lord in a vision and said to him, Joseph, son of David, fear not to take Mary thy wife, for that which $\left\{\begin{array}{l}\text{is}\\ \text{will be}\end{array}\right\}$ born of her is from the Holy Spirit.

21. *She shall bear thee* a son, and $\left\{\begin{array}{l}\text{thou shalt}\\ \text{she shall}\end{array}\right\}$ call his name Jesus: for he shall save his people from their sins.

22. Now all this is come to pass, that it might be fulfilled which was spoken by the Lord through the prophet, saying,

23. Behold, the virgin shall be with child, and shall bring forth a son, and they shall call his name Immanuel; which is, being interpreted, God with us.

24. And Joseph arose from his sleep, and did as the angel of the Lord commanded him, and took unto him his wife;

25. And knew her not till she had brought forth a son: and he called his name Jesus.

22. Now this which happened was that there might be fulfilled that which was spoken by the Lord in Isaiah the prophet, who had said,

23. Behold, the Virgin shall conceive and shall bear a son, and they shall call his name Emmanuel, which is by interpretation, our God with us.

24. But when Joseph arose from his sleep he did as the angel commanded him, and took his wife, and she

25. *Bare him a son*, and *he called* his name Jesus.

On comparing these two accounts, it appears that they closely agree, except in verses 16, 21, and 25, where in the Syriac Gospel the ordinary text is so changed as to represent that the birth of Jesus was altogether natural. Whereas the ordinary text says simply, " Mary *of whom was born Jesus. . . . And she shall bring forth a son . . .* and till *she had brought forth a son,*" the Syriac Gospel says, " Joseph *begat* Jesus," " she shall bear *thee* a son," and " she bare *him* a son, and he called his name Jesus." It requires but slight attention to see that the changes here introduced are all in the Syriac version, making the ordinary text the original; for, while the ordinary text is consistent throughout, the Syriac version is inconsistent in that it has left intact several passages which clearly imply the miraculous conception.

To get the full force of the argument, it is important also to notice that the language of the verses into which these significant changes have been made is such that slight alteration would produce the result so far as those verses were concerned. But to eliminate the whole idea of the miraculous conception, the heretical copyist would have had to change the whole texture of the paragraph, which he did not dare to do.

For example, in the Syriac version the eighteenth verse retains the assertion that Mary "was found with child from the Holy Ghost," and that, "when they [Joseph and Mary] had not come together"; while in the nineteenth verse it is inconceivable that Joseph should have been minded quietly to divorce Mary if he had reason to believe the child was his. At any rate, this is not what a just man would have thought of doing. Again, in the twentieth verse, the vision of the angel of the Lord to tell him not to fear to take Mary is entirely out of place if Jesus was his son in natural order, and not through the Holy Spirit, as is asserted in the last clause of the verse. The retention of the twenty-third verse, containing the prophecy of the virgin birth, is another of the inconsistencies of the new Syriac version.

Thus, from even a hasty examination, there would seem to be little doubt that the newly discovered Syriac version is a bungling halfway attempt to change the meaning of the orthodox text which already had the field, and which the boldest heretic did not dare to deal with freely. The supposition that the ordinary text should have grown out of the new Syriac version con-

NEWLY DISCOVERED EXTERNAL EVIDENCES. 235

tradicts all our knowledge of the action of the causes and motives which lead to and permit the textual changes which occur in sacred literature. The reference of this text, therefore, to the heretical sect of "Adoptionists" represented by Cerinthus at the close of the first century is based upon substantial evidence.

That this new Syriac version preceded the Curetonian can also easily be shown; for, while in the main the text of the two is evidently the same, it is equally evident that the Curetonian revision was by an orthodox hand, who contented himself with the simplest method by which the text could be brought back into harmony with the current view. For example, in Matt. i, 16, where the new Syriac version reads, "Joseph, to whom was betrothed the Virgin Mary, begat Jesus Christ," the Curetonian Syriac omits the repeated Joseph, and by a slight change eliminates the representation that Jesus Christ was begotten by Joseph, making it read, 'To whom was betrothed the Virgin Mary, and bare Jesus Christ.'' That this was a modification of the new Syriac version appears from comparing both with the orthodox version, which reads, "And Jacob begat Joseph, the husband of Mary, of whom was born Jesus who is called Christ." The relationship of the new Syriac to the Curetonian is seen in the introduction into both of the "Virgin Mary" and the phrase "to whom was espoused." In the orthodox version Joseph is called the husband, since espousal and marriage were not so sharply defined among the Jews as they are in modern civilization.

In i, 25 there is similar evidence that the Curetonian text was derived from that which was the basis of the new Syriac, for in both the clause in the orthodox version "and knew her not till" is omitted, the new Syriac version reading, "And she bare him a son"; while the Curetonian, though omitting the significant clause quoted from the orthodox text, brings the verse into line with it by a slight transposition of letters, so that it reads, "And she bare him, [viz.] the Son." But the Curetonian text, while omitting the phrase in the twenty-fifth verse "and he knew her not till," has substituted in its place the clause "and he was living with her in purity till."

This is by no means the whole of the argument, for there is much else bearing in the same direction, as, for example, the overanxiety of the Curetonian revisers to support the theory of Mary's virginity. Where the orthodox version in i, 25 tells us that Joseph took "his wife," the Curetonian reads, took "Mary"; and in i, 20, where the orthodox version read, "Fear not to take to thee Mary thy wife," the Curetonian read, "Fear not to take to thee Mary thy spouse"; and again, i, 19, where the orthodox text read, "Joseph her husband," the Curetonian reads simply "Joseph." *

Any one familiar with the principles of textual criticism can see that the order of development in this interesting case has been from the orthodox version to the slightly but imperfectly altered text of the new Syriac version, from which, with slight but imperfectly wrought out counterchanges, has been derived the text of the Curetonian Syriac. But as the Curetonian Syriac is demonstrably earlier than the Peshito, and by its conformity to Tatian proved to belong to the first half

---

* See Prof. J. Rendel Harris in Contemporary Review, vol. lxvi, p. 654 *et seq.*

NEWLY DISCOVERED EXTERNAL EVIDENCES. 237

of the second century, the new Syriac text is thrown back to the very beginning of the century, and the orthodox text is pushed back into the first century, and is thus proved to have the indorsement of the apostolic age itself.

A fourth discovery of equal importance with the preceding is that of a portion of the so-called "Gospel of Peter."* This is a fragment discovered by the French Archæological Mission at Cairo, in 1887, in a package which came down from the Christian tombs in Akmin in Upper Egypt, but was not published till 1892. The larger part of the writing in this package or book consists of a discussion in Greek arithmetic. The portion of the Gospel of Peter preserved is that extending from the account of the washing of Pilate's hands to the return of the disciples to Galilee after the resurrection, making in all about sixteen hundred words.

4. The Gospel of Peter.

Like Tatian's Diatessaron, the Gospel of Peter was chiefly known in modern times by the references to it which are found in the early Church fathers. It was mentioned by Eusebius,† who says that Serapion, Bishop of Antioch about 190, found copies of it in the mountain district of Rhossus, where it had evidently been in use for some time. Serapion is said to have described it as incorporating the errors of the Docetæ, who denied the reality of Christ's human body. He says also that some portions of the history were somewhat amplified in it.

The discovery of a portion of the original amply

---

* This, also, may be found in Ante-Nicene Fathers, vol. ix.
† H. E., iv, 12.

confirms the correctness of this representation. The Gospel of Peter was not an original Gospel. But, like Tatian's Diatessaron, it is a compilation from the four Gospels, weaving the separate accounts into one story, and colouring them slightly by occasional interpolations and slight changes in the interest of the Docetic heresy. For example, in the account of the crucifixion it adds a clause stating that Jesus " kept silence as having no pain "; while the last words of Jesus from the cross, " My God, my God, why hast thou forsaken me?" is changed into "My might, my might, thou hast forsaken me."

But the important point to be noticed here is that the compiler of the Gospel of Peter made use of the fourth Gospel as well as of the first three, thus demonstrating not only its existence, but its recognition by the churches at the time of the compilation, whatever that was.

Upon the first publication of this fragment, the early date of its compilation was cogently argued by Prof. J. H. Thayer.* The most convincing evidence consists of a passage in Justin Martyr's First Apology (i, 35), which was evidently quoted from this Gospel of Peter. " In detailing the fulfilment of prophecy in Christ's career, Justin says, ' Ridiculing him, they set him on the judgment seat and said, " Judge for us."' It had been previously thought by some scholars † that Justin got this incident from some apocryphal source. That opinion seems now to be established.' For it is evident that Justin derived this form of statement from

---

* See The Boston Commonwealth, December 31, 1892.
† For example, Hilgenfeld, Die Evangelien Justin's, p. 241.

NEWLY DISCOVERED EXTERNAL EVIDENCES. 239

this very Gospel of Peter, which, in its account of the mockery, says, "They clothed him with purple, and set him on a seat of judgment, saying, 'Judge righteously, King of Israel.'"

Justin Martyr's familiarity with the Gospel of Peter, therefore, throws that document back into the first half of the second century, a date which is now pretty generally accorded to it. Thus it becomes an additional witness of great power to the existence of the fourth Gospel in the first quarter of the second century, for it is scarcely possible that that Gospel should have reached such a plane of equality with the others as to be used in a heretical compilation made in the second quarter of the second century, unless it had been generally recognised for a considerable period before.

The result of this abundant and new direct evidence is to shorten the historical interval to be spanned between the apostolic period and the known acknowledgment of the four Gospels fully fifty years. The force of the evidence is all the stronger from the significant fact that it has all been in one direction. Whenever the new documents have been discovered they have uniformly confirmed the traditional belief in the early acknowledgment of the Gospels.

The Traditional View confirmed.

It was freely said, for example, during the third quarter of the nineteenth century that if we could but discover Tatian's Diatessaron it would be found that Tatian did not regard the fourth Gospel as on an equality with the other three. But we have discovered the Diatessaron, and we find that it does just what the agnostic critics said it would not do. It was freely said by these same critics that if we should discover the so-called Gospel of Peter we should find in it an absence of close dependence upon the four Gospels. But a portion of it has been discovered, and we find that it, too, is nothing but a compilation with evident heretical comments. Thus it becomes more and more clear that the four Gospels already in the early part of the second century had the field all to themselves. It is largely these facts which have compelled Harnack to acknowledge that the agnostic critics of the past fifty years have been following phantoms of their own creation. The traditional or, better, the *historical* view concerning the dates of the New Testament literature were correct.

But as there are two other lines of argument in support of the same conclusion, further comment must be deferred until they have been presented.

NOTE.—Though without important positive bearing upon the question in hand, the great interest elicited by the recent discovery of a few purported new sayings of Jesus requires a few words of comment. Early in the year 1897, Messrs. Grenfell and Hunt, of Oxford, found in the ruins of Oxyrhynchus, on the edge of the Libyan Desert, a hundred and twenty miles south of Cairo, with other Greek papyri, a single leaf containing seven or eight passages, each beginning with the words "Jesus says," and without any connecting narrative. Their translation is as follows, the periods indicating the existence of words which are undecipherable:

1. ". . . and then shalt thou see clearly to cast out the mote that is in thy brother's eye."

2. "Jesus saith, Except ye fast to the world, ye shall in no wise find the kingdom of God; and except ye keep the Sabbath, ye shall not see the Father."

3. "Jesus saith, I stood in the midst of the world, and in the flesh was I seen of them, and I found all men drunken, and none found I athirst among them, and my soul grieveth over the sins of men, because they are blind in their heart. . . ."

4. "... poverty. ..."

5. "Jesus saith, Wherever there are ... and there is one ... alone, I am with him. Raise the stone and there thou shalt find me, cleave the wood and there am I."

6. "Jesus saith, A prophet is not acceptable in his own country, neither doth a physician work cures upon them that know him."

7. "Jesus saith, A city built upon the top of a high hill, and stablished, can neither fall nor be hid."

This discovery has given rise to an endless amount of discussion and conjecture as to whether we have here a fragment of some of those numerous efforts to which Luke refers* as having been put forth in his time to record the doings and sayings of Christ. It requires, however, but a brief examination to see that, however this may be, there is no indication in this fragment that anything of importance has been omitted by the evangelists in their compendious accounts of the life of Christ.

The first of these sayings agrees exactly with Luke vi, 42. The second is new and peculiar, and, on a literal interpretation, is so out of harmony with the well-known teachings of Christ as to suggest strongly that it was modified in the interests of some of the early heretical sects of Jewish proclivities. Christ did not urge fasting. The third saying has the appearance of a compilation. "Was seen in the flesh" is identical with 1 Tim. iii, 10; "drunken," with Matt. xxiv, 49; "thirst," with Rev. xxi, 6, xxii, 17, etc. The general tenor of the saying is like that of John i, 10. The fourth is too defective to be of any value. The fifth is likewise defective in the first part. The last part is likely enough an original saying of Jesus, but really adds nothing of importance to what we already have. The sixth saying contains an addition to the familiar passage in Luke, "No prophet is acceptable in his own country"; but the addition is not of importance. If genuine, the compilers of the Gospels did not show bad sense in omitting it. The seventh saying certainly obscures the figure in Matt. v, 14 by mixing two diverse conceptions, and has the weakness of a secondary modification.

There is certainly nothing in this fragment to make it likely that it is a portion of the λόγια κυριακά (*sayings of our Lord*), which

---

* Luke i, 1; Acts i, 1.

Papias says were written in Hebrew by Matthew, and upon which he is said to have commented;* for in all probability that was nothing else than the entire Gospel of Matthew itself, since both in classical and New Testament usage the word λόγια, "oracles," has a much more comprehensive sense than the word λόγοι, "words."

Upon the whole question of the completeness of our Gospels and of their representation of Jesus, Prof. J. H. Ropes has given the best statement we have seen:

"The question that springs to the mind of every one, especially when such a discovery as these 'Logia Jesu' is put into one's hands, is whether new light is about to break on the Gospel traditions, whether the little region of our knowledge is to be enlarged by new traditions carried by missionaries to Egypt and there loyally repeated and at last written down, or from books brought perhaps from remote spots in Palestine or Asia Minor by Egyptian travelers and kept as doubtful treasures in some dusty library in a city up the Nile. If Papias should be found, the direct tradition that he preserved would probably be found to have been excerpted by Eusebius, who was in the habit of substantially exhausting the information of his authorities. His value would come from the more searching methods of our historical science, which draws inferences where the ancients only extracted positive statements. But such a discovery as this leaf of words which 'Jesus saith' opens larger possibilities. Perhaps these are genuine, perhaps some of the ten preceding leaves of the mutilated book may contain more and may yet be found. May it be that the Gospels are in danger of being superseded by these newcomers, or, to put it more reasonably, that our idea of our Lord could be considerably modified by some new knowledge?

"It may be confidently replied that this is wholly unlikely. It is probable that the canonical Gospels have preserved practically all the tradition of the evangelical history which came beyond the borders of Palestine at all. The writers of the second, third, and fourth centuries were profoundly interested in all that could be learned of the life of Christ. They occasionally mention extra canonical sayings that they have picked up here and there, and reverence for the Gospels does not prevent them from transmitting

---

* Eusebius, H. E., iii, 39.

such. But of these all that can possibly be thought genuine do not amount to twenty, and no one of them is sure enough or important enough to change our conception of Jesus and his teaching. One gets strongly the impression from studying these remains that the work of the writers of our Gospels, the laboriousness of which we seldom realize, was done with a thoroughness which practically exhausted the sources of knowledge at their disposal. We have, doubtless, not indeed a complete account of Jesus' teaching, but yet a complete account of the topics on which he taught and of the ideas which he most emphasized.

"And it is further to be noted that outside tradition can seldom or never have such certainty as that contained in the Gospels of the New Testament. Our reliance on them depends partly on their early date, now well ascertained, but also on the guarantee of the Catholic Church. They contain the history as those churches which had heard the apostles preach received it. They were accepted because they offered not new traditions but old, and the writers were in a sense the agents of the churches. The perpetual tradition of the church accredits them as it does not any other documents whatever. But the final test must be the consistency and intelligibility of the account of Jesus and his teaching which the Gospels furnish. The real difficulty with all such traditions as these Logia, or the other extra-canonical sayings of Jesus that have been collected, is that they lack the support which in a large mass of material the several parts give to one another, and that they have no context to make them intelligible. No one can tell what surprises may be in store, but of rivals to the Gospels there can be no question, and of valuable direct light on the life of our Lord there can be comparatively little hope. Indirect light, ancient documents which will make clearer to us the conditions in which our Gospels were written and how they were collected,. and information about the complex life of the early Church, we may hope for in considerable abundance."[*]

---

[*] See The Congregationalist for August 19, 1897, pp. 253, 254.

CHAPTER VIII.

THE TESTIMONY OF TEXTUAL CRITICISM.

The Problem.
IT is well known that we have none of the original manuscripts of any of the books of the New Testament. The oldest copies in the possession of scholars are supposed to have been made about the year 350 A. D.—that is, about three hundred years after the date usually assigned to the writings of most of the books. It is a matter of no less interest than importance to ascertain how we can assure ourselves that the text we now have is correct, so that we can rely upon it for doctrine and reproof. For, even if we possessed manuscripts purporting to be original and claiming to have the signature of an apostle, we should still be called upon to prove that the claim was authentic and the signature genuine, which might be found harder than to prove by circumstantial evidence both the genuineness of the document itself and a reasonable degree of accuracy in its transmission.

It requires but little attention directed to the work of textual critics to perceive that it is something far more than mere comparison of manuscripts and versions and patristic quotations. The results of criticism are attained by strict adherence to scientific principles of induction. Here, as everywhere in science, the true light which penetrates the unknown is derived from the facts which are known. As, in the realm of physical science, the investigator is called upon to produce a known cause which is open to observation, and from this is expected to be able to account for the phenomena under consideration, so the textual critic is called upon to account for the variations of manuscripts upon such natural principles that the true condition of the original text shall be established beyond reasonable doubt. The true text is that which will most naturally account for all the variations.

The starting point for the textual critic is his knowledge of the limited capacity of the human mind, and of the motives which control the actions of men. Man's mental force is so connected with the ever-changing elements of his physical organization that his best intentions are never exactly carried out. There is thus a physical basis for a large portion of the variations in the specific acts which men put forth. The astronomers are familiar with this fact in the necessity they are under of finding the personal equation of each observer. The eyes of no two observers are exactly alike, nor is the acuteness of the vision of any one person an absolutely uniform quantity. An astronomer was recently heard to remark that before making important observations he found it advantageous to rest his eyes by going into a dark room and looking for a while into the blank space before him. It is well known that proof readers can not so readily detect mistakes when they are wearied from overwork, or any other cause, as when their minds are fresh; while, on our railroads,

The Known Causes of Variation.

great care has to be taken not only to eliminate from the employees those who are partially deaf and colour blind, but to avoid the adoption of signals which are likely to be mistaken for one another, and to guard against everything which may dull the senses of the employees, and so interfere with their alertness in reading the signals and in descrying any impending danger. The limitation of the hours of labour becomes, therefore, a question of the public welfare, and the prohibition of the use of intoxicants by the employees becomes an economical necessity.

The infirmities under which the human mind operates in the reproduction of manuscripts are such that it is not possible for a person to make two copies of an extended document which shall be exactly alike. In both of them there will be mistakes, and each will differ to some extent from the other. Even in printed documents which have been subjected to the searching ordeal of proof reading mistakes are sure to occur. For example, the first edition of the King James's translation of the Bible was printed in 1611. On comparing this with the editions printed in 1613, more than four hundred variations are brought to light, taking no account of differences in spelling. Among these variations are some which are very considerable. In the edition of 1613 the whole clause " and put my finger into the print of the nails " (John xx, 25) is omitted. In another place two whole verses were omitted; while in the edition of 1611 twenty-one words in Ex. xiv, 10 were accidentally repeated. The edition of 1613 also was unfortunate in more than one instance in omitting the word " not " where it completely re-

Observed Instances.

versed the meaning. In this edition, 2 Tim. iv, 16 reads, "I pray God that it may be laid to their charge." In 1632 an edition appeared which omitted the word "not" in the seventh commandment, and in the same year another edition, which made 1 Cor. v, 9 read, "Know ye not that the unrighteous shall inherit the kingdom of God." The edition of 1611 reads in Gen. xxvii, 44, "until thy brother's fury *turn* away"; the edition of 1613 substitutes "*pass* away." In Mark xii, 13 the edition of 1611 reads, "and they *send* unto him certain of the Pharisees," while in the edition of 1613 it is changed to the past tense—"they *sent*," etc. In Heb. x, 23 the true reading is, "the profession of our *hope*." Through a misprint, this stands in all the later copies of King James's Version "the profession of our *faith*." And in Job xxix, 3 the edition of 1613 has changed the "*walked* through darkness" of the first edition to "*shined* through darkness."*

With such illustrations of human liability to error before him, the task of the textual critic is to determine, if possible, both the limit and the law of the tendency. He is to eliminate the error and correct the texts by tracing the variations to their probable cause. In the cases just enumerated the omission of the clause in John xx, 25 is readily explained by the fact that the words " print of the nails " occur twice in successive lines:

Except I shall see in his hands the *print of the nails* and put my finger into the *print of the nails*, and thrust my hands into his side, I will not believe.

This would naturally confuse the type-setter, since he might easily think that the second occurrence of the

---

* See Critical Essays of Ezra Abbot, p. 223 *et seq.*

phrase was the point he had reached on taking off his eyes from the manuscript to concentrate his attention upon the work of selecting and arranging the type for the first. The same confusion occasioned by two similar endings produced the opposite result in Ex. xiv, 10. In this case the type-setter encountered the words "children of Israel" twice:

And when Pharaoh drew nigh, the *children of Israel* lifted up their eyes, and, behold, the Egyptians marched after them; and they were sore afraid: and the *children of Israel* cried out unto the Lord.

But when he returned from setting it up the second time, his eye fell on the first sentence, and the second was repeated without further thought. Mistakes of this kind are as frequent as they are natural. The Greek word *homoeoteluton*—meaning similarity of ending—is technically used to describe them.

The omissions of the word "not" referred to are evidently pure blunders, but of such a sort that they could ordinarily have been detected from the nature of the context. No one would seriously think that Paul had asserted that the unrighteous should inherit the kingdom of God. The substitution of "sent" for "send" in the edition of 1613 is traceable, however, to a well-known mental tendency. It is slightly easier to make the tenses of a narrative conform than it is to maintain the liveliness of conception involved in the use of the historical present. In narrating the events of the Saviour's history, it is easier to say "they *sent* unto him the Pharisees" than to say "they *send* unto him the Pharisees." It is more in accordance with our ordinary conceptions, and therefore easier to speak of the profession of our *faith* than it is of the profession of

THE TESTIMONY OF TEXTUAL CRITICISM. 249

our *hope*. In Job xxix, 3 the substitution of "walk" for "shine" can be accounted for by the occurrence of the words "darkness" and "light," which would suggest "shine," and by the fact that the word "shine" occurs in the line immediately above it.

Thus a close analysis of these known variations from the edition of 1611 in the edition of 1613 would approximately reveal the causes producing them. So limited, however, is the material in this comparison that in many cases the cause would not be clear. Our inference respecting it would often be based upon only a slight amount of probability. In other instances, however, the probability would be so great that it would amount almost to a certainty.

With this brief preliminary examination of a well-known instance of variation in different reprints of the same work, where both are before us and their relations to each other are well known, we can more intelligently advance to the broader consideration of the variations in the early manuscripts of the New Testament. In doing this we shall find that these variations have as real a physical basis as do the aberrations of the stars in their courses, and that they are as subject to scientific classification and treatment as are the facts of the astronomer or geologist.

The Documentary Evidence.

The documentary evidence from which to reconstruct the autographs of the New Testament consists of three classes: 1, Early manuscript copies, or codices; 2, early translations; 3, early quotations. Before proceeding further it will be profitable to take a brief survey of these external sources of information.

There are four manuscripts of pre-eminent value in this discussion. They will be described, not necessarily in the order of their importance, but in the order of their nomenclature, for it has been agreed upon by textual critics to refer to the oldest class of manuscripts by the capital letters of the English alphabet. As, however, one of the most important of all the codices was discovered after the first letters of the English alphabet had been appropriated, scholars found it convenient to designate this by the first letter of the Hebrew alphabet.

1. Greek Manuscripts.

(1) א (Aleph) is the celebrated CODEX SINAITICUS, discovered in 1859 by Tischendorf in the library of the Convent of St. Catharine on Mount Sinai. This contains the whole of the New Testament, written in capital letters upon leaves of beautiful vellum. The pages are thirteen and a half by fourteen and seven eighths inches square, and the writing is in four columns of forty-eight lines each. There are scarcely any marks of punctuation, no breathings and accents, and no separation between the words, the last letter of a word oftentimes beginning a new line. Frequently recurring words are also often written in an abbreviated form, and the manuscript bears marks of having been revised and corrected by three or four later hands. From the character of the manuscript, its date has been assigned to the middle of the fourth century. Indeed, it is considered to be quite possible that it is "one of the fifty copies of the Bible which in the year 331 the Emperor Constantine ordered to be executed for Constantinople

THE TESTIMONY OF TEXTUAL CRITICISM. 251

under the direction of Eusebius," the great Church historian.

(2) A, the CODEX ALEXANDRINUS, now in the British Museum, was obtained from the Patriarch of Constantinople, who is thought to have brought it from Alexandria. It came to England as a present to Charles I. It contains nearly all of the New Testament, and is written in capital letters upon quarto leaves of vellum, about thirteen by ten inches. There is no division of words, and scarcely any punctuation. This manuscript is assigned to the beginning or middle of the fifth century.

(3) B, CODEX VATICANUS.—At what time this manuscript came to Rome is not definitely known. It contains the whole of the four Gospels and nearly all the rest of the New Testament. Its page is a quarto. The text is written in three columns, forty-two lines to a column. There are no intervals between the words, except at the end of the paragraphs. It is known to have been in the Vatican Library since 1475. Its date is supposed to be about the same as that of the Sinaitic Codex—namely, about 350.

(4) D, or CODEX BEZÆ, has both a Greek and a Latin text in parallel columns. It was obtained by the distinguished scholar Beza from a monastery in Lyons when that city was sacked in 1562. In 1581 Beza presented it to the University of Cambridge, England, where it now constitutes one of the treasures of their library. It is a quarto volume, ten by eight inches, with the Greek text on the left-hand page and the Latin on the right hand. There are thirty-four lines to a page. It was probably executed about the middle of the sixth century, but it represents a much earlier text.

There is preserved a large number of other copies both of the whole and of parts of the New Testament. But in their variations they are all so grouped around these that in the brief space allowed for the consideration of the facts here we shall find it profitable to limit our statements chiefly to these four representative manuscripts.

Besides the manuscripts, however, there are the early translations and the quotations of the early Christian Fathers which furnish independent evidence of what was the original text. Of the versions, the four most important are the Old Latin, known to have been in use in northern Africa at the close of the second century, the Old (or Curetonian) Syriac, traceable to the early part of the second century, the two Egyptian versions (the Thebaic and Memphitic) of about the same date. But we do not have copies of these versions that are any earlier than those already referred to of the original text. They testify, however, to the readings current when the translations were made.

2. Early Translations.

The quotations from the early Christian Fathers are most important in bearing positive testimony both to the existence and to the character of the early variations in the text of the New Testament.

3. The Quotations.

ORIGEN, who was catechist in Alexandria about 230 A. D., wrote voluminous commentaries and apologetic treatises in the Greek language. His quotations are very abundant, and he pays special attention to the variations of texts that were already in existence.

TERTULLIAN, a Latin father in the vicinity of Carthage at the close of the second century, also wrote

THE TESTIMONY OF TEXTUAL CRITICISM. 253

extensively and quoted most liberally. From his writings we learn much directly concerning the condition of the Greek text, to which he often refers, but more concerning the Old Latin version, which was in use among his people, and concerning which a good part of our information comes from his quotations.

IRENÆUS, a Greek missionary from Asia Minor, who spent the larger part of his life in Lyons, France, and became bishop of that city about the year 170, wrote an extensive treatise against the heretics of the time, and both freely commented upon certain variations in the texts which were in circulation, and showed by his own quotations the existence in his time of well-defined classes of various readings.

CLEMENT of Alexandria was the catechetical teacher at Alexandria preceding Origen, who was his pupil. Clement wrote much in the Greek language, and had occasion to quote and comment upon a considerable portion of the New Testament. His work in Alexandria began before the close of the second century.

JUSTIN MARTYR comes to notice about the year 140, having been born in Palestine near the beginning of the second century, and suffering martyrdom in 165. In his two Apologies and in the Dialogue with Trypho —all composed about 150—he interweaves a large number of quotations from the Gospels, and thus incidentally bears witness to the readings which were current at that time.

MARCION was a noted heretic contemporary with Justin Martyr. He discarded the Old Testament, and published an edition of the Gospel of Luke so mutilated as to adapt it to the support of his heretical views. No copy of this is in existence, but it can be largely reconstructed from the quotations made by Tertullian and Epiphanius in their successful efforts to controvert Marcion's heresies. These quotations bear important testimony to the state of the text in the New Testament in the early part of the second century.

From a comparison of the readings supported by these and other witnesses, a scientific basis is laid for estimating their value, and of determining the history of the variations and the originals from which they sprang. Upon this examination and comparison is based the science of textual criticism, whose rules of procedure are, as already remarked, as well ordered and as securely based as those of any other inductive science. We shall find it advantageous to pause here a little in our argument to consider the method by which textual critics reach their conclusions.

Among the rules of textual criticism, two are of such special importance that they cover nearly the whole ground. These are: 1, The shorter reading is most likely to be the original reading; 2, the harder reading is most likely to be the original. These rules serve as the ordinary touchstone by which both the general value of a manuscript and the correctness of a particular reading are mainly determined. It should be borne in mind, however, that the rules are based upon the cumulation of a great number of probabilities, each one of which might be successfully challenged if it stood alone. The reasons underlying these have already been hinted at. In proceeding we will first show more fully the application of the rules and the reasons underlying them, and then note how they are really confirmed by some of the apparent exceptions.

The Rules of Textual Criticism.

THE TESTIMONY OF TEXTUAL CRITICISM. 255

The rule that ordinarily the shorter text is the original arises from the fact that there are known to be in operation several causes tending to secure the amplification of a statement in the course of copying, while there are few causes tending to produce the opposite result. So definite are the causes tending to produce amplification that their effect can be roughly estimated, just as the mathematician can estimate the chances of any particular arrangement of dice in successive throws when he knows how the dice are loaded. In fact, the mind of the ordinary scribe when engaged in copying a manuscript is loaded with several well-known, distinct tendencies leading to amplification. With a considerable degree of certainty, therefore, this rule can be used as a critical test of the value both of manuscripts and of single readings.

The Scientific Basis.

As already intimated, the physical basis of this rule is the inertia of the human mind. The most conscientious copyist can never quite free his thoughts and actions from the influence of preconceptions and habitual lines of movement. Indeed, few are aware until their attention is called to it how complicated is the process of obtaining ideas from the written or printed page. At every step the reader imposes his own interpretation upon the language, and always to a greater or less extent reads not only the lines, but between the lines. The transcriber is therefore, in proportion to his intelligence, sure to become to some extent an interpreter and corrector.

Rev. Dr. Riggs, who translated the Bible into the Armenian language, relates that when he was putting it through the press in New York he had six compositors employed, five of whom spoke English and had no knowledge of the Armenian language further than what would enable them to select the letters from the case. Their work was therefore almost wholly mechanical. The sixth compositor was a native Armenian, who understood the copy which he was setting up. But this native Armenian made more mistakes than did all the others put together. The English-speaking compositors did not know enough to make a mistake in Armenian, while the Armenian's mind was so constantly active that it was continually making trouble. While they could not read between the lines if they would, he could not help doing so.

Reading between the Lines.

During the exciting political campaign of 1896 large posters were put up all over a small town in Ohio announcing that a certain speaker was to demonstrate the folly of free silver by the aid of stereopticon illustrations and calcium light. When the lecturer arrived it was found that he never resorted to this means of enforcing his ideas, and was not at all prepared to do so. But not only had this been announced on the posters, it was repeated in various items in the local paper. Very naturally, inquiry was set on foot to account for the mistake, for evidently it could not be causeless. It was soon found that a letter commending the lecturer stated that he "illumined his speeches with most interesting illustrations." Unconsciously the committee had read between the lines, and had added a most natural interpretation of the text. The writer of the recommendation was a literary man of poetical temperament, to whose thought calcium light was not at all necessary for the illumination of a political address. Whereas the committee, in thinking of the wants of an ordinary audience and of the devices which were in common use, were having calcium light continually in their minds. Innocently enough, therefore, they in their announcement stated explicitly what they thought the language of the recommendation meant. The production of that letter naturally explained the mistake.

In estimating what additions and changes in the text are likely to be made by transcribers, it is necessary to start with a correct knowledge of the mental characteristics of this important class of persons. Upon this point we can do no better than to quote the discriminating words of Westcott and Hort:

Mental Characteristics of Copyists.

> Every change not purely mechanical made by a transcriber is in some sense of the nature of a correction. . . . Those which bear any relation to sense would never be made unless in the eyes of the scribe who makes them they were improvements in sense or in the expression of sense; even when made unconsciously, it is the relative satisfaction which they give to his mental state at the time that creates or shapes them. Yet in literature of high quality it is, as a rule, improbable that a change made by transcribers should improve an author's sense or express his full and exact sense better than he has done himself. It follows that, with the exception of pure blunders, readings originating with scribes must always at the time have combined the appearance of improvement with the absence of its reality. If they had not been plausible, they would not have existed; yet their excellence must have been either superficial or partial, and the balance of inward and essential excellence must lie against them.*

---

* The New Testament in the Original Greek, vol. ii, p. 27.

Any person who has had much to do with ordinary proof readers and reporters can readily appreciate the correctness of these remarks. Usually the intentions of these important members of the literary fraternity are good, but their mental horizon is necessarily somewhat narrowed by their occupation. So exclusively is the attention of proof readers given to the mere proprieties of speech that they have a distinct tendency to sacrifice strength of utterance to supposed elegance of diction; while they are peculiarly liable to misapprehend technical terms and the profounder forms of expression used by the master minds whose addresses they are set to report or to prune. The point is well illustrated by the experiences of a lecturer who had appropriately used the word "infinitesimal"; but the reporter, who was unfamiliar with mathematical expressions, came to him on the next day with his report already printed in the paper, and, displaying it, asked if he had not been correct in changing the word "infinitesimal" to "infinite."

Doubtless more than one person has had trouble in keeping proof readers from changing "juridical" into judicial. There is a well-known passage in the Old Testament * which speaks of the "sound of the *going* in the tops of the mulberry trees" as the signal upon which the children of Israel were to rise and smite the hosts of the Philistines. But a very capable proof reader, who was less familiar with the Bible than with some other things, insisted on changing the copy of this in a sermon which he was reading to "the sound of a *gong* in the tops of the mulberry trees."

---

* 2 Sam. v, 24; 1 Chron. xiv, 15.

THE TESTIMONY OF TEXTUAL CRITICISM. 259

Jesus I know, and Paul I know, thinks the proof reader when coming to unfamiliar words, but who are you? and so the change is innocently made in the supposed service of truth.

It is thus easy to see that the natural tendency of a scribe in copying a manuscript would be to add explanatory words, or make modifications which would remove what appeared to him an infelicity or obscurity in the statement. For example, in Matt. xxv, 6 a certain class of texts read, "Behold, the bridegroom *cometh*"; whereas another class (א, B, D) omits the "cometh," and reads simply, "Behold, the bridegroom." Now the longer of these readings simply gives explicit statement to what any one can see is implicitly contained in the shorter reading. From what we know of the mental habits of scribes, we can but think it much more likely that this word "cometh" should have been added in process of transcription than that it should have been omitted. Again, in Matt. xviii, 28 some texts read, "Pay *me* what thou owest," while others (א, B, D) omit the "me" and read simply, "Pay what thou owest." Here again it is readily seen that a scribe would be more likely to *insert* "me" than to *omit* it; for of course that is what is meant, and the mind of the scribe would naturally give explicit statement to the obvious meaning contained in the shorter form.

Examples of Amplification.

Influence of "Assimilation."

This tendency of the transcriber to amplification would manifestly be intensified when the same passage occurs in other portions of the Bible in a fuller form than is found in that which is being copied. In such cases the general tendency to amplification is re-enforced by the independent and additional tendency to *assimilate* the two accounts.

A good instance occurs in Matt. ix, 13, where the version of 1611 reads, "I am not come to call the righteous, but sinners *to repentance.*" In the Revised Version, as in ℵ, B, D, the words "to repentance" are omitted. The same passage occurs in Mark ii, 17 with the same variations in the versions and manuscripts. But in Luke v, 32, where also the same passage occurs, the words "to repentance" are retained in the Revised Version and in all the manuscripts, and no one has ever doubted that the words were originally there. On both the principles just stated, therefore, it is easy to see why these words should be added to Matthew and Mark in the course of transcription, but it is not easy to see why they should be omitted. Two causes are in the field to secure their addition, but none to secure their omission. First, the idea of the full expression is implicitly contained in the abbreviated form. The whole story of Christ's work emphasizes the truth that when he called sinners it was *to repentance.* In adding those words to this sentence the scribe was but stating explicitly what was implicitly involved. And, secondly, the actual occurrence of the full expression in Luke, with which the scribes were familiar, greatly strengthened the tendency in this particular instance. Its presence in Luke would seem to justify the conviction in the copyist's mind that the omission had occurred by mistake, and hence would tend to secure the addition.

The influence of assimilation is perhaps still better seen in the case of a more considerable addition to the text, whose history has been carefully worked out by that prince of American textual critics, the late Prof. Ezra Abbot, premising, however, that in our statement of the case we will expand his symbols into phrases that will be self-luminous:

"In Matt. xx, 22 the common version reads, 'Are ye able to drink of the cup I shall drink of [and to be baptized with the baptism that I am baptized with]?' and in verse 23, 'Ye shall indeed drink of my cup [and be baptized with the baptism that I am baptized with].' The clauses here bracketed are wanting" in the oldest manuscripts (ℵ, B, D) and in those which have evidently been copied from the oldest manuscripts, and in most of the copies of the Old Latin version as well as of the Vulgate, in the oldest Syriac version, in the earliest Egyptian version, and in the quotations of Origen, and several other of the earlier Church Fathers. "Origen (in the early part of the third century) expressly notes the fact that they were found in Mark, and not in Matthew. In Mark x, 38, 39 none of the manuscripts or versions omit them. But in Matthew" only one manuscript of the oldest class contains them. They are found, however, in a great number of the later copies of Matthew (mostly those of the ninth and tenth centuries), and in a few copies of the Old Latin and in the later Syriac versions, and in the quotations of some of the later Church Fathers.

"Now, if these clauses belonged originally to the text, they must have been omitted by accident or by design. They could not have been omitted accidentally in so many and so independent very early authorities, including all, so far as we know, that represent the second and third centuries. In the twenty-third verse, the last word in the Greek, indeed, agrees in the last four letters with the word which ends the preceding clause, but there is no such occasion for accidental omission in verse 22. Nor can we discover any motive for intentional omission of the clauses. On the other hand, their insertion is readily explained by their existence in Mark. We conclude, then, with confidence, that the clauses in question did not belong to the original text." *

These are but a few specimens of the assimilation which has evidently occurred in hundreds of places in preparing later copies of the Gospels. The tendency of the copyists to assimilate them to one another is natural and, to a certain degree, irresistible. It was probably greatly assisted also by the early construction of harmonies of the Gospels, like Tatian's Diatessaron. The extent to which this tendency to assimilation has operated in a particular class of manuscripts becomes, therefore, a means of determining the relative age of the readings which they contain. The more frequently a manuscript has been copied during an uncritical period the greater will be the number of texts in which the influence of the tendency will be manifest. That assimilation of parallel accounts will be the general rule is inferred, therefore, by a strictly scientific process of reasoning from cause to effect.

Another cause operating to amplify the text in the process of transcribing it is found in the difficulty of distinguishing on the margin of a manuscript between a correction and an annotation.

Marginal Annotations.

The habit of making notes on the margin of one's

---

* Critical Essays, pp. 231, 232.

manuscript is probably as ancient as the art of writing; while the hazard of their being confounded with the original copy is as old as the trade of the copyist. But marginal notes have a stamp of their own, and in general can be recognised by their character. They are usually attempts to explain some difficult matter (or what seemed to the scribe a difficult matter) in the text. For example, the fourth verse of the fifth chapter of the Gospel of John contains the kind of material of which marginal notes are naturally made. It has a striking resemblance to the ordinary productions of an expositor. The passage occurs in the account of the healing of the lame man at the pool of Bethesda. Here was doubtless an intermittent spring into which the sick were accustomed to be plunged for the healing of their various bodily infirmities. In this verse the explanation is put forward that "an angel went down at a certain season into the pool and troubled the waters." But the whole can be omitted without any disturbance to the sense. We are not surprised, therefore, to find that the oldest manuscripts and versions do omit it, and that most of the older Church Fathers are ignorant of it. This being the case, the probability is strong that it is an explanatory marginal note of some commentator incorporated into the text by a conscientious scribe.

Up to this point the reasoning has been largely theoretical. From our knowledge of the natural tendencies affecting the minds of copyists, we have concluded that the manuscripts which are characterized by the shorter and the harder reading more nearly represent the autographs than do the fuller and

Direct Evidence of the Influence of these Tendencies.

more polished copies. It remains to verify this inference more extensively by comparing the texts which upon these principles are supposed to be the more correct representative of the originals with what are otherwise known to be older readings.

With reference to many passages in the New Testament, we have evidence of their earlier forms in their quotation by the writers of the second and third centuries, and in the versions which were made during this same early period. Specially important are the quotations from Origen, who, as already said, flourished during the first half of the third century, or one hundred years before the date of the Sinaitic and Vatican manuscripts; while other Christian writers determine for us in many instances the form of the text in use during the latter part of the second century. If our principle be correct, we ought to find that those manuscripts which habitually contain the shorter and harder readings are generally supported by the early versions, and by the quotations from the writers of the second and third centuries; and this we find to be the fact. In illustration, it will be necessary to dwell at length only upon one or two instances.

In Matt. xix, 17 there is in the received text a clear instance of the influence of the tendency both to assimilation and to the critical removal of an apparent difficulty in the reading. The received text in Matthew agrees exactly with the parallel verses in Mark (x, 18) and Luke (xviii, 19), which read: "Why callest thou me good? None is good save one, even God." But ℵ, B, D have a different and seemingly more difficult reading in Matthew. These read: "Why askest thou me concerning that which is good? One there is who is good." On turning to the known early versions and quotations, we find that they support this harder reading. Origen expressly calls attention to the fact that the form of the question in Matthew is different from that in Mark and Luke, and that Matthew represents the Saviour as asking the young man why he inquired of him concerning that which is good. This form, witnessed to by Origen, is found in the Vulgate, the Old Latin, the older Syriac, and the Coptic and Ethiopic versions. Thus in this instance the verification is all that could be asked. The text which had been pronounced to be best both by internal evidence and by its occurrence in the oldest manuscripts is proved also to be the reading of the earliest writers. But the variation in Matthew is by no means an impossible reading or one that is devoid of sense; nor is it in contradiction to the reading found in Mark and Luke; for it is not to be supposed that the conversation between Jesus and the rich young man was limited to the few words that are given to it in the report of the evangelists.

Another illustration may be taken from Mark iii, 29, where in the received text from which King James's Version was made it is said that "he who shall blaspheme against the Holy Ghost hath never forgiveness, but is in danger of eternal damnation." In the Sinaitic, Vatican, and Beza manuscripts (א, B, D), however, and in the class which they represent, it reads that he shall be in danger of eternal *sin*. Now, it is easy to see that this reading is a little more difficult to understand than is the other. At first thought the superficial reader would naturally suppose that the idea of condemnation rather than of sin was appropriate with the word eternal, and was really necessary to fill out the sense. The occurrence of this harder reading in ℵ, B, D is both a water mark of the antiquity of their text and is an important testimony to both the correctness and antiquity of the reading " eternal sin." Subjecting it now to the test of verification by an appeal to the earliest versions and quotations, we are positively assured that it is an old reading, for it is found in the Old Latin, the Memphitic, the Gothic, and Armenian versions, and is the reading of Cyprian, Augustine, and Athanasius.

And thus in thousands of instances it will appear that the readings characteristic of the class of manuscripts represented by the Sinaitic and Vatican are supported by the more valuable ancient versions and by the quotations found in the writings of the earlier Church Fathers.* Thus these manuscripts as a class are proved to contain a text which is old as well good. Having thus established their general character as witnesses, their testimony becomes of great weight in doubtful cases where other evidence is wanting. The agreement of these texts, however, is not an absolute criterion, for it is possible that they all incorporate some common error in the earlier copies from which they were made. But their agreement in a reading establishes a presumption in its favour which can be disturbed only by most weighty considerations. There can be no reasonable doubt that when ℵ, B, and D agree they represent with great faithfulness the text which was in general use by the Christians of the second century. But even these texts do not always agree, and

---

* Tregelles on the Printed Text of the Greek Testament, p. 148.

THE TESTIMONY OF TEXTUAL CRITICISM. 267

they all very frequently disagree with the Alexandrian manuscript.

Recurring now more specifically to the four early manuscripts of the New Testament already briefly described—namely, the Sinaitic (ℵ), the Alexandrian (A), the Vatican (B), and that of Beza (D)—we find that they represent three, if not four, well-defined classes of specific readings whose chronological relations can be determined by evidence of various kinds.

Chronological Classification of the Manuscripts.

The Alexandrian Codex (A) is the basis of the so-called received text from which King James's Version was made, and is supported in its readings by the great mass of Greek manuscripts of the New Testament now in existence. As compared with the three other early manuscripts mentioned, however, this codex quite uniformly has the smoother and the longer readings. A large number of these longer readings have evidently originated through some editorial revision which had in view the variations of earlier texts, and which made systematic effort to combine and preserve them. This has given rise to a large number of "conflate" readings —that is, of readings which, instead of representing one only of two variations, contains them both in combination.

For example, in Mark viii, 26, ℵ and B read simply, "Do not even enter into the village," while D reads, "Do not tell it to any one in the village." A combines the two, reading, "Neither go into the village nor speak to any one in the village." Again, in Mark ix, 49, ℵ and B read, "For every one shall be salted with fire," while D reads, "For every sacrifice shall be salted with salt." But A combines the two, reading, "For every one shall be salted with fire, and every sacrifice shall be salted with salt."

Again, in Luke ix, 10, B and D read that Jesus and his disciples went into "a city called Bethsaida," while ℵ and the Old Syriac versions read "into a desert place"; but A reads, "into a desert place of a city called Bethsaida," which is evidently made up from the other two. In Luke xxiv, 53, ℵ and B read that the disciples were "continually in the temple *blessing* God," while D reads "*praising* God"; but A and its great company of companions combine the two, and give the reading of the received text, "continually in the temple *praising and blessing* God." Summing up the results of eight typical instances of conflation in the text, Westcott and Hort * give a table showing that, while A and the received text exhibit the conflation in every case, ℵ, B, and D exhibit it in no one of the cases; and so of the old versions, neither the Old Latin, the Old Syriac, nor the most ancient Egyptian version contains the conflated readings, while the later revision both of the Latin and the Syriac do contain them in nearly every instance.

And thus by a wide induction of facts it is most clearly proved that soon after Christianity became the state religion, or toward the close of the fourth century, there was some sort of an editorial revision of the texts of the Gospels. This was made probably in Antioch, which was then one of the most important centres of religious culture, and was generally adopted by the Greek-speaking portion of the state Church, and, under

---

* New Testament in Greek, vol. ii, p. 104.

THE TESTIMONY OF TEXTUAL CRITICISM. 269

the influence of the new condition of things, was more carefully copied than during the previous centuries. The writings of the celebrated Chrysostom, the "golden-mouthed" preacher of Antioch and Constantinople, during the close of the fourth century, give abundant testimony to the familiarity of the public during his time with the smoother, longer, and combined readings transmitted through the Alexandrian Codex (A) and its companions.

In tracing back the history of these separate elements which, having been combined in the latter part of the fourth century, became the basis of the received text, we find at least two well-marked lines of variation already in existence during the early part of the second century which are so characteristic and widely distributed that they must have originated as variations at a considerably earlier period, thus bearing testimony to the existence of the originals at the very beginning of the century, if not much earlier.

As already noted, Codex Bezæ (D) contains many peculiar readings which were widely distributed in the western part of the Roman Empire, and hence is called the Western text.

This codex, while containing a few striking interpolations of considerable length, bears every internal mark of being in most respects close to the original; but many of its peculiar readings are found in the quotations of writers in the second century. The quotations of Irenæus and of his pupil Hippolytus clearly show that the main peculiarities of this Western text were in existence soon after the middle of the second century; while the quotations of the heretic Marcion, who came from Pontus to Rome about the middle of the second century, and of his teacher Justin Martyr, who was put to death in Rome about the year 165, carry these readings back to the first part of the second century. The wide distribution of these characteristic Western readings is further shown by the fact that in some of his writings Origen, who represented the Alexandrian school in the early part of the third century, gives a prominent place to them.

The writings of Justin Martyr and of the heretic Marcion contain a large amount of incidental but positive evidence that as early as the middle of the second century many of the characteristic variations of Codex Bezæ (D) were already in circulation. For example, in Matt. xxv, 41, where the received text has the word *poruesthe* (πορεύεσθε) for "depart," Justin agrees with D, the Old Latin, Irenæus, Tertullian, and Origen in the use of its synonym *hupagete* (ὑπάγετε).*

<small>Evidence from Justin Martyr's Text.</small>

In Luke iii, 22 the accepted text reads, "Thou art my beloved Son, in thee I am well pleased"; whereas D and many Latin fathers read, "Thou art my Son, this day have I begotten thee," and this is the reading found in Justin Martyr.†

In Luke x, 16 the reading of the received text is, "He that *rejecteth* me, *rejecteth* him that sent me." But D, with the Old Latin and the Old Syriac version, reads, "The one who *heareth* me, *heareth* him that sent me," and this is the reading of Justin Martyr.‡

In Luke xiii, 27 the reading of D is "workers of unlawfulness" (*anomias*, ἀνομίας), instead of "workers

---

* Dialogue with Trypho, chap. lxxvi.   † Ibid., lxxxviii, ciii.
‡ First Apology, chaps. xvi, lxiii.

THE TESTIMONY OF TEXTUAL CRITICISM. 271

of unrighteousness" (adikias, ἀδικίας), as in ℵ and B. In this case also Justin agrees with D.*

In Luke xii, 48 Justin agrees with D as against most other manuscripts, in the form of the comparative in the clause "to whom they commit much, of him they will ask the more," and in the use of a compound verb instead of a simple one. Justin and D read *pleon* (πλέον) for *perissoteron* (περισσότερον); also *apaiteesousin* (ἀπαιτήσουσιν) for *aiteesousin* (αἰτήσουσιν), making it read, "to whom God has given more, of him shall more be required." †

In Luke xx, 24 Justin and D agree in using the general word for "coin" (τὸ νόμισμα) for the specific word "penny" (δηνάριον), making the question "Tell me, Whose image does the *coin* bear," instead of "Whose image and superscription does the *penny* have." ‡

Luke xxii, 42, 44 are omitted by ℵ, A, B, and many other manuscripts, but they are contained in D and in the Old Latin, the Old Syriac, and in some Egyptian manuscripts, while they are expressly cited by Justin Martyr,# and are inserted by an early reviser into the margin of ℵ. The verses, "And there appeared unto him an angel of heaven strengthening him." "And being in an agony he prayed more earnestly: and his sweat became as it were great drops of blood falling upon the ground," are certainly not "a product of the inventiveness of scribes." If not a part of the original copy of Luke, they must be a genuine fragment preserved for awhile outside of the Gospel, or more likely incorporated by Luke himself into a second edition. The important

---

* First Apology, chap. xvi.
† Justin Martyr, First Apology, chap. xvii.   ‡ Ibid.
# Dialogue with Trypho, chap. ciii.

thing to notice here is that Justin Martyr had the verses in his manuscripts in common with the widely distributed old versions.

Luke xxiii, 34 is another one of the most touching utterances of Christ which is omitted by some of the best manuscripts—namely, by B, D, and by one of the early revisers of ℵ, and by some manuscripts of the Old Latin version, and of the early Egyptian versions, but it is contained in the original ℵ, in A, and nearly all other manuscripts, in all the Syriac versions and in most copies of the Egyptian versions.

These instances conclusively show that many established variations in the text were in existence in widely scattered documents which were freely circulating about the middle of the second century. Some of them clearly exhibit what would be called, in the words of Prof. Sanday, "an advanced though early stage of corruption." While Justin's quotations from the Gospels, agreeing as they do in so many cases with D and the Old Syriac and Old Latin versions, carry the date of the variations well back at least toward the beginning of the second century. "The coincidences are too many and too great all to be the result of accident, or to be accounted for by the parallel influence of the lost Gospels." *

Evidence from Marcion's Text. Marcion's edition of Luke, which was issued about the middle of the second century, bears equally positive testimony with the quotations of Justin to the textual variation which had obtained currency in the early part of the second century.

---

* The Gospels of the Second Century, p. 136.

In Luke v, 14 Marcion reads, "that it might be a testimony to you," instead of a testimony "to them," in this agreeing with D.

In Luke v, 39 "and no man having drunk old wine desireth new: for he saith, The old is good," is omitted both by Marcion and by D, but is retained by most other manuscripts and versions.

Luke xii, 14, Marcion, in company with D, and the Old Syriac version, omits the word "divider," and says simply, Who made me a "judge" over you.

In Luke xii, 38 Marcion agrees with D, Irenæus, and the Old Syriac version in having a conflate text. In these documents it reads, " [And if he shall come in the evening watch, and shall find them doing so] and if in the second, and in the third he shall come and find them so, blessed are they." The clause in brackets was common to Marcion, D, and the Old Syriac, thus witnessing to its great antiquity. But it does not occur in ℵ, A, or B.

In Luke xvi, 12 A and D read, "Give you what is *your* own"; but B reads, "Give what is *our* own," and this with a slight variation is Marcion's reading —that is, he uses the first person instead of the second person.

In Luke xxi, 18 "And not a hair of your head shall perish" is omitted by Marcion, and in company with him is the Old Syriac version, which also omits it.

In Luke xxi, 27 Marcion in company with D and the Old Syriac version prefixes the word "great" to power, making it read that the Son of man shall come "in a cloud with great power and great glory," instead of "power and great glory."

These are but specimens of a large class of readings which demonstrate the existence of the Gospels in the very first part of the second century at least. While the meaning of the passages is not seriously affected, the slight variations, such as are naturally made in copying manuscripts, are abundant and already fixed when Marcion issued his edition of Luke about the middle of the second century. This class of variations has been well compared in their significance to the fossils which determine the geological age of the rocks. There must have been time for the deposition. The readings had already been established in Marcion's day, as is shown by the wide range of texts and versions which incorporated them. The words of Prof. Sanday, commenting upon this evidence, are abundantly justified:

In the year 140 A. D. Marcion possesses a Gospel which is already in an advanced stage of transcription—which has not only undergone those changes which in some regions the text underwent before it was translated into Latin, but has undergone other changes besides. Some of its peculiarities are not those of the earliest form of the Latin version, but of that version in what may be called its second stage (e. g., xvi, 12). It has also affinities to another version kindred to the Latin and occupying a similar place to the Old Latin among the churches of Syria. These circumstances together point to an antiquity fully as great as any that an orthodox critic would claim.*

I think it is a safe proposition to assert that, in order to bring the text of Marcion's Gospel into the state in which we find it, there must have been a long previous history, and the manuscripts through which it was conveyed must have parted far from the parent stem.†

---

* The Gospels of the Second Century, p. 235.
† Ibid., p. 236.

THE TESTIMONY OF TEXTUAL CRITICISM. 275

The testimony of textual criticism to these classes of early variation in the manuscripts of the four Gospels has a most important bearing upon the date of the books themselves. They show that already in the early part of the second century the text of the four Gospels was treated by orthodox and heretic alike with all the reverence which was bestowed upon it in subsequent periods of Church history. It can be established by abundant evidence, strictly scientific in its character, both that the text of the New Testament which was current in the second century was not that of the autographs, and that at the same time it differed so little from the autographs that no serious changes could have been made in them. The fact that Origen and Irenæus were themselves textual critics endeavouring to determine what was the true reading in various cases shows that some time had elapsed between the writing of the autographs and the writing of the copies which were open to their inspection. This of itself would beyond all reasonable doubt throw the composition of these books back into the first century or into the apostolic age itself, where tradition has usually placed them.

The Inevitable Inference.

An irresistible confirmation of this inference is derived from a comparison of the extent of textual variations in the Gospels during the second century and that which had taken place at the same time in the Epistles of Paul which every one acknowledges to have been written a little after the middle of the first century. The textual variations of the Gospels which appear in the second century are fully as great as those in the Pauline Epistles, thus revealing an approximate similarity of date.

In the words of Westcott and Hort, the coincidences between the Vatican and Sinaitic manuscripts are so numerous and of such a nature that they can be due only to "the extreme and, as it were, primordial antiquity of the common original from which the ancestries of the two manuscripts have diverged, the date of which can not be later than the early part of the second century, and may well be yet earlier." And again, "The books of the New Testament, as preserved in extant documents, assuredly speak to us in every important respect in language identical with that in which they spoke to those for whom they were originally written."

Lest, however, the extent of these variations should be overestimated, it is proper to add that the uncertainty is constantly growing smaller, and in no case does it seriously affect the main teaching of the book. Where the reading of a single passage is still in doubt, the removal of that passage from the context would not essentially change the result, for the teachings of the New Testament are not suffered to depend upon a single thread of argument. On the contrary, they have all the breadth of support which is furnished by varied expression in a wide range of literature.

Narrow Margin of the remaining Uncertainty.

The variations in one manuscript offset those in another, and out of the whole the original text emerges with a surprisingly small amount of uncertainty. According to the latest and best authority, seven eighths of the words of the New Testament have passed the ordeal of textual criticism without question, and of the remaining one eighth only a small fraction are subject to reasonable doubt, so that fifty-nine sixtieths of the words of the New Testament as they came from the original authors are known with practical certainty. And even of the one sixtieth open to question the larger part of the doubt pertains to changes of order in the words, and other comparative trivialities, so that, according to Westcott and Hort, "the amount of what can in any sense be called substantial variation is but a small fraction of the whole residuary variation, and can hardly form more than a thousandth part of the entire text." *

The *number* of the "various readings" frightens some innocent people, and figures largely in the writings of the more ignorant disbelievers in Christianity. "One hundred and fifty thousand various readings"! Must not these render the text of the New Testament wholly uncertain and thus destroy the foundation of our faith?

The true state of the case is something like this. Of the one hundred and fifty thousand various readings, more or less, of the text of the Greek New Testament, we may, as Mr. Norton has remarked, dismiss nineteen twentieths from consideration at once as being obviously of such a character, or supported by so little authority, that no critic would regard them as having any claim to reception. This leaves, we will say, seven thousand five hundred. But of these, again, it will appear on examination that nineteen out of twenty are of no sort of consequence as affecting the sense; they relate to questions of orthography, or grammatical construction, or the order of words, or such other matters as have been mentioned above, in speaking of unimportant variations. They concern only the form of expression, not the essential meaning. This reduces the number to perhaps four hundred, which involve a difference of meaning, often very slight, or the omission or

---

* The New Testament in the Original Greek, vol. ii, p. 2.

addition of a few words, sufficient to render them objects of some curiosity and interest, while a few exceptional cases among them may relatively be called important. But our critical helps are now so abundant that in a very large majority of these more important questions of reading we are able to determine the true text with a good degree of confidence. What remains doubtful we can afford to leave doubtful. In the text of all ancient writing there are passages in which the text can not be settled with certainty, and the same is true of the interpretation.*

---

* Prof. Ezra Abbot, in Critical Essays, pp. 208, 209.

CHAPTER IX.

INTERNAL EVIDENCES OF THE EARLY DATE OF THE FOUR GOSPELS.

From every point of view the four Gospels are most remarkable literary productions. They have secured most astonishing effects by the simplest literary methods. One of the most surprising of their effects has been the suppression of all rivals. The Gospels sum up all that is known of the life and words of the great Founder of the Christian religion. Outside of them scarcely a dozen sayings or deeds of Christ have been recorded. Yet, in the words of the writer of one of these Gospels, the world could not contain the books which should record all that he said and did during the years of his ministry.

The full significance of this phenomenon appears only when considered in connection with the incompleteness of the histories and the strength of the general desire to have the missing portions of Christ's biography supplied by some means. According to the author of the third Gospel, many efforts had been made in his day to write this biography. But the event has shown that these efforts were unsatisfactory to the world, for scarcely a fragment of any of them has been preserved. In the process of natural selection only the four Gospels have survived. So speedily did they obtain possession of the field that either they prevented other rivals from arising or they prevented them from obtaining currency.

When we consider the early spread of Christianity over the whole extent of the Roman Empire, the foregoing fact becomes of the very highest significance. Within sixty years of the death of Christ churches were planted throughout all Syria and Asia Minor and Greece and in Egypt and Italy, while within a century northern Africa and western Europe were the seat of flourishing Christian communities. That in any of these widely spread communities there should not be preserved any considerable fragment of the history of their Master, except such as is found in the four Gospels, is a most striking testimony to the completeness with which these histories occupied the field.

So striking is this fact that it is difficult to resist the conviction that the four Gospels had the prestige of official documents. We can not, however, maintain that there were any formal councils which adopted them, for of this there is not only no evidence, but overwhelming evidence to the contrary. The conditions were rather those in which a law prevails by general consent. Apparently the weight of authority by which the several Gospels were promulgated was so great and their conformity to known facts was so complete that no one could have the hardihood to put forth any competitors. If they were really believed to issue from the circle of the apostles, and so were thought to have the eye-witnesses chosen by Christ himself as their sponsors, this pre-eminence is perfectly natural. But on any other theory it is in the highest degree unnatural and improbable.

THE EARLY DATE OF THE FOUR GOSPELS.

But it is not necessary to rest our belief upon such a generality alone. Minute examination of the Gospels, and comparison of their representations with the known tendencies of human nature and the known conditions of the times, amply sustain the conclusion that the Gospels are a trustworthy contemporary record of the events attending the establishment of the Christian religion. In every respect the Gospels bear the water-marks of genuine history.

Freedom from Puerilities.

The success with which the four Gospels are made to adhere to a single exalted purpose is convincing evidence that the writers were restrained by the near presence of the facts which they record. Writing as they do the history of the most marvellous being that it ever entered the imagination of man to introduce upon the earth, the self-control which they exhibit is super-human, except on the theory that they were the narrators of facts which were near at hand, and were so fixed in the public mind that they could not be easily augmented or tampered with. From the point of view of the ordinary biographer, the four Gospels are extremely defective. They contain scarcely anything to gratify the ordinary curiosity. They tell us nothing about the personal appearance of Christ. Painters and sculptors are left absolutely without information for guidance in their efforts to portray his form and mien.

The reticence of the Gospels concerning the childhood of Christ illustrates this self-restraint in most remarkable degree. The whole period from his birth to the beginning of his ministry at thirty years of age is passed over with the narration of a single incident. We are told by the writer of the third Gospel simply that "the child grew and waxed strong, filled with wisdom; and the grace of God was upon him." Then there is narrated the brief story of one of his accustomed visits to Jerusalem at the time of the Passover, when he was inadvertently left behind by his parents on their return and was found with the learned teachers in the temple hearing them and asking them questions which astonished all. This interesting and characteristic story is closed with the simple statement that he "advanced in wisdom and stature and in favour with God and men." * This is followed † in Matthew and Mark by the incidental statements of his neighbours that Jesus was known to them simply as a carpenter and the son of a carpenter, whose brothers and sisters were still remaining quietly at home.‡ With these exceptions, there is absolute silence with respect to the history of his early life.

The Childhood of Jesus.

The natural tendencies of unregulated minds cherishing the conception in history of a being capable of such supernatural power as is freely ascribed to Jesus are amply shown in the apocryphal Gospels. In these the infancy of Jesus is filled with prodigies strikingly out of harmony with the uniform exalted purposes of Christ's mission as represented in the New Testament. For example, in the Gospel of Thomas,# which is one

The Apocryphal Gospels.

---

* Luke ii, 40–52.   ‡ Mark vi, 3.
† Matt. xiii, 55 ; Mark vi, 3.
# Early enough in date to be quoted by Irenæus.

of the earliest of the apocryphal Gospels, and was certainly in existence during the second century, we are told that when Jesus was five years old he miraculously purified a muddy stream to obtain clay from which to make playthings on the Sabbath day. When with other children he was engaged in fashioning sparrows out of the soft clay, a devout Jew rebuked the parents of Jesus for allowing him to break the Sabbath. Whereupon Jesus, to show his power, imparted life to the lumps of clay, and they flew off into the sky. At another time a boy who had rudely run against him was struck dead by Jesus, and the parents who complained of this were made blind.

When Jesus was six years old the Gospel of Thomas narrates that " his mother gave him a pitcher and sent him to draw water and bring it into the house. But he struck against some one in the crowd, and the pitcher was broken. And Jesus unfolded the cloak which he had on and filled it with water and carried it to his mother."

A little later we are told that when the father of Jesus had made a couch for a rich man he found that the cross pieces were too short. But Jesus remedied the error by taking hold of the pieces and stretching them out to the proper length.

Another characteristic story relates to his experience at school, where he was put under a teacher to learn his letters. But when the teacher had written the alphabet for his pupil, he found himself unable to impart any information to him. Whereupon he took him back to his father, saying: " I can not endure the sternness of his look. . . . This child does not belong to earth. . . . I made a struggle to have a scholar, and

I was found to have a teacher. My mind is filled with shame, because I an old man have been conquered by a child. . . . Therefore I beseech thee, Brother Joseph, take him home. What great thing he is, either God or angel, or what I am to say, I know not."

In striking contrast to these puerilities, the miracles ascribed to Jesus in the four Gospels are all limited *The Contrast.* to the period of his ministry, and are subordinated to the exalted purpose of supporting the claims put forth by him as a teacher of truths which can be adequately enforced only by supernatural means, and which are eminently worthy of supernatural indorsement. A noteworthy characteristic of these miracles of the Gospel history is that, with two exceptions, they are never done except for the distinct beneficent purpose of helping others who were in trouble. Jesus is not represented as performing any miracle for his own advantage. He could multiply the loaves and fishes for the weary multitude when far away from home, but he himself sat helpless beside the well of Sychar awaiting the return of his disciples from the village near by to bring him bread to eat, and asking of a disreputable Samaritan woman to draw water from Jacob's well to quench his thirst.* When tempted in the wilderness, Jesus indignantly refused to prostitute his miraculous power by turning stones into loaves of bread to satisfy his hunger at the end of a forty days' fast.

---

* John iv, 7.

THE FREEDOM OF THE GOSPELS FROM COMMENTS BY THE WRITERS.*

But this freedom of the Gospels from puerilities is only a specific incident to a more general fact—namely, that to an extent absolutely unique in literature the Gospels are limited to the simplest possible narrative of facts undiluted by note or comment; while the occasions throughout the Gospel narratives where the reader naturally desires additional information to gratify his curiosity are as numerous as the instances themselves which are narrated. What, for example, can exceed the mystery surrounding the various appearances of Christ after his resurrection! For forty days he is represented as being alive after rising from the grave, but he only meets with his disciples a few times and in widely separated intervals and places. There is absolutely nothing in the narrative to satisfy our curiosity with regard to where he was during these intervals or concerning the manner of his separating from the disciples after the various recorded meetings.

On the morning of his resurrection, in the early twilight, he meets the devout women who were on the way to his sepulchre, and makes himself known to them, but permits only the briefest interview, telling them to go and tell his brethren that they could see

---

* In this section I am indebted for many suggestions to the interesting volume entitled Internal Evidences of the Genuineness of the Gospels, by Prof. Andrews Norton (Boston: Little, Brown & Co., 1855); also to Sanday's Lectures on Inspiration and to Prof. Huidekoper's Indirect Testimony of History to the Genuineness of the Gospels.

him if they would go to Galilee. There is, however, no attempt to expand the narrative by detailing the incidents of this first interview, upon which the imagination would fondly like to linger. Nor is there any attempt to gratify our curiosity respecting the whereabouts of Jesus during the intervals which separated his various subsequent appearances. He no more mingles freely with his disciples; he no more returns over the lonely road to Bethany to enjoy the ministrations of the fond household of Lazarus and his sisters.

Mystery of his Resurrection Body.

It is scarcely possible for us to exaggerate the mystery surrounding the movements of Jesus during this entire interval between the resurrection and the ascension. How mysterious, for example, is everything connected with his appearance to the two disciples on the way to Emmaus on the day of his resurrection! Dazed and heart-broken, two unknown disciples were wandering off a few miles to the west of Jerusalem on the road leading to Joppa. An unknown traveller joins them, and journeys with them a distance of some miles, entering into their conversation concerning the thrilling events of the past few days. But so great is their confusion of mind that they do not recognise in this lonely traveller the familiar form of their Master until their eyes are opened, after their frugal repast, at the moment of his departure from them.

Upon returning to Jerusalem that same evening, these two disciples joined the eleven as they are gathered together in a secret place rehearsing how their Lord had risen from the dead and appeared to Peter. " And as they spake these things, he himself stood in the midst.

of them . . . and said unto them, Why are ye troubled? and wherefore do reasonings arise in your hearts? See my hands and my feet, that it is I myself: handle me, and see; for a spirit hath not flesh and bones, as ye behold me having. . . . And while they still disbelieved for joy, and wondered, he said unto them, Have ye here anything to eat? And they gave him a piece of a broiled fish and he took it, and did eat before them." * Whereupon there follows a week of mysterious silence.

Without any attempt to fill in the history of the interval, the writer of the fourth Gospel records another appearance at Jerusalem upon the eighth day after the resurrection. At this time the sceptical Thomas is present with the others, and has his doubts dissipated; when again silence for an unknown time rests upon the scene. Still disheartened and dazed by the marvellous events which are unfolding before them, the disciples have returned to their former haunts on Lake Galilee, and have taken up their former occupations of fishermen. Here again, unannounced and with his absence unaccounted for, the lonely form of their risen Saviour appears upon the shore of the lake, and invites them to breakfast with him upon food which he had evidently prepared with his own hands.

After another unknown interval Jesus again meets his chosen disciples at an appointed place upon one of the mountains of Galilee, giving to them the grand commission to go into all the world and make disciples of all the nations, and renewing his promise to be with them alway, even unto the end of the world. Again a silence closes over the scene until he reappears

---

* Luke xxiv, 36-43.

to them in Jerusalem, and leads them out to Mount Olivet, and for the last time expounds to them the Scriptures which foretell " that the Christ should suffer, and rise again from the dead the third day, and that repentance and remission of sins should be preached in his name unto all the nations, beginning from Jerusalem. . . . And he led them out until they were over against Bethany, and he lifted up his hands and blessed them. And it came to pass, while he blessed them, he parted from them, and was carried up into heaven." *

The naïve simplicity of this narrative, or rather of these four narratives, is unparalleled in the literature of the world. If it had been the product of human design or the record of human delusions, the story would not have been left in such an unfinished condition. As it is, no effort whatever has been made to answer the thousand and one curious questions that arise in the mind of every reader respecting the movements and whereabouts both of Christ and of his disciples during the intervals between his various appearances between the resurrection and the ascension. If imagination had been lively enough to furnish what we have, it would have been sure to furnish more. The only reasonable explanation of the limitations set to the narrative is that it is a bare statement of facts too great and mysterious to be understood at the time, and too serious to be tampered with afterward.

Not the Work of Imagination.

If ever there was a history in which the writers would be justified in expressing their indignation at the treatment of the hero whose life work they were

---

* Luke xxiv, 46–50.

THE EARLY DATE OF THE FOUR GOSPELS. 289

depicting, it is that of Christ who came to his own and his own received him not, and who, though represented to be the long-expected deliverer of his people, was despised and rejected of men, and was compelled to suffer the torture and death of the vilest malefactors. From what we know of commentators and preachers from that time to the present, this suppression of all feeling on the part of the writers of the four Gospels shows beyond controversy that they were writing under a restraint which was not felt by any of the writers with which we are acquainted since the first century of our era. The moment we strike into the circle of the writers of the post-apostolic age we find ourselves in the company of commentators with all the peculiarities incident to their efforts to explain and smooth away the *prima facie* difficulties apparent in the Gospels, and to enforce and enlarge upon the meaning of the facts which are recorded.

Undesigned Coincidences.

The Gospel histories are not a narrative of isolated facts whose truth is incapable of verification by circumstantial evidence, but, on the contrary, they are in a remarkable manner open to comparison with contemporary history. The degree to which all their incidental references to facts fit into known history constitutes in itself a demonstration of the contemporary character of the records.

The New Testament was not written in the dark ages, nor in an unknown corner of the earth, but in one of the most enlightened periods of ancient civilization and in the very centres of that civilization. By reason both of its own character and of the character of the times in which the history was enacted, the New Testament is peculiarly open to cross-examination, and through this to verification of the general correctness of its historical assertions. The field opened in such an investigation is so large that there is room barely to touch upon it. Nevertheless a few points are so salient that a brief statement of them can be made effective.

In our hymns and in other religious literature the words "kingdom" and "church" are synonyms.* In the couplet

>I love thy kingdom, Lord,
>The church of thine abode,

one can readily see how the two words coalesce in meaning. There is, however, an easily recognisable difference in the ordinary significance of the words. The phrases "kingdom of heaven" and "kingdom of God" convey a less definite idea than that involved in the word "church." The church is an attempted realization of the kingdom on earth. This realization began in local Christian assemblies which were organized after the death of Christ in the wake of apostolic preaching. It would be natural, therefore, that the word "church" should not come into general use until the thing itself had come into existence. We should look also to find the more general term in use during Christ's life.

Use of the Words "Church" and "Kingdom."

An examination of the New Testament shows that, while the word "kingdom" in the sense of the invisible

---

* See the argument more fully worked out by Prof. W. E. C. Wright in the Bibliotheca Sacra for October, 1895, pp. 747-749.

church occurs more than a hundred times in the Gospels, the word "church" is found in them but twice, and in one of those instances the genuineness of the word is open to serious doubt. Whereas, the extent to which, a little later, the word "church" was used to express the modified conception which came in with the visible organization of believers is no less surprising than instructive both in the Acts and in the Epistles. In Acts, "church" occurs twenty-one times, and in nearly all cases refers to the local congregation, while the word "kingdom" occurs only eight times. In Romans the word "church" occurs five times—all in the sixteenth chapter—while "kingdom" occurs but once. In 1 Corinthians "church" occurs twenty-two times, and "kingdom" but five times. In 2 Corinthians "church" occurs nine times, "kingdom" not at all. In nearly all these cases the word "church" is used in its narrow, local significance.

On the other hand, in Ephesians and Colossians, while the word "church" occurs thirteen times and the word "kingdom" but three times, "church" has in every instance its more general meaning, corresponding to the kingdom of God.

An irresistible inference from these facts is that the one hundred or more passages in the Gospels where the word "kingdom" is used became fixed in their literary form before the other books of the New Testament were written. This uniform choice of the word "kingdom" in no less than one hundred instances, and the failure to use the synonymous word "church" except in two instances, proves beyond all reasonable doubt either that those passages were put into writing at the time of their utterance or that they were recalled to memory at a later period by writers who were bent on reproducing the exact words of their Master, and whose memories were so vivid that they could recall them with phenomenal accuracy. Even the fourth Gospel, which all admit was written as late as the last decade of the first century, uses the word "kingdom" five times without using "church" at all, although the word "church" occurs three times in the Third Epistle of John, and twenty times in the Apocalypse. In all these cases, however, the word "church" when used by John refers to the local, visible body. This uniform practice by the writers of the Gospels of putting the word "kingdom" in the mouth of Jesus rather than the word "church" can be explained by no other cause than the attraction upon their minds of a controlling central fact. The experiences with their Master were photographed upon their minds so clearly that they could not be obscured by any experiences of later life. It is entirely beyond the bounds of belief that biographies manufactured at second hand should have adhered so singularly to this recondite but most appropriate distinction in the use of two synonymous words. On the supposition of the composition of the Gospels from the original records of eye-witnesses, the incidental coincidences are profound and natural. On the supposition that there was a conscious design on the part of the writers to maintain this distinctive use of the synonyms, a most improbable incongruity is introduced into the problem; for if there is one thing in a literary point of view more characteristic of the Gospels than another, it is the naturalness and freedom from artificiality with which their story of the most remarkable events in the world's history is told.

A second example which we can profitably dwell upon somewhat at length presents itself in the peculiar use in the New Testament of the phrase "Son of man." This phrase is used as a designation of Jesus thirty-two times in Matthew, fourteen times in Mark, twenty-six times in Luke, and ten times in John, making in all eighty-two times, while it is fairly distributed through all four of the Gospels. A noticeable thing also in connection with the use of the phrase is that it is a favourite with Christ himself. Indeed, he is scarcely ever represented as designating himself by any other appellation. In John there are three or four instances of styling himself "Son of God," and several instances in which he speaks of himself merely as "the Son." But the phrase in designation of himself which the disciples are represented as hearing fall most frequently from his lips was "the Son of man." They heard him say, "The Son of man hath not where to lay his head," "The Son of man is Lord even of the Sabbath," "The Son of man shall send forth his angels," "The Son of man shall come in the glory of his Father," "The Son of man hath power to forgive sins," "The Son of man shall be betrayed," "The Son of man is come to save the lost," "The Son of man shall be lifted up," "Ye shall eat the flesh of the Son of man," "Ye shall see the Son of man ascend," "Now is the Son of man glorified," and so forth.

From this frequent use of the appellation by Jesus to designate himself, and his evident avoidance of the use of other appellations, the superficial observer would be led to expect that this would be the favourite designation which his disciples would apply to him. But, on the contrary, with two or three exceptions, the disciples are represented as never designating their Master by that favourite term, and even those exceptions prove the rule. Stephen, indeed, in the supreme moment of martyrdom, when the heavenly vision broke upon his view, exclaims, " Behold, I see the heavens opened, and the Son of man sitting on the right hand of God." * The writer of the Apocalypse also is recounting a heavenly vision when he describes the form of one who is " like unto the Son of man." † But elsewhere, except when represented as upon the Saviour's own lips, the phrase is not found in the whole New Testament.

For such a phenomenon there must be a cause. It can not be by accident either that the use of the phrase was discontinued by the disciples or that it was so faithfully retained in the Gospels and excluded in the other literature.

Only the most profound and philosophical attention to the matter can bring to light the reasons which led Jesus to choose the appellation and his followers to avoid it. Jesus appropriately chose the appellation because, while implying the exalted condition of his pre-existent state, it expressed his complete assumption of humanity and the perfect humiliation of his earthly condition. Viewed from the heavenly standpoint of his own higher consciousness, the remarkable thing was that he had come down to earth and had assumed the conditions and limitations of humanity, and was a son of man, tempted in all points as we are. But to his disciples, while the humanity was evident enough, the supernatural phenomena were the ones which demanded

---

* Acts viii, 56.   † Rev. i, 13; xiv, 14.

THE EARLY DATE OF THE FOUR GOSPELS. 295

expression. Thus it came about that without comment these two modes of speaking of him, which are so expressive of profound distinctions, were preserved. Nothing but a simple-minded effort to report things exactly as they occurred could have secured this unstudied harmony.

Another equally striking case occurs in the use and disuse of the word "disciples." In the first three
<small>Use of the Words "Disciples," "Brethren," and "Saints."</small> Gospels this is used one hundred and sixty times to designate the followers of Christ; in the fourth Gospel it occurs seventy-eight times; in Acts, thirty times; while in the other books of the New Testament it does not occur at all. But in them the same persons are designated as "brethren" or "saints." Now, it is easy to see, on prolonged reflection, that there is a natural and logical reason for this change of terms in the unfolding of that remarkable history. While Christ was with his followers they were, with reference to him, "disciples"; but after his ascension and the formation of the Church their principal relations were with each other and with the outside world. Therefore "brethren" and "saints" are the natural words to express what was uppermost at that time in their conscious daily experiences. But it is extremely improbable that any later historian would have kept those distinctions in his mind when writing the history at second hand, especially in composing such inartificial narratives as the Gospels are.

Another instance of a similar sort appears in the account of the blood and water which is said to have issued from the Saviour's side when pierced by the soldier's spear. This is a very singular physiological fact, and is introduced in such a way that no one can suppose the writer knew its full significance. The story reads that when the soldiers came to the group upon the cross to break their legs and thus hasten their death before nightfall, they perceived that Jesus was already dead, and hence refrained from mutilating his body in that manner. This the writer looked upon as a fulfilment of the prophecy that "a bone of him should not be broken." "Howbeit one of the soldiers with a spear pierced his side, and straightway there came out blood and water." This, too, is looked upon as fulfilling the prophecy "They shall look on him whom they pierced." The issuing of the blood and water, however, is not referred to as the fulfilment of any prophecy or antecedent expectation, but is introduced, like many other incidents recorded in the fourth Gospel, merely as a vivid reminiscence which could not without effort be omitted in the narrative.

<small>The issuing of Blood and Water from the Saviour's Side.</small>

So frequent are these pictorial incidents related in the fourth Gospel that they add greatly to the impression of historical accuracy given to the story as there related. It is the writer of the fourth Gospel who fixes the day of Christ's baptism; it is he who determines the hour of his calling the two disciples to follow him; it is he who mentions the green grass on which the multitude sat down when miraculously fed; it is he who describes the position of the disciples at their last supper with Jesus, and makes mention of their gestures; it is he who recalls the darkness into which Judas went out from the supper; it is he who mentions the lanterns and torches carried by

<small>Minuteness of John's Observations.</small>

THE EARLY DATE OF THE FOUR GOSPELS. 297

those who arrested Jesus; it is he also who relates the changing positions of Peter at the time of his denial of Christ, and the means by which Peter obtained access to the hall. And so on, "we find everywhere in this Gospel the air and manner of an eye-witness and participant in the scenes recorded." Everything fits in perfectly with the theory that the Gospel was written by John in his old age when the incidents of early life are peculiarly vivid. The book reveals everywhere the memory of an old man which retains with photographic distinctness the scenes of his early personal experience.

It is thus, apparently, that John has preserved for us this most significant circumstance of the issuing of blood and water from the Saviour's side when pierced by the soldier's spear. But in this most incidental and unwitting manner he has here given us what serves as the report of a post-mortem examination over the body of the crucified one; for, according to the highest medical authority, the phenomenon mentioned is extremely rare, but might reasonably be supposed to occur in connection with death from rupture of the heart under stress of intense mental anguish. In such cases death occurs almost instantaneously, and the amount of blood which issues from the heart into the pericardium is considerable, sometimes amounting to a quart or more. When collected thus it speedily separates " into its solid and liquid constituents, technically called crassamentum and serum, but in ordinary language blood and water. Several instances have been adduced of the common use of this language even by medical writers, and it is not less natural than common, since the crassamentum contains the greater part of the

Marginal note: Equals a Post-mortem Examination.

solid and more essential ingredients of the blood, while, with the exception of albumen, the serum consists chiefly of water." *

The appearance here described by the writer of the fourth Gospel is one which is too unusual to have been familiar either to the writer or to those who at a later time transcribed the Gospel. It can not be the error of the copyist, but bears every mark of being a distinct reminiscence whose significance was not then understood. But now, to the physiologist of modern times, the whole scene is perfectly comprehensible, and becomes full of meaning. The Roman spear which pierced the side of Jesus as he was hanging upon the cross in an upright position set free the coagulated blood which had poured out into the pericardium through a rupture of the walls of the heart, occasioned by the mysterious but intense mental excitement of the sufferer. Thus in this incidental description the writer spoke better than he knew.

In accordance with this significant reminiscence of the writer of the fourth Gospel, it is to be observed that various remarks in the other Gospels prepare us for this conclusion. The full reports which are given of the last week of the Saviour's life in Jerusalem, when he saw the clouds gathering from which was to pro-

The Sorrow of Passion Week.

---

* Stroud, The Physical Cause of Christ's Death, pp. 108, 145, 146, with the indorsement of Dr. Simpson, p. 11. In support of this view of the case, Dr. W. W. Keen, Professor of Principles of Surgery and Clinical Surgery in Jefferson Medical College, Philadelphia, has recently lent the weight of his high authority (see Bibliotheca Sacra, July, 1897, vol. liv, pp. 469–484, article Further Studies on the Bloody Sweat of our Lord).

ceed the thunderbolt that at last descended upon his head, reveal every occasion for the intensest mental anguish such as would in a literal sense strain the heart to its utmost. At his triumphal entry to the city upon the preceding Sunday, loud cries and tears burst from him as he contemplated its approaching doom;* while in the mysterious agony † in Gethsemane, 'where he was greatly amazed, and sore troubled, and exceedingly sorrowful even unto death, Luke ‡ records that, "being in an agony, he prayed more earnestly: and his sweat became as it were great drops of blood falling upon the ground." Here the bloody sweat is a well-recognised physiological accompaniment of those forms of mental agony which, according to the representation, weighed upon the Saviour during all his ministry and pre-eminently during the last week of his earthly life. It is in accordance with this interpretation that at the supreme moment of agony upon the cross, and at the point of death from the actual rupturing of his heart, he should utter the loud and piercing cry which is reported by three of the evangelists.#

If, however, this view of the cause of Christ's death be rejected, as it is by many eminent authorities, another explanation of the phenomenon is readily at hand —namely, that the water issued from the pleural sac, where it had accumulated in the last few hours as a consequence of some unrecorded injury which Jesus had received during the buffetings of his trial. It is not by any means unheard of that a large amount of water should thus accumulate within a few hours after a

---

* Luke xix, 39–44.   † Mark xiv, 33, 34.   ‡ Luke xxii, 44.
\# Matt. xxvii, 50; Mark xv, 37; Luke xxiii, 46.

300   CHRISTIAN EVIDENCES.

severe blow to the side. The location of this membrane surrounding the lungs is such that the thrust of the spear which penetrated the heart of one hanging as Jesus did upon the cross would at the same time rupture the pleural sac. In either case the phenomenon would give positive assurance of the death of the victim, and the cause be too recondite to have suggested the narrative.

THE GOSPELS REFLECT THE GENERAL CONDITIONS OF THE APOSTOLIC AGE.

Another line of evidence pointing with irresistible force to the origin of the Gospels during the apostolic era is to be found in the strictness with which the four Gospels limit themselves to the facts known to exist during the period to which they relate. The whole literary atmosphere of the four Gospels is that of the early part of the first century. There is scarcely a word or mental conception or historical allusion in any of the Gospels which indicates, on the part of the writers, a knowledge of the condition of things which existed subsequent to the destruction of Jerusalem.

It is impossible for the historian or man of letters to exaggerate the social, religious, and historical importance of the capture of Jerusalem by the Roman army under Titus A. D. 70. From this time forth the sacred city ceased to be the religious centre of the Jews. The magnificent temple which for centuries had been the chief attraction to Jewish pilgrims from all over the world was utterly destroyed. The smoke of their offer-

The Destruction of Jerusalem.

THE EARLY DATE OF THE FOUR GOSPELS. 301

ings no longer arose from the sacred altars upon Mount Moriah. From that time to this Gentiles have not ceased to profane the sacred inclosure. Since that time the solemn feasts have not been celebrated there with the pomp and show of Herod's time. The schools of the prophets have been discontinued in the courts of the temple. The scribes and Pharisees and Sadducees and Herodians no longer figure in the picturesque and exciting scenes which marked the earlier half of the century. Faithful devotees like aged Simeon and Anna were no longer found waiting at Jerusalem in confident hope of the redemption of Israel.

It would be scarcely possible for any historian writing at second hand subsequent to this great turning point in the world's history, and describing the scenes in Jerusalem and other parts of Palestine previous to that event, not to betray the later point of view from which he was contemplating the facts. But we look in vain in the first three Gospels for the least intimation of this later point of view; while in the fourth Gospel also, which was confessedly written after that event, in the very last part of the century, the whole atmosphere of the narrative is that of the first half of the century—a phenomenon which can be accounted for only on the theory that the writer as a young man was a participant in the scenes enacted sixty years before, and either by notes or by the peculiarities of memory characteristic of old men when dwelling upon their younger days, or by inspiration, was able to limit his thoughts to the definite facts of those earlier experiences.

For the enforcement of this important truth it is

only necessary to dwell upon a few typical examples. In doing this, special significance will belong to illustrations taken from those portions of the third Gospel which have by some been regarded as later additions to the original story. It would be impossible, however, to conceive of language which should more perfectly breathe the spirit of the times and exclude every suggestion of a later period than that which is found in the first two chapters of Luke. Herod is king in Judea; Zacharias of the course of Abijah is priest in Jerusalem, and his wife Elisabeth was of the daughters of Aaron. In the order of his course Zacharias enters the temple to burn incense, when the angel appears to him and announces that his own son, yet to be born, was to be the forerunner of the Christ who was to go forth in the power of Elijah, according to the word of the prophet. At the same time Joseph and Mary, though reckoned among the families of Bethlehem, are living at Nazareth, and receive the announcement that one is to be born to her who is yet a virgin, who shall be called the Son of the Most High, and who was to sit upon the throne of his father David.

Illustrations from Luke.

The two exquisite hymns of these favoured women —the Magnificat and the Benedictus—could scarcely have originated at any later time than that assigned to them. They are composed almost entirely of fragments of the Old Testament woven together into forms of sublimest beauty. But it is evident that not the least shadow of the events of later times has fallen upon them. How redolent of the expectations of the period are the closing sentences of the one and the opening sentences of the other!

He hath holpen Israel his servant,
That he might remember mercy
(As he spake unto our fathers)
Toward Abraham and his seed for ever.

Blessed be the Lord, the God of Israel;
For he hath visited and wrought redemption for his people,
And hath raised up a horn of salvation for us
In the house of his servant David
(As he spake by the mouth of his holy prophets which have been since the world began).

The birth of Christ is fearlessly assigned by Luke to the time of the enrolment under Augustus Cæsar, made when Quirinius was Governor of Syria, thus introducing an apparent discrepancy which only the results of latest scholarship have been able to explain.

The Census of Quirinius.

The discussions over this apparent discrepancy are extremely significant. The best attested reading and translation of the passage is, "Now it came to pass in those days there went out a decree from Cæsar Augustus that all the inhabited earth should be enrolled. This was the first enrolment, made when Quirinius was Governor of Syria"* (Luke ii, 1, 2). Although this has the appearance of being a definite attempt on the part of the writer to fix accurately (according to his promise in the introduction) the date of Christ's birth and the circumstances which led to its occurrence at Bethlehem, it has been from the earliest time the subject of ceaseless disputes.

---

* See an able discussion of the census of Quirinius, by Prof. W. M. Ramsay, the Expositor, April and May, 1897.

In Acts v, 37 an enrolment is spoken of, or rather "the enrolment"—that is, the great enrolment or the well-known enrolment which was made under Quirinius about the year 6 A. D.* But from the time of Tertullian, in the early part of the third century, it has been persistently maintained by some that the earlier enrolment was not made when Quirinius was Governor of Syria.† Tertullian expressly says, "At this very time a census had been taken in Judea by Sentius Saturninus." This officer we know to have been Governor in Syria B. C. 9–7. Doubtless Tertullian, having access, as he would, to Roman records, ascertained that an enrolment, ordered by Augustus Cæsar, was begun in Syria under the administration of Saturninus.

That the first census of Augustus Cæsar was initiated at this time is rendered highly probable by the recent discovery that a series of enrolments were made by the Roman Empire in Egypt at intervals of fourteen years. Such enrolments are positively proved to have taken place in Egypt running back from the year 229–230 to the year A. D. 89–90. From that period to 6 A. D. (the period of the enrolment referred to in Acts v, 37), we have no direct evidence upon the point. But as that occurred upon a multiple of fourteen, and as so many other features in the organization of the Roman Empire are known to date from the activity of Augustus Cæsar's fertile mind, there can be no reasonable doubt that the policy of making a census once in fourteen years was permanently adhered to. That would bring the census previous to the one mentioned in Acts in

---

* See Josephus, Antiq., xvii, 13, 5.
† See Tertullian, Against Marcion, iv, 19.

the year 8 B. C., making its initiation at the close of the governorship of Saturninus, as Tertullian affirms. Now, we know from Josephus that Quirinius, who had charge of the census in A. D. 6, had been "governor" or consul in Syria at a previous period,* while Zumpt has shown that at about the time at which the birth of Christ is now assigned—namely, 4 B. C.—Quirinius was somewhere in the East, and, for all we know, was executing this census as Luke has said. At any rate, we know nothing to the contrary. Thus there is no positive evidence to contradict Luke, while there is much evidence to corroborate his statement. Luke must have been a very incompetent blunderer to have committed at his time the error which some attribute to him. His general habit of accuracy, however, is such that so patent a blunder upon so easily established a historical fact is in the highest degree improbable; while it is still more improbable that any one who was fabricating history from imperfect information at a later period should have introduced such an apparent discrepancy as is here presented. For, the census is not executed according to later Roman methods by the direct agents of the empire, but indirectly, according to the native tribal system, and under the direction of a native king. There is therefore this additional mark of truthfulness in the account, that the method of execution incidentally coincides with the transitional stage of government which we know to have been in operation at the period indicated, but which disappeared shortly after.

The motives leading Joseph and Mary to Bethlehem are those which could have appeared to exist only

---

* Antiq. xvii, 13, 5.

before the destruction of Jerusalem. After that event there would have seemed to be no inducement for this couple to have made the journey from Nazareth to Bethlehem for the sake of retaining their enrolment there.

The Birth of Christ. The appearance of the angels to the shepherds is likewise most redolent of the spirit of the times to which it is assigned. Christ the Lord, it is announced, is to be born to them that day in the city of David, whither they repair with haste, to find the infant Saviour lying in the manger.

In due time, when the days of purification according to the law of Moses are fulfilled, the infant is brought to the temple at Jerusalem, where the sacrifices according to the law of Moses are performed in his behalf. It is then that Simeon, a righteous and devout man, who was looking for the consolation of Israel, and upon whom the Spirit of the Lord was moving, received the Saviour into his arms, and blessed God, and said, "Now lettest thy servant depart, O Lord, according to thy word in peace, for mine eyes have seen thy salvation"; while to the mother he said, "Behold, this child is set for the falling and rising up of many in Israel, and for a sign which is spoken against." Here also we find Anna the prophetess, the daughter of Phanuel, of the tribe of Asher, who departed not from the temple, worshipping with fastings and supplications night and day, and coming up that very hour she gave thanks unto God, and spake of him to all of them that were looking for the redemption of Jerusalem.

From beginning to the end of these introductory chapters there is not the least trace of the colouring of later times. Nothing can be more certain from a literary point of view than that they are contemporary documents which have come down to us unmodified since apostolic times. As one proceeds in reading the Gospel, he finds nothing to impair this impression.

In the third chapter we are set down " in the fifteenth year of the reign of Tiberius Cæsar, Pontius Pilate being Governor of Judea, and Herod being Tetrarch of Galilee, and his brother Philip Tetrarch of the region of Iturea and Trachonitis, and Lysanias Tetrarch of Abilene, in the high priesthood of Annas and Caiaphas," when "the word of God came unto John, the son of Zacharias, in the wilderness." Such minuteness of description reveals the easy hand of a contemporary writer perfectly familiar with complicated events which have passed under his own observation. In keeping with this, the description of the work of John the Baptist is throughout entirely in the costume of the times into which he is introduced. The expectations of the people who came to his baptism were pre-eminently those of that particular portion of the first century of our era to which he is assigned. The publicans and the soldiers introduced are also in perfect harmony with the scene, while the reference to Herod and Herodias are such as would not have been thought of by any one but a contemporary writer.

The Time of his Ministry.

In the account of the temptation in the fourth chapter—the scene which is laid upon the pinnacle of the temple, whence the Son of God is asked to cast himself down—bears every mark of a simple narrative by a contemporary author. In the same chapter also the account of the beginning of his ministry in Nazareth, where "he entered, as his custom was, in the synagogue on the Sabbath day and stood up to read," is too graphic and natural to suggest anything but the account of a contemporary. The miracles at Capernaum, where again he was attending the synagogue on the Sabbath day, are too simply told and too delicately representative of the conditions of the time and place to be anything but genuine.

Especially in the fifth chapter is the account of the miracles most lifelike and accurate in its setting. The leper was told to show himself to the priests and offer for his cleansing according as Moses commanded, while the Pharisees and doctors of the law had come out from every village of Galilee and Judea and Jerusalem. The opposition of the scribes and Pharisees is such as could not have been thought of in the latter part of the century.

In the sixth chapter, likewise, the activity and confidence of the scribes and Pharisees, so characteristic of the first half of the first century, while their institutions were in a most flourishing condition, appears in every paragraph.

In the seventh chapter the presence of the centurion and his kindly relation to the Jews is pertinent only to that time; while the message which John the Baptist sent from his prison house by two of his disciples to Jesus, and the reply of Jesus, with the references of the historian to the conduct of the publicans, the Pharisees, and the lawyers, are all in the local colouring of the time and place to which they are assigned.

In the third verse of the eighth chapter there is a most instructive undesigned coincidence in the mention of Joanna, the wife of Chuza, Herod's steward.

THE EARLY DATE OF THE FOUR GOSPELS. 309

This faithful woman is again barely mentioned in Luke xxiv, 10 as among those to whom the Saviour appeared on the morning of his resurrection, as they were bearing spices and ointments to embalm his body. Here she is one of those who "ministered to him of their substance." No one but a contemporary would have preserved this relation of Chuza to Herod's household, while it is a natural explanation of Herod's familiarity with the work of Jesus as related in Matt. xiv, 1 and Luke ix, 7. It is significant also that the seat of this Herod's (Antipas) jurisdiction was in Galilee, where most of Jesus's work was done.*

In passing over the later chapters, it is sufficient to note the lifelike character and the purely local colouring of the account of the rejection of Jesus and his disciples by the Samaritans "because his face was as though he was going to Jerusalem" (ix, 53), and of his references to Chorazin, Bethsaida, and Capernaum in chapter x. In the same chapter also the parable of the good Samaritan is intensely local in all its suggestions. A similar remark is due with reference to the denunciations of the Pharisees and lawyers and of their opposition to him in the latter part of this chapter and in the beginning of the next.

In the thirteenth chapter the reference to the Galileans whose blood Pilate mingled with their sacrifices, and of the recent destructive fall of a tower in Siloam, are characteristically local in their colouring, as is the reference to the journey to Jerusalem, and to the Pharisees and Herod in the latter part of the chapter.

---

* See Blount's Undesigned Coincidences, p. 263.

21

In all subsequent chapters again the Pharisees and the lawyers appear at Jerusalem in the character which only befitted the period which preceded the destruction of the city. Especially are these portraitures accurate in the delineation of Christ's visits to the temple during his last week at Jerusalem and of the struggling elements which come to the surface during the trial and the crucifixion. The only possible occurrence of an anachronism in this account occurs in the reference to the destruction of Jerusalem in Luke xix, 43, 44, xxi, 20, 21, 24, where it is alleged that the description is too definite to have been prophetic, and hence could have been written only after the event.* An examination of the passages, however, gives little reason for this suggestion. The first of the passages reads: "For the days shall come upon thee, when thine enemies shall cast up a bank about thee, and compass thee round, and keep thee in on every side, and shall dash thee to the ground, and thy children within thee; and they shall not leave within thee one stone upon another, because thou knewest not the time of thy visitation."

Prophecy of the Destruction of Jerusalem.

The second reads: "But when ye see Jerusalem compassed with armies, thou knowest that her desolation is at hand. Then let them that are in Judea flee unto the mountains; and let them that are in the midst of her depart out; and let not them that are in the country enter therein."

If there is anything in these passages implying a later date than that of the destruction of Jerusalem,

---

* But see Rom. xi, 25.

THE EARLY DATE OF THE FOUR GOSPELS. 311

they could be most readily accounted for as interpolations or modifications of single texts through the processes with which we have been made familiar in textual criticism. But an examination of them does not seem to show any necessity even for this. The descriptions of the siege and destruction of the city accords with what was familiarly known as habitually taking place in the capture of a walled city defended by brave inhabitants, while in one respect the description is very clearly what would not have been made after the fall of the city. In the twenty-first verse of the twenty-first chapter we find the exhortation, "Let them which are in Judea flee unto the mountains." It is well known, however, that during a lull in the siege the Christians fled to Pella, and Eusebius * speaks of an oracle which commanded the Church in Jerusalem during the siege "to leave and dwell in a city of Peræa, called Pella." It is therefore worthy of note that Luke has not altered this command to suit the incident, as a later historian would have been likely to do, but retains the exact phraseology of Matthew and Mark, "Let them that are in Judea flee unto the mountains," adding also, "and let them that are in the midst of her depart out; and let not them that are in the country enter therein."

In this connection also it is worthy of special note that the fourth Gospel, which is acknowledged to have been written twenty-five years after the destruction of Jerusalem, makes no reference whatever to the prophecy, so carefully recorded in each of the first three Gospels. This circumstance illustrates one

Historical Character of the Fourth Gospel.

---

* H. E., iii, 5, 3.

of the most striking characteristics of the fourth Gospel when its late date is taken into consideration; for in this case we have the extremely difficult task imposed upon an author of writing a history sixty years after the occurrence of the events, while excluding all extraneous references and all subsequent facts, and limiting one's self to a pure narrative of the times without admixture of mental conceptions formed from later points of view. This is the remarkable feat accomplished by the writer of the fourth Gospel. A proper appreciation of its significance will greatly enhance the impression of genuineness which is made by a careful perusal of the work.

The fourth Gospel does indeed begin with a paragraph which shows intimate acquaintance with the philosophic disquisitions which became prevalent among Greek-speaking Jews in the latter part of the century through the writings of Philo, who had much to say about the "Logos" or "Word" of God. All the use, however, which John makes of this phraseology is to rescue it from its perversion, and to preserve it in a corrected sense for the use of later Christian philosophers.

With the nineteenth verse of the first chapter the history of the ministry of Jesus is begun, and henceforth the topic is adhered to with scrupulous care to the very end of the book. With a success which is phenomenal the writer transports his readers to the period, and limits himself to a plain statement of facts uncoloured by the reflection of later events and of later mental conceptions. To this statement there is only one exception. It does appear that John is writing for an audience that is distant from Palestine and is unfamiliar with its former geographical names, and with the local customs of the times. In many places, therefore, we meet in the fourth Gospel with supplementary words and phrases evidently designed to give the explanation which the writer perceived would be called for by those into whose hands his Gospel would first fall. For example, in ii, 6 he says that the six waterpots of stone which are spoken of in connection with the miracle of making the water wine at Cana in Galilee, were "set there after the Jews' manner of purifying." In v, 2 he says that the name of the sheep gate was called "in Hebrew" Bethesda. In vi, 1, after speaking of the Sea of Galilee, he adds the phrase, "which is the Sea of Tiberias." In ix, 7 the word "Siloam" is stated to mean "by interpretation" sent. In x, 22, after speaking of the feast of dedication, he adds that it was "in the winter." In xi, 18, after referring to Bethany, he explains that it was "nigh unto Jerusalem, about fifteen furlongs off." In ii, 13 and xi, 55 he takes pains to say that the Passover is a "feast of the Jews." Any one can see at a glance that these explanatory remarks would only be made by a writer who had in view the wants of readers who were considerably separated in time and space from the event.* But they are not such as to change at all the colouring of the narrative, and, while perfectly natural in a writer at the close of the century, it is worthy of special note that the first three Gospels were not influenced either in the original writing or in the transmission by this natural tendency of later times. We have, therefore, in this contrast of John and the first three Gospels additional testimony

---

* See also the use of the word "Jew," ii, 8, 33.

to the early date of the first three, and to the scrupulous care with which in general they were transmitted by the scribes.

In reference to the internal marks that the writer of the fourth Gospel was an eye-witness, sufficient evidence has already been presented. It is pertinent here merely to call attention, by way of supplement, to the success with which the author has kept out extraneous matter. From beginning to end the scenes described and the political and social conditions brought to light are those which are known to have existed at the time of Christ's ministry, and to have passed away soon after. There is no shaping of the story with reference to its bearing upon subsequent questions. The historical part thus bears the clearest marks of being strictly historical, and not an expanded and modified story, such as would have been composed by ordinary historians a century after the event.

John an Eye-witness.

A single illustration may be taken from the ninth chapter, which contains the account of the healing of the man who had been blind from his birth. At every turn the description is of the most lifelike character, and is absolutely true to the times so far as we know them, and absolutely free from the modifications natural to the reflections of a later period.

The account begins with the passing of the blind man which suggests to Christ's disciples the question whether his blindness was the result of his own sin or that of his parents. In addressing Jesus, the disciples use the Hebrew word "rabbi." After disabusing them of their false opinion as to the cause of this misfortune to the blind man, Jesus proceeds to moisten some clay with his spittle and to anoint the blind man's eyes with it, commanding him to go and "wash in the pool of Siloam." Upon returning, the blind man came with his sight restored, which made him an astonishment to all his friends and neighbours who had been familiar with him as a beggar by the wayside. So astonished were they that they could scarcely believe their eyes, and doubted whether it were indeed really he or some one that looked like him. When called upon to tell how his eyes were opened, he repeated in the simplest way his story, whereupon there was a general desire to know where Jesus is, but the blind man can not tell them.

Upon the blind man's being brought before the Pharisees, they endeavoured to persuade him that Jesus was to be blamed for healing him on the Sabbath, and to them he repeats, in the simplest way, the account of his healing, reasoning that Jesus could not be a bad man, else God would not have given him power to perform such a miracle. He must therefore be a prophet.

At this juncture a party of Jewish agnostics began to deny that the man had ever been blind, and called upon his parents to prove the fact. They, however, in the most positive manner, testified to his blindness from birth, but say they know nothing about how he has been healed, adding emphatically, "Ask him; he is of age; let him speak for himself." This short answer of the parents, it appears, is to be accounted for by their fear of the Jews, who had agreed that they would put out of the synagogue any man who should confess that Jesus was the Christ.

Upon this, the blind man was recalled and put under

oath to tell the whole truth. But he was not now so positive as before that Jesus might not be a sinner, simply taking a negative position, saying that he does not know whether he is or not, but he does know that the miracle has been performed upon him. But he refuses to tell them the story over again, and insists upon his right to do as he pleases about telling them, and inquires of them tauntingly why they want to hear the story again after he has told it to them twice, " Would ye also become his disciples? " Upon this the Pharisees deride him with being a disciple of Jesus, while they are disciples of Moses. " But as for this man Jesus we know not whence he is." This arouses the blind man, who tells them that they ought to know that God does not hear sinners, and that " if this man were not from God he could do nothing." Whereupon they lose their patience and cast him out as an incorrigible sinner.

After all this, the blind man meets Jesus again, who asks him if he believes on the Son of God (or, as many ancient manuscripts have it, the Son of man). The blind man says, " And who is he, Lord, that I may believe on him? Jesus said unto him, Thou hast both seen him, and he it is who speaketh with thee. And he said, Lord, I believe. And he worshipped him. And Jesus said, For judgment came I into this world, that they which see not may see; and that they which see may become blind. Those of the Pharisees which were with him heard these things, and said unto him, Are we also blind? Jesus said unto them, If ye were blind, ye would have no sin; but now ye say, We see: your sin remaineth."

Of the numerous extended discourses recorded in

THE EARLY DATE OF THE FOUR GOSPELS. 317

the fourth Gospel, it need only be remarked that, however much they show the colouring of John's own mind, there is no evidence that they are not faithful representations of the original impressions made upon his mind at the time of their delivery; for clearly they have not been distorted by any effort, either conscious or unconscious, to adapt them specifically to the later developments of Church history, while the uniform high plane of thought along which they move stamps them as belonging to that original vein of high revelation which characterizes the discourses of Christ elsewhere reported. In none of them are there any marks of that speculative weakness so common in the writers of the post-apostolic age. At the same time there is an originality about it which equally separates it from the post-apostolic writings whose dependence upon the Gospels is always evident, even upon superficial examination.

The Discourses.

PROF. HUIDEKOPER'S ARGUMENT.

A powerful argument was carefully worked out by the late Prof. Frederick Huidekoper upon The Indirect Testimony of History to the Genuineness of the Gospels, of which we can give no better account than to present a brief summary, simply premising that the argument is based upon the freedom of the Gospels from the influence of post-apostolic ideas and events, thus bringing it into line with the whole trend of the present chapter.

1. He calls attention first to the fact that "the Christian authorship of the Gospels was contrary to

the controversial wants of the early Christians, and so embarrassed them in their arguments with heathens that it is morally impossible they could have fictitiously assigned such authorship to them." For purposes of controversy the early Christians would have found it extremely convenient to have been able to appeal to Jewish or heathen records of Jesus, and among the apocryphal writings such documents appear as the Acts of Pilate, Letter from Pilate to Tiberius, Correspondence of Abgarus with Christ, Alleged Correspondence of Seneca with Paul, Alleged Letter of Marcus Antoninus, and others. But none of these will stand comparison at all with the four Gospels, and are universally rejected by all classes of critics.

Profane Authorship not claimed.

2. "Of all the controversies in which Christians were engaged, whether between themselves or against Jews or heathens, not a trace appears in the Gospels." These controversies, as we know from the Epistles, were very bitter; especially bitter was that between the Jewish and the Gentile Christians which led to the council at Jerusalem, whose results are recorded in Acts xv, 7. Indeed, the attitude of the judaizing element in the Church was extremely bitter, as one can learn from the Epistle to the Galatians. But of all this conflict not a trace appears in any allusion to be found in the four Gospels. The same is true concerning the controversies which inevitably arose between the Jews and the Christians and between the heathen and the Christians, as well as between the Gnostics and the orthodox Christians of the second century. Of these controversies we have abundant evidence in the

No Trace of Later Controversies.

THE EARLY DATE OF THE FOUR GOSPELS. 319

writings of Justin Martyr, Irenæus, Theophilus of Antioch, and Tertullian, but the four Gospels know nothing of these controversies, and were not in the least degree affected by the controversial atmosphere which pervaded the last part of the first and the whole of the second century.

3. "Of the opinions prominently asserted and defended by the early Christians, or by particular schools among them, and which they rode as hobbies, not one appears in the Gospels." Of these opinions, those concerning heathen deities and their supposed relation to the evils of the world; those concerning idolatry and the sin of sacrificing to idols; those concerning Christ's mission to the under world; the resurrection of the flesh; the millennium; the restoration of Jerusalem; the destruction of Rome; the return of Nero; and the personal appearance of Christ, were all of them hotly contested in post-apostolic times; but the Gospels are altogether neutral in their attitude toward them.

Early Christian Schools unrecognized.

4. "Of the customs to which the early Christians attached importance, or to which they were wedded, we find nothing in the Gospels, except the baptismal formula of the second century." These customs relate to such questions as the mode of observing the Sabbath, the observance of Sunday as a day for religious gathering, and the eating of blood. It would certainly have been most natural, on the theory of the late origin of the Gospels, to have found in them some more specific justification for the observance of Sunday than they contain.

Early Christian Customs unknown.

5. "The peculiar designations for God used by Christians in heathen lands are absent from the Gospels." In the early patristic literature most laboured efforts are constantly made to distinguish the God of Christianity from the prevalent heathen conception of deity. These writers call him "the true God," "the soul God," "the unoriginated God," "the imperishable God," "the Maker of the universe," "the Parent of all things," "the Father of the universe," etc. But in the Gospels there is no reflection of anything but the common Jewish methods of designating Deity. "They show no traces of Christian effort to prevent heathen misconception."

Opposition to Heathenism not developed.

6. "The terms by which Christians were designated" in heathen lands are absent from the Gospels, as were the terms which were used by Christians to express the ideas which arose in the early development of the Church. We have already dwelt at some length upon the occurrence in the Gospels of the phrases "Son of man," "kingdom of heaven," and "disciples," and of the absence from the Gospels of the synonym for these phrases which occur so abundantly in the Epistles. To this we might have added a considerable list of phrases and words which are adduced by Prof. Huidekoper in illustration of his point. Among the most conspicuous of these is the phrase "Jesus Christ," which does not occur in the Gospels, where he is "almost universally called Jesus, a term which occurs more than six hundred times. If the word Christ be at any time employed it is as an official title, usually with the prefix the, and we also find Jesus the Christ. The exceptions

Absence of Later Phrases.

THE EARLY DATE OF THE FOUR GOSPELS. 321

confirm rather than militate against the inference to be drawn from this usage." These exceptions are John i, 17, which is a doctrinal reflection of John in his old age, and illustrates how natural the phrase had become in the early development of Church history. The phrase occurs also in Matt. i, 1 and 18 and Mark i, 1, both of which also in the introduction of their history naturally reflect the use of later times. But in the history itself the phrase is carefully avoided, the only exception being Mark ix, 41.

Other phrases frequent in later apostolic times, but avoided in the Gospel narrative, are "Christians," the origin of which is related in Acts xi, 26, and which occurs later in Acts and in the Epistles, but nowhere in the Gospels; "unbeliever" and "lawless," words frequently used in the Epistles to describe the heathen, but never used in the Gospels; and the word signifying "devout man," and its cognate signifying "godliness" ($εὐσεβής$, $εὐσέβεια$). These occur frequently in the Acts and the Epistles, but are unknown in the Gospels.

7. "We find various questions about public games, slavery, and other things, in which the Christians were deeply interested, but on which the Gospels attribute no remark to the Master." Early in the history of the Church the wickedness of these games became the subject of remark. In the persecutions of which we have record the Christians were frequently thrown into the arena to be tortured and put to death by wild beasts. But "in the Gospels we find from the Teacher of teachers no word on the subject of these games; no condemnation of them as barbarities; no answer put into the mouth of his followers which might

Antagonistic Heathen Institutions unrecognized.

aid them in escaping; no word of encouragement to assist them in enduring these atrocities."

8. The wars under Nero and Hadrian by which Jerusalem was desolated, and during the last of which a temple of Jupiter Capitolinus was erected on the site of Solomon's temple, are not referred to except in the indefinite prophecy of Jesus concerning the destruction of Jerusalem, to which we have already alluded.

Miscellaneous Omissions.

There is an absence also in the Gospels of any intimation of the systems of Greek philosophy with which the churches became early familiar as they spread throughout the Roman Empire. Nor is there any allusion which would indicate acquaintance with the views of natural science prevalent among the people surrounding the Gentile churches. Nor do we find the influence of any of the later emperors or of Greek culture in general reflected in any way in the four Gospels.

Conclusion.

In view of this array of facts, there is irresistible force in Prof. Huidekoper's concluding remarks:

It is morally impossible if the Gospels had been fictitious, or were slowly growing under the hands of Christians, that they should have omitted all the topics of chief interest to those who wrote them.

If we now turn to the spurious records which Christians forged, we can to some extent test the truth of the preceding remarks. The test is imperfect, because these spurious records were not strictly original compositions, but (setting aside the Letter of Lentulus) simply an effort to reproduce facts concerning Jesus—especially the miracles—as recorded in the Gospels, basing them, however, on non-Christian evidence. Had these documents aimed to originate a life of the Master rather than to substantiate

THE EARLY DATE OF THE FOUR GOSPELS. 323

one which already existed, they would have had a much wider field for introducing the peculiarities of other countries or later times. In these records we find Jesus charged with destroying the Sabbath and effecting cures by magic. Articles of clothing, belonging to official position, are mentioned by their heathen names; the terms Lord's Day and Palm Sunday are introduced as if in use during the ministry of Jesus; we find the Roman standards doing homage to Jesus; we find twelve persons in Judea charged with being proselytes and maintaining that they are born Jews—a subject of dispute natural in localities outside of Judea, but unlikely to affect simultaneously twelve witnesses in Jerusalem; we find crucifixion treated as a Jewish form of punishment; the results of Christ's mission to the under world are plainly stated; a description of his personal appearance is given at length; the appeal to the Old Testament as having foretold the crucifixion and resurrection of Jesus admits but one interpretation; and the pseudo-predictions foretell the destruction of the temple with a sufficient description of those who were to destroy it.

There is yet an indirect argument to be drawn from a condition of things nineteen or twenty years after the ministry of Jesus. Six different writers—heathen, Jewish, and Christian—concur in implying or referring to a widespread excitement at that date among Jews, the blame of which was thrown to some extent on Christians. The writers are Tacitus, Suetonius, the author of a Jewish Sibylline production, Paul, Luke, and Eusebius. There can hardly be a question that these writers, with the exception perhaps of Paul and Luke, wrote independently of each other. Their concurrence implies that at the date mentioned Christianity had taken considerable hold in Italy. The allusions, moreover, to the excitement and to some circumstances connected with it are, in the Acts of the Apostles and in Paul's letters to the Thessalonians, so incidental that they can only have been written by persons who lived through it, and whose readers were familiar with it. Writers of a later date would not have expected such allusions to be understood. These allusions establish the fact that the documents were written by persons then living, and each of these documents implies a then accepted history of Jesus, essentially such as we find in the Gospels.

Summary.

Thus we are led by three independent lines of argument to the conclusion that can not well be shaken that we have in the four Gospels a record of facts which was accepted by the Christians of the first century as the basis of their conception of the person and work of Christ and of their consequent religious faith. These, and none others, were the records of Christ's life which they carried with them as they were dispersed in all directions throughout the vast Roman Empire. Such uniformity in documentary evidence of widely distributed localities could not have been secured by dispersion from any centres of influence which arose subsequent to the first century. Whatever be the problems concerning the history of Jesus Christ, they must be solved by the condition of things which existed in the apostolic age. The newly discovered documents, especially Tatian's Diatessaron and the new Syriac version of the Gospels, both revealing the established beliefs of the early part of the second century, enforce the evidence, which was already sufficient, that all four of our Gospels were regarded as sacred books by the Christians early in the second century, and so point irresistibly to their origin in the first century.

An examination of the general style of the Gospel narratives, and of the numerous undesigned coincidences in their incidental use of phrases and reference

THE EARLY DATE OF THE FOUR GOSPELS. 325

to the existing historical and social conditions, amply justifies the conclusions indicated by the external evidence.

While, finally, that minute examination which has been made necessary by the scientific efforts of the textual critics to establish the original text on scientific principles has lent its powerful aid to the confirmation of these other independent conclusions that the four Gospels are all first century documents, proceeding from the apostolic age. This conclusion may now be taken as proved beyond all reasonable doubt.

As already remarked, the value of this new evidence is enhanced by the fact that it is all in the same direction. The newly discovered evidences have all supported the earlier dates which have been assigned to the Gospels. No evidence has come to light of a contrary character. When we consider the variety of the new witnesses and the diversity of places from which they have come, this is certainly very remarkable, and is enough to dispel all lingering fear that, after all, we had been mistaken in the confidence which had been so long reposed in the old line of Christian evidences. The new in no respect opposes the old, but re-enforces and supports it at every point.

To those familiar with geological lines of reasoning, a striking analogy presents itself in the likeness of many of the points adduced from textual criticism and the other circumstantial evidence, to the stray fossils by which the age of geological strata are determined. Rocks which are otherwise indistinguishable in their texture may be recognised and assigned to their position by a very few fossils imbedded in them; and so the horizon of these texts and versions and compilations may confidently be determined by the chance expressions and historical allusions contained in them which reflect the literary conditions of the time at which they were written. These documents may be compared to conglomerate rocks, the age of whose separate pebbles is more or less easily capable of determination. The Gospels do not contain pebbles of any kind from the post-apostolic age. The conditions of life subsequent to the destruction of Jerusalem are so peculiar and so well known that they could be readily recognised if they were present, and at the same time they were so pervasive that they could scarcely have failed to have impressed themselves upon historical writers who felt at liberty to use any freedom at all in their representation of the historical facts with which they were dealing. The internal evidence abundantly supports the external evidence that all of the Gospels are products of the apostolic age.

Indeed, so strong is this evidence that the destructive and agnostic criticism of the New Testament which has prevailed so extensively during the past fifty years may be fairly said to have received its deathblow in the closing decade of the nineteenth century, so that Harnack, its last and ablest representative, has formally surrendered the field with the following most significant words, to which reference has already been made:

. The oldest literature of the Church in all main points and in most details, from the point of view of literary criticism, is genuine and trustworthy. . . . The chronological succession in which tradition has arranged the original documents of Christianity is, in all essential points from the Epistles of St. Paul to the writings of

Irenæus, correct, and compels the historian to keep clear of all hypotheses concerning the course of events which conflict with this succession.

It will remain for us briefly and directly to consider the probability that such histories as are presented in the four Gospels could have arisen in the apostolic age except in connection with actual events occurring substantially as they are recorded.

CHAPTER X.

POSITIVE RESULTS OF THE CUMULATIVE EVIDENCE.

CHRISTIANITY is a member of the historical branch of the family of inductive sciences. The foundations upon which it rests are similar to those upon which all the other members of the family rest. If it seems to give more prominence to faith than other sciences do, and less to sight, it is because it rises to a higher circle of conclusions, and touches a higher class of interests than any which they attempt to reach. In this it pays tribute to the noblest endowments of the human mind, and prepares the way for the attainment of the highest results of civilization. A generation which can not grasp historical lessons, and which can not seize and act upon those more subtle forms of probable evidence which underlie historical reasoning, disowns its heaven-born heritage, and becomes infantile in its character and retrograde in its movements. Inductive philosophy pays abundant tribute to all the methods of reasoning which are involved in the study of Christian evidences.

<small>Christianity rests on a Scientific Basis.</small>

Is chemistry an experimental science? So is Christianity. But neither is exclusively so. If chemistry deals more largely with experiment than do the other sciences, it is because its field is more restricted. If the chemist walks principally by sight, it is because he does not walk far, but is content to grovel about among elementary things. But chemistry is by no means wholly an experimental science. The chemist, like every one else who lifts himself at all above the present, obtains his highest conceptions of truth by *reasoning* upon the facts of experiment and observation. The experiment gives to his sight but the isolated fact in an isolated crucible. Through memory and his general confidence in the record of other men's work he reaches, by a course of reasoning, the higher generalizations which have made his science so productive in the material development of modern civilization.

Christianity more than Experiment.

Nor is the chemist always content with moderate flights into the realm of the unseen. Assuming the solidarity of the universe, and believing in a unity of all things, which can come only from the purpose of an infinite Creator, the chemist reaches up to the stars with the spectroscope, and from the lines which it furnishes infers the existence in the most distant worlds of the very same elements which he encounters in his everyday experiments. On the other hand, penetrating the realm of the infinitely divisible, he obtains visions of the weight and movement of ultimate molecules of matter which are incalculably beyond the discerning power of his microscope. After taking these lofty flights of imagination, it ill becomes the chemist to make light of that scientific faith which is the "evidence" of other things unseen; for all inference is really faith, being the evidence of things not seen. He who can attain the higher flights of faith reached by modern chemistry and physics has no reason to be disturbed that other sciences attempt to rise a little above the earth on which they mainly tread.

To a still greater degree is the astronomer limited to what he sees with the mind's eye. The universe is the astronomer's crucible, but every element in it is infinitely beyond the power of human manipulation. The facts of astronomy are such as are obtained only by distant observation. The Ptolemaic system of astronomy does not differ so much from the Copernican in its facts as in its interpretations. We accept modern astronomy because it seems to us a more rational interpretation of the facts. The element of rationality when traced down to its ultimate basis rests upon the assumption that there is a divine economy in the universe. There is a law of parsimony in accordance with which there are no unnecessary causes introduced for the production of phenomena. The success with which man is able to make discoveries through the guidance of this principle, and by it to predict the future and infer the unseen, abundantly verifies the assumption. In bestowing upon man the higher powers of thought the Creator has given him the key which successfully unlocks the secrets of the universe. The difference between modern astronomy and the astronomy of the savage is merely a measure of the difference between the development of the civilized mind through its co-operative and historical methods and the development of the savage who lives in isolation both from his contemporaries and from his predecessors; while the measure of the brute's mental capacities is seen in its apparent utter

Astronomy more than Observation.

RESULTS OF THE CUMULATIVE EVIDENCE. 331

inability to discern any meaning in the starry heavens spread out above him.

In geology we rise a step higher among the inductive sciences. Geology belongs wholly to the realm of natural history. The science of geology is an attempt, through interpretation of the fragmentary effects which are within reach of present observation, mentally to reconstruct the causes which have operated in the past. In the strict sense astronomy also would have to be reckoned among the historical sciences, for the messages which come to us even from so near a body as the sun are three minutes old when they arrive; while those which come to us from the more distant nebulæ started upon their journey long before the building of the pyramids or the rise of civilization in the valley of the Euphrates. But in geology the breadth of the grounds of our confidence in inductive reasoning is brought far more clearly to light than it is in chemistry and astronomy. In geological reasoning we both determine the present and forecast the future through our inferential belief in the existence and co-operation of past causes. Few results of human thought are more sublime than those which have resulted in the correlation of geological phenomena.

Geology more than a Record of Facts.

The geologist deals far more with consequential facts than he does with those that are open to direct observation. A few geologists like Dana and Darwin have enjoyed the privilege of circumnavigating the globe. But no one can examine a great manual of geology without seeing at once that the author's success is attained by the skill with which he uses the observations of others. He has learned how to rely upon human testimony, and that in the case of a great multitude of witnesses whom he has never seen. Indeed, if the geologist of the present were not able to stand upon the shoulders of those who have preceded him, and to secure a higher point of vision by means of the record of their work, the science would admit of no progress whatever. And thus at every point shall we find that modern science is resting upon the general trustworthiness of human testimony. While it is true to a certain extent that the first duty of a scientific man is to doubt the testimony of others, and even of his own senses, this is certainly not the whole of his duty. It is as necessary to avoid captious doubt and unreasonable criticism as it is to cherish that limited amount of suspicion which will secure a thorough cross-questioning of the witnesses. Until one pauses to look specially into the matter, he can hardly be aware how much of geology he takes on faith and accepts upon evidence which is so general as to defy analysis.

Following out this same line of thought, it is to be noted that Christian apologists are greatly indebted to the advocates of Darwinism for the respect which they have created for the scientific use of probable evidence.

Darwinism the Deathblow to Empiricism.

From the view point of the empiricism which had come to prevail in botany and zoology, it was natural that Darwinism should be discarded by the French Academy as too theoretical to be called scientific. But botany and zoology had, under a false application of the Baconian method, descended well-nigh to the level of mere botanical and zoological bookkeeping, from which the reasoning faculties were almost entirely excluded; while it was denied that the numerous and cumulative facts pointing, on every principle of design, to the same natural origin of species which had already been accorded to varieties, could lead to any valid conclusions. From this thraldom to mere empiricism Darwin has freed the scientific world, and in so doing he has done much to reveal the true nature of a great mass of false assumptions respecting the true standards of proof which were coming in to embarrass Christian apologists and to mislead the general public concerning the foundations of Christian belief.

Especially is Darwin's example a valuable object lesson in his method of dealing with paradoxes and objections. The question that overwhelms the ordinary student of Darwinian evolution is, How can these things be? How is it possible that there should be such potency in an infinitesimal germ that its influence should, after lying in abeyance for hundreds of generations, suddenly be felt in every portion of the new organism which has sprung from it in line of direct descent? Yet such are some of the facts with which his doctrine of heredity has to deal. The theory of Pangenesis with which this great master endeavoured to explain the mystery served only to magnify it, and by its very boldness to daze the mind of friend and foe alike. In his efforts to explain away the innumerable difficulties of his theory, Drawin incurred the reputation of being the prince of wrigglers. Knowing well the impossibility of seeing everything with perfect clearness, and the necessity of believing much which we can not explain, he wisely contented himself with retorting * that he was less of a wriggler than some others. Writing to Sir

---

* Life and Letters, vol. ii, p. 239.

Joseph Hooker after perusing Herbert Spencer's Principles of Biology, he says: "I feel rather mean when I read him [Spencer]; I could bear and rather enjoy feeling that he was twice as ingenious and clever as myself, but when I feel that he is about a dozen times my superior, even in the master art of wriggling, I feel aggrieved."

It is important to keep these minor uncertainties of science in mind when we come to face the numerous *prima facie* objections that can be urged against the Gospel histories. It were foolish to attempt to deny that there are many difficulties in the way of accepting these accounts of the origin of Christianity in all their particulars. But it should be remembered, and all modern science emphasizes the statement, that in no department of human inferences and beliefs do we have a perfectly clear field in which we may avoid all objection. We are not permitted anywhere to choose between practical beliefs which are encompassed with objections and practical beliefs which are wholly unencumbered by doubts. But if we exercise our reasoning powers at all, our infirmities are such that we must choose the least of two evils and decide upon a balance of probabilities. The demand for unattainable certainty leads in military matters to inactivity; in business affairs, to stagnation; in science, to empiricism; in philosophy, to agnosticism; and in religion, to scepticism.

[margin: Minor Uncertainties do not invalidate the Main Conclusion.]

FINAL SUMMARY.

In light of our previous discussions it will be profitable, in conclusion, briefly to sum up, in accordance with the principles of inductive science, the evidence upon which our faith in Christianity may properly repose, and which may serve as a reasonable basis for religious acitivity.

Christianity is not an untried experiment or a new thing in the world. Every one who comes in contact with Christian civilization soon learns that the best things in it claim to have their origin in the belief in the reality of Christ's character and work and mission as they are portrayed in the four Gospels. Without fear of contradiction we may assert that the noblest men and women with whom we come in contact are in the great majority of cases those who have made Christ their pattern and have believed what is recorded in the Gospels concerning him and his relations to mankind.

Christianity known by its Fruits.

As the experiences of life enlarge, and the inadequacy of the world to satisfy one's noblest aspirations becomes more and more evident, the adaptation of Christianity to one's increasing spiritual wants becomes more and more clear and impressive. This is evident not alone or principally in the Christian standard of morals and duty, but pre-eminently in the motives which Christianity furnishes to inspire hope in a race depressed with a sense of its weakness and shortcomings. Christianity has the same kind of adaptation to the spiritual longings of mankind that food has to the appetite of the hungry.

Nor is the larger outlook any less convincing. It means much that, defective as Christian civilization confessedly is, it is the only civilization worth having. It is the only civilization by whose natural influences the rights of man are respected, freedom of thought is maintained, intellectual progress is secured, and justice and morality are successfully incorporated into the fundamental laws of the nations. Say what we please by way of criticism, it does not take one long to perceive that the civilization of Europe and America is infinitely superior to that of the Orient. It is equally clear also that Western civilization is not the cause but the product of Christianity. Even John Stuart Mill was compelled to admit that " religion can not be said to have made a bad choice in pitching on Jesus as the ideal representative and guide of humanity; nor, even now, would it be easy even for an unbeliever to find a better translation of the rule of virtue from the abstract into the concrete than to endeavour so to live that Christ would approve our life." *

Upon some such general basis of experience as this is every man set out to examine more critically the foundations of his belief in the historical character of the accepted life of Christ. The vast multitude go no further in these inquiries, but rest in the beliefs which have been so widely entertained by the wisest and best people with whom they come in contact, and which are so fully authenticated by their general adaptation to the wants of society, and their fitness to meet the deep necessities of the believer's own soul. Nor is such con-

Christianity commends itself.

---

* Essays on Religion, pp. 253, 254.

fidence unscientific. So far as they go, these evidences of adaptation are satisfactory. They are too intricate and comprehensive to be altogether dissevered from the truth. Indeed, the popular belief in Christianity is as well founded, and founded upon the same kind of general trust in expert evidence, as are the popular beliefs in the Copernican system of astronomy and in the general credibility of any portion of ancient or modern history. But to preserve this basis of confidence it is necessary for the leaders of thought in every generation to verify the foundations anew and to give close attention to the details of the argument. The work of the apologist can never be dispensed with so long as men are called upon to give a reason for the faith that is in them respecting any body of scientific study.

The facilities for this scholarly verification of the truth of the Christian records increase with every decade. Fifty years ago there was a painful lack of literature spanning the century from the destruction of Jerusalem, about the year 70, to the beginning of the literary activity of Irenæus, about the year 170. Indeed, aside from the Apologies of Justin Martyr, which were written about the middle of the second century, and a few fragments from Papias, there were scarcely any trustworthy writings extant dating from the early part of the second century from which direct proof could be obtained concerning the existence of the four Gospels; and the evidence from Justin Martyr was mostly confined to the first three Gospels, from which his quotations were very abundant, for his quotations from the fourth Gospel were so few and so inexact that there was large opportunity to question whether

Growing Strength of the Historical Argument.

he had the Gospel of John before him or not. Both the disposition and the opportunity to question Justin's acquaintance with the fourth Gospel have continued down to the last quarter of the nineteenth century. Because Justin Martyr does not refer to the evangelists by name, but uses a more general title, "memoirs of the apostles," which lumps them all together, there was much plausibility in the contention that the four Gospels, and especially the fourth Gospel, were not in existence in the early part of the second century, but that in place of them there was a common body of tradition from which the substratum of our present Gospel was derived. But it was maintained that the mythical or legendary additions were so great that the real facts were nearly buried out of sight.

The discoveries of the last twenty-five years, however, have done much to bridge over this chasm in the direct evidence. Tatian's Diatessaron, or Harmony of the Four Gospels, has been discovered. This settles beyond controversy the fact that in the first part of the second century the fourth Gospel was received by the churches as on a par with the other three, and that all four were thus early accepted as the only authoritative record of Christ's earthly life. Again, within the past few years a heretical Syriac version of the Gospels has been discovered whose translation was evidently made in the early part of the second century. This again bears witness to the same fact—namely, that early in the second century the four Gospels had the whole field to themselves, and that nobody thought of making any wholesale changes in them; for, while there are clear indications that both Tatian and the translators of this

The Recent Discoveries.

RESULTS OF THE CUMULATIVE EVIDENCE. 339

Syriac version cherished certain heretical views concerning the nature of Christ, the most which they attempted to do in support of their views was to make slight changes in the text in one or two places where the motive is clearly evident, and which are so incongruous that they can easily be eliminated by the textual critic.

The text of this new Syriac version shows that it preceded even that of the Curetonian Syriac, which must have been in existence early in the second century. It can be plausibly urged that the Curetonian was derived by correction from the new Syriac, but not that the new Syriac was derived from the Curetonian; while it is still more clear that the new Syriac is derived from the ordinary text by making poorly disguised changes in it in the interest of a heretical sect which at the close of the first century denied the miraculous conception of Jesus. From this comparison alone it is proved beyond reasonable doubt that the body of the text of the Gospels was generally accepted very early in the second century, thus bringing the recognition of the fourth Gospel down to within twenty or twenty-five years of the life of John.

Finally, the recently discovered fragment of the so-called "Gospel of Peter" also bears indubitable testimony to the recognition of the fourth Gospel as on an equality with the other three in the very first quarter of the second century. For the "Gospel of Peter" preceded Justin Martyr. This is clear from the fact that Justin Martyr evidently made use of its peculiar phraseology. This "Gospel," too, while a compilation in the interest of a heretical sect, shows no knowledge of any facts concerning Christ's life that are not recorded in the four Gospels, and the fourth Gospel is used in the compilation equally with the others.

Thus the arguments from external documents in favour of the genuineness of the four Gospels is cumulative in its character, and is now much stronger than it was a half century ago. Indeed, the recent discoveries leave scarcely any basis for even unreasonable criticism to challenge the statement that all four of the Gospels were generally accepted at the close of the first century with the same reverence which is paid to them by the Church at large at the present time.

Through comparison of the various texts which were in circulation in different parts of the world in the second century we are led, upon independent lines, to the same conclusion. Variations in the texts were already the subject of discussion by Irenæus in the latter part of the second century; while it is clearly evident in Origen's time that the variations in reading which mainly characterized the three great classes into which the texts upon examination fall were already established at the beginning of the third century. Certain variations in the texts had at that time become, in geological phrase, "fossilized." Those which were perpetuated in Alexandria were different from those which were perpetuated in the West, and these were different still from those perpetuated in the Syriac churches in the East. No reasonable account of the origin of these variations can be given without assuming a lapse of time which would throw the writing of the Gospels back into the very first of the second century, or, more reasonably, into the first century itself. These textual variations accord readily with the theory

Textual Criticism bears witness to the Early Date of the Gospels.

RESULTS OF THE CUMULATIVE EVIDENCE. 341

of the apostolic origin of the four Gospels, but are very difficult to account for upon any theory which places them later than the apostolic period.

All this external evidence is amply supported by every line of internal evidence brought out by close inspection of the Gospels themselves. They have every mark of genuineness.

Internal Marks of Genuineness.

The documents used appear to be histories written by eye-witnesses testifying to commonly received facts. In a remarkable degree the witnesses have withdrawn their own personality from the narratives and have confined themselves to a simple statement of facts, exclusive of all notes and comments. The four Gospels have throughout the air of genuineness. They seem to be the story of unsophisticated witnesses. There are no motives of self-interest apparent to distort the narrative. The writers are indifferent to the seeming discrepancies which, on first comparison, raise superficial difficulties. The narratives are also full of local references to the geography and history and the social and religious condition of the time which furnish abundant opportunity for cross-questioning the witnesses and for determining the environment of the writers.

All these lines of investigation unite with the external evidence to indicate that the Gospels were written during the apostolic period, and have come to us substantially unchanged in their form. The picture which we have of Christ is the impression which was made by him upon the generation of men with whom he lived and worked and died. So strong was that impression that time has been unable to change it. So well defined and clear was the portraiture of the four evangelists that no subsequent hands have ever dared to paint another picture, and have scarcely had the courage to retouch this in any important detail. The four Gospels have the field, and, so far as we can see, they have always had it. Even Papias, in the early part of the second century, who boasts that he had access to witnesses who had vivid recollections of the apostles themselves and of their teaching, does not deign to add anything to the record which we have in the four Gospels.

It is in vain to say that this evidence is vague and indefinite; for, as compared with the evidence upon which we accept the ordinary facts which regulate our daily lives, the evidence is not vague or indefinite. It is as fully verified as that upon which we venture to eat our daily bread or conduct our daily business affairs. The Christians of the first century were the natural guardians of the documents which record the facts upon which they staked their all in the matter of religious belief. Such guardianship is better than that of Church councils. It is the guardianship afforded by the general consent of those who were called upon to sacrifice most upon the establishment of the facts, and it is the general consent of communities so widely scattered that a high degree of uniformity could not have been artificially secured. The documents have all the weight that attaches to official records found among the public archives of a nation. There can be no reasonable doubt that the portraiture of Christ as we have it in the four Gospels is the portraiture accepted by the contemporaries of Jesus. As the writer of the third Gospel has expressed it, these are the things

The Statute of Limitations.

which were "most surely believed" among the first generation of Christians.

The necessities of social organization demand in civil law the enactment of "statutes of limitations." These provide that the general acknowledgment of a purported fact for a certain period shall be considered as conclusive evidence of it. If, for example, a man has remained in undisturbed possession of land for a certain number of years, it is presumed that he has a valid title to it, and no one is allowed to dispute his claim. While the basis of these statutes is largely one of expediency, it is in good part one of truth. The proper time to dispute a title is when all the witnesses are accessible. If one waits to establish a claim until all or many of the original witnesses are dead or far removed, the presumption is overwhelming that he does not have a good case. Otherwise why should he not have made his attempt earlier, when there was ample room for rebuttal? Pretended evidence raked up after general interest in the subject has declined, and after the original witnesses are no longer within reach, has a very suspicious look on the face of it. Since the very necessities of social life demand there should be some end of litigation, the law steps in and, in its statutes of limitations, forbids the reopening of questions which have been long settled by general consent.

It is freely admitted that the action of a legislature in fixing the boundaries of its statutes of limitations is, to a certain extent, arbitrary. There is no hard-and-fast line where the division between what is absolutely settled by general consent and what is not can be drawn. In other words, human enactments upon this point, as upon all others, are only approximately correct. But the statutes rest upon a most important principle of human evidence. In general, possession is really nine points of the truth as well as of the law.

While it is true that this principle does not apply with absolute force to the evidences of Christianity, it is true to this extent, that any one who proposes to disturb the faith which rests upon that of the apostolic era assumes a very heavy responsibility. He should admit that an overwhelming burden of proof rests upon him. To establish his case, he must bring forward something more than conjectural evidence.

Not a restriction to True Liberty.

If it be said that this position unduly limits investigation, it is proper to reply that no impartial investigator plans to free himself from the restrictions imposed upon him by the clearest evidence which is attainable. Any one is at liberty to deny that England is an island. But he is not at liberty to ignore the evidence to the contrary which is already in possession of the world. Apparently the idea which many have of liberty of thought is that they shall be at liberty to ignore all the strongest evidence and be permitted to base their conclusions on such residue of uncertainties as are left after the main witnesses have been rejected. While this method of procedure may be satisfactory to themselves, they need not wonder or complain if the world in general stands aloof from them and prefers the larger freedom of the truth itself as supported by the best class of evidence.

The confidence which the Church has reposed in the beliefs concerning the life of Christ which were formed by the first generation of Christians is based upon the highest kind of evidence. They were the original witnesses. Their testimony is limited to the plainest statement of facts. It is testimony sealed by the very blood of the witnesses. How different the testimony is from what would have originated in any form of delusion or intentional deception appears from even the imperfect analysis of it which we are attempting to give.

The question, therefore, which we are brought to face is, Were the Christians of the first century labouring under a delusion? The answer again is to be obtained by inspection.

Were the Apostles deluded?

We have everything in the crucible for direct analysis. We have, on the one hand, the human nature of the first century with its well-known environments, and we have the portraiture of Christ in the four Gospels. Is the original of this picture from heaven or is it a natural product of the first century? The first impulse of many who look upon the portraiture is to say that the picture is too beautiful to be true. And if regarded as a mere work of the human imagination, it certainly is so. But, on the other hand, it can be said with even greater emphasis that the portraiture of Jesus accepted by the early Christians is too beautiful not to be true. It claims to be a picture unfolded upon the earth by a heavenly artist; and so far is it above the conceptions of the human imagination that the truthfulness of the lineaments is their most reasonable explanation.

The sublime portraiture of Jesus Christ in the New Testament is produced by the simplest and most inartificial means. It is a straightforward, simple story, consisting of facts selected from the experiences of a human life which was shorter than the average, and which was violently cut off in the midst of its development. According to the story, a being in possession of extraordinary supernatural power comes into the world, and develops from infancy to manhood under all the conditions of ordinary human life. Yet this supernatural power is in its exercise so subordinated to the highest order of spiritual laws that a composite picture is formed possessed at once of the highest conceivable sublimity, and yet of the most perfect human sympathies. In him the supernatural and the natural are made to abide in perfect harmony. In him the supernatural is made to interpenetrate the natural without producing any incongruity and without developing into a monstrosity. Though represented as having dwelling in him the whole power of the Godhead bodily, Jesus Christ is still consistently represented as in full possession of the natural powers and attributes of humanity, and is tempted in all points as we are. He was a Jew by birth and by his whole environment, scarcely ever having travelled beyond the restricted bounds of his native land. He was the Messiah of Jewish prophecy, and yet not the Messiah which the Jews were expecting. He was regarded as superhuman by his followers, having unlimited power over the forces of Nature, and yet he was constantly thrown upon the sympathy and dependent upon the charity of these same believing friends and disciples. Having no earthly home, he sought the shelter which others could provide, and in the last hour committed his mother to the care of the disciple who was fortunate enough to possess a home of his own. Able to feed the multitude upon bread which needed only his blessing to make it exhaustless, he still was de-

The Sublimity yet Simplicity of the Portraiture.

pendent upon the bounty of benevolent women for his daily sustenance. Abundantly able to smite the rock and cause living waters to gush out, as in the wilderness, he sat at the mouth of Jacob's well thirsting for water which was beyond his reach, and besought the help of the first person who came with a bucket and line to draw it up from the depths. Asserting that legions of angels were at his command for deliverance, he yet suffers death upon the cross, and listens unmoved to the infuriated cry of the multitude, "He trusted in God; let him deliver him now, if he desireth him."

This combination of natural and supernatural elements in the portraiture of Christ is in the highest degree impressive and convincing. In ordinary experience the human mind is incapable of so combining these elements as to secure a congruous character. In all cases, except in that of Jesus Christ, the attempt to impose supernatural qualities upon the framework of ordinary humanity has produced a monstrosity. The supernatural has overtopped and crushed the natural. The superhuman has monopolized the human, and the product has been far from perfect, considered from either point of view.

Christ above the Power of Human Invention.

In the case of Jesus Christ the same would be true except for the unity which is given to his person by the sublime conception which is presented of his mission and spiritual work. In discussing the question of the sinlessness of Christ, those who deny it, fairly make out a case if only we grant to them the concessions which they ask concerning his supernatural character and mission. If Christ was simply a man, his character is far from perfect. The authority and the prerogatives which he assumed were those which it is not proper for a man to assume. In his claims to be the Messiah of the Jews; in his pains to concede in use of the phrase "Son of man" that he was human; in the violence with which he denounced the scribes and the Pharisees; in his announcements to particular men and women that their sins were forgiven; in the absoluteness of his assertions that he represented the will of God in the world; in the absoluteness of his claims to know what was going on in the hearts of men; in the boldness with which he essayed to perform miracles; in the complacency with which he received the worship of men; in his assertions that he was to be the final judge of all men; and in many other ways Christ is made to assume prerogatives that are superhuman. And yet such is the grandeur of his mission that there is no incongruity in the total conception of his person and work as presented in these remarkable biographies. Even those who have been most disposed to magnify the defects of Christianity in its practical results have been overwhelmed with admiration at the character of Christ as portrayed in the Gospels.

The emphatic words of Rousseau are both so beautiful and so true that it is well for every succeeding generation to imprint them upon their memory: "Shall we suppose the evangelical history a mere fiction? Indeed, my friend, it bears no marks of fiction. On the contrary, the history of Socrates, which no one presumes to doubt, is not so well attested as that of Jesus Christ. Such a supposition, in fact, only shifts the difficulty without obviating it; it is more inconceivable that a number of persons should agree to write such a history than that one should furnish the subject of it. The Jewish authors were incapable of the diction, and strangers to the morality contained in the Gospel. The marks of its truth are so striking and inimitable that the inventor would be a more astonishing character than the hero."

To similar effect are the weighty words of Napoleon as, from the solitude of St. Helena, he compared his own career with that of the founder of the Christian religion. "I search in vain in history," says he, "to find the similar to Jesus Christ, or anything which can approach the Gospels. Neither history, nor humanity, nor the ages, nor Nature offer me anything with which I am able to compare it or to explain it. Here everything is extraordinary. The more I consider the Gospel, the more I am assured that there is nothing there which is not beyond the march of events and above the human mind."

Still more appropriately is the truth expressed by Channing, the founder of American Unitarianism: "In proportion to the superiority of Jesus to all around him was the intimacy, the brotherly love, with which he bound himself to them. I maintain that this is *a character wholly remote from human conception.* To imagine it to be the production of imposture or enthusiasm shows a strange unsoundness of mind. I contemplate it with a veneration second only to the profound awe with which I look up to God. It bears no mark of human invention. It was real. It belonged to and it manifested the beloved Son of God."

Or, in the words of another, "*It would require a Jesus to forge a Jesus.*"

Remembering that the privilege and duty of shaping

our practical conduct by the ideals presented in Christian history are not dependent upon the mathematical demonstration of its truth, but upon its proof to a high degree of probability, the case is made out with reference to our attitude toward Christianity "beyond all reasonable doubt." The historical proof of Christianity rests upon a much firmer basis than can be found underneath the great mass of beliefs which inspire and direct the general activities of the human race. To abandon, for hypercritical reasons, our belief in the main correctness of the original documents of Christianity which have come down to us from the first century is to cut loose from the line of historical progress, and unnecessarily doom ourselves to spiritual death by a slow process of mental starvation.

The Privilege of Believing.

INDEX OF BIBLICAL PASSAGES.

	PAGE
Acts ii, 25	142
v, 37	304
xi, 26	321
Deuteronomy ii, 25	141
Genesis ii, 14	133
vii, 4; viii, 15	137, 138
xiii, 18	167
xiv, 14	167
xix, 24, 28	125
xix, 26	168
xxiii, 2	167
xxxvii, 28	120
xli, 54, 57	141
John i, 17	321
i, 19	312
ii, 6, 13	313
ii, 15	118
iii, 3–5	219
iv, 7	282
v, 2	313
v, 4	168, 263
vi, 1	313
ix	314 et seq.
ix, 7	313
x, 12–14	169
x, 22	313
xi, 18, 55	313
xix, 31–37	296

	PAGE
John xx, 19	119
Joshua xiv, 15	167
xix, 47	167
Judges i, 10	167
xviii, 27–29	167
1 Kings x, 23, 24	141
Luke i, 54, 55, 68–70	303
ii, 1, 2	303
ii, 40–52	282
iii	307
iii, 22	270
iv	307
v–viii	308
v, 14	273
v, 30	118
v, 32	260
v, 39	273
viii, 3	309
ix, 7	309
ix, 10	268
ix, 10, 13	309
x, 16	270
xii, 14	273
xii, 38	273
xii, 48	271
xiii, 27	270
xvi, 12	273
xviii, 19	264
xix, 43, 44	310
xx, 24	271

	PAGE		PAGE
Luke xxi, 18	273	Mark ix, 41	321
xxi, 20, 21, 24	310	x, 18	264
xxi, 27	273	x, 38, 39	261
xxii, 42, 44	271	Matthew i, 1, 18	321
xxiii, 41	121	ix, 13	260
xxiii, 34	272	x, 30	64
xxiv, 31	119	xii, 42	141
xxiv, 36–43	287	xiii, 55	282
xxiv, 46–50	288	xiv, 1	309
xxiv, 53	268	xviii, 28	259
		xix, 17	264
Mark ii, 17	260	xx, 22, 23	261
iii, 29	265	xxi, 12	118
vi, 3	282	xxiv, 36	165
viii, 26	267	xxv, 6	259
ix, 49	267	xxv, 41	270

SUBJECT AND AUTHOR INDEX.

Abbot, E., quoted, 219, 247, 261, 277.
Absurdities, 18.
Acquired characteristics, inheritance of, 97.
Adams, Prof., faith of, 26.
Adoptianism, theory of, 230.
Agassiz, A., an extreme creationist, 105.
Agnosticism, true and false, 2; of Herbert Spencer, 2; of Prof. Huxley, 3; concerning the future life, 17; significance of pure, 24; of Sir William Hamilton, 27; of Darwin, 110; excessive, suicidal, 185, 199; Gladstone on, 199.
Akabah, Gulf of, 126.
Alexandrinus, Codex, 251; character of, 267.
America during the Glacial period, 144 et seq.; destruction of species in, 146.
Amplification of text, 256, 259 et seq., 262.
Annotations, marginal, 168, 262 et seq.
Apocryphal Gospels, 282 et seq.
Apostolic age, general conditions of, 300.
Ararat, mountains of, 135.
Aristides, Apology of, 221.
Ark, Noah's, 133, 134.

Armenian monastery at Venice, 224, 226.
Assimilation, influence of, on texts, 259 et seq.
Astronomy, more than observation, 330.
Atoms, character of, 4; manufactured articles, 5; Huxley's faith in, 5; implied omnipotence of, 38; are they indivisible, 40.
Augustine, hospitable to traducianism, 104.
Automaton, man not an, 68; an animal perhaps not an, 184.

Baarlam and Josaphat, tale of, 224.
Barnes, quoted, 205.
Bar-Salibi on Tatian, 225.
Benevolence, an absolute duty, 172.
Bensly, Prof., cited, 229, 230.
Bernoulli, John, opposition to Newton, 29.
Berosus on the ark, 134.
Beyond reasonable doubt, chapter on, 172-200.
Bezæ, Codex, 251; character of, 269.
Blankenkorn, on the Dead Sea, 127.
Blood and water, from the Saviour's side, issue of, 296 et seq.
Bloody sweat, 299.
Blount, his Undesigned Coincidences, cited, 309.

Blunt, W. T., on the effect of winds on the level of the Great Lakes, 123.
Bonnet's theory of incasement, 43, 59.
Bourne, G. C., on complexity of cell theory, 56 *et seq.*
Brethren, use of the word, 295.
Buckland, his Reliquæ Diluvianæ, 151.
Buffon, theory of incasement, 43.
Burkitt, Mr., cited, 229, 230.
Butler, on probability the guide of life, 185, 188.
Butterflies, protective colouring of, 96, 98.

Caspian Sea, gas and oil wells of, 128.
Catharine, Convent of St., 220, 228.
Causes, created, secondary, 68; reality of, 69; secondary, 190.
Cave deposits at Palermo, 154.
Cayley, Prof., faith of, 26.
Cells, elective affinity of, 47; minuteness of, 48.
Cell theory of life, 45; complexity of, 56; Bourne's representation of, 56 *et seq.*
Census of Quirinius, 303.
Cerinthus, heresy of, 230.
Challis, J., theory of gravitation, 36.
Channing's tribute to Christ, 349.
Chemistry, more than experiment, 329.
Choices, subordinate, beset with uncertainty, 172.
Christ, his escape at Nazareth, 118; drives out money changers, 118; mysterious appearances, 119, 285, 286; resurrection of, central, 190; childhood of, 282; in the apocryphal Gospels, 283; beneficent character of miracles of, 284; resurrection body of, 286; cause of death of, 297; sorrows of, 298; bloody sweat of, 299; date of birth, 305; time of ministry, 307; use of the appellation, 320; Mill's appreciation of, 336; sublimity of the apostolic conception of, 345 *et seq.*; portraiture of, above the power of human invention, 347; Rousseau's tribute to, 348; Napoleon's, 349; Channing's, 349.
Christianity, presumptions in favour of, 188; scientific basis of, 328 *et seq.*; more than an experiment, 329; known by its fruits, 335; commends itself, 336; cumulative proof of, 337; supported by recent discoveries, 338; sustained by textual criticism, 340; has every internal mark of authenticity, 341.
Christians, number of, in the second century, 208.
Church and kingdom, contrasted, 290 *et seq.*
Chuza, a member of Herod's household, 39.
Ciasca, Father, discovers Diatessaron, 228.
Civilization, superiority of, 22; early development of, 139; hazards of, 187.
Clement of Alexandria, 205, 253.
Conservation of energy, 13, 32.
Continuity of Nature, 9.
Cope, on relation of mind to matter, 75; on survival of the fittest, 93.
Copyists, mental characteristics of, 257 *et seq.*
Creation, implied by Darwin, 7; asserted by Croll, 9; by Clerk Maxwell, 9; a free act, 19; out of nothing, 41; limitations of, 110.
Creationism, 104.

SUBJECT AND AUTHOR INDEX. 355

Credibility of the biblical miracles, 165.
Criticism, textual, chapter on testimony of, 244–278; principles of, 254 et seq.; scientific basis of, 255 et seq.
Croll, on geologic time, 8; postulates creation, 9.
Crucifixion, date of, 209.
Cumulative evidence, positive results of the, chapter on, 328–350.
Curetonian Syriac version, 229, 235 et seq., 252, 339. See VERSIONS, OLD SYRIAC.

Darwin, C., definition of evolution, 7; on pangenesis, 44, 333; gemmules, 46; on elective affinitive of cells, 47; on Parthenogenesis, 48; method of dealing with difficulties, 109; on recent destruction of species, 146; defects of, 198; criticism of Spencer, 334.
Darwin, G. H., on geological time, 8.
Darwinian argument, limitations of, 6; Principia of, 42.
Darwinism and design, chapter on, 89–117; not a system of philosophy, 90, 107; ultimate assumptions of, 92; involves design, 102; and the law of parsimony, 107; the deathblow to empiricism, 332.
Davis, J. D., on the Noachian deluge, 133–138.
Dead Sea, depression of, 125 et seq.; gas and oil wells of, 128, 129; salt deposits of, 127, 169.
Deism, insufficiency of, 23, 65, 81, 86; defined, 63, 89; sublimity of, 65.
Deluge, the Noachian, 132–165; cuneiform account of, 133 et seq.; the two compared, 133 et seq.; universality of, 140 et seq.; credibility of, 143; and the Glacial period, 143–165; summary concerning, 164.
Delusion, the apostles not the subject of, 281 et seq., 345.
Design and Darwinism, chapter on, 89–114; special and general, 91; complexity of, 91, 112; comprehensiveness of, 111.
Design, can not be excluded from Nature, 9.
Diatessaron. See TATIAN.
Difficulties, Darwin's mode of dealing with, 109.
Disciples, use of the word, 295, 320.
Discoveries of the nineteenth century, 202.
Discrepancies in the evidence concerning Lincoln's Gettysburg address, 196.
Docetæ, heresy of the, 238.
Doubt, benefit of the, 184, 186, 188; excessive, suicidal, 185, 350; affects all human affairs, 192; concerning the authorship of Lincoln's Gettysburg address, 193 et seq.; concerning a speech of General Grant, 195; equivalent to insanity, 199.
Doubt, reasonable, 166; judicial charge respecting, 180.

Earthquakes in the Dead Sea region, 130; in the Sierra Nevada Mountains, 131.
Easter, time of, 216.
Egyptians, Gospel according to the, 206.
Emerson, on the destruction of Sodom and Gomorrah, 127.
Emmaus, Christ at, 286.
Endless existence of present order of things, 6.
English Bible, variations in early copies of, 246.

Epistles of Paul, variation in tests of, 275.
Ephraem Syrus, commentary on Tatian, 227.
Ether, vibrations of, 37.
Evidence, amount necessary to proof, 177, 180; weight of, affected by the seriousness of the conclusion, 183, 187 *et seq.*; need not be demonstrative, 185; presumptive, 188; not invalidated by minor discrepancies, 196.
Evidences of the early date of the four Gospels, internal, chapter on, 279-327.
Evil, existence of, not inconsistent with benevolence of God, 17.
Evolution, Darwinian, 6; Spencerian, 7; Lamarck's theory of, 51; Weismann's theory of, 51; relation of, to design, 89; indefiniteness of, 89.
Experimental evidence limited, 329 *et seq.*
External evidences of Christianity, as they stood in 1875, 202; newly discovered, chapter on, 201-243.

Faith, freedom of, 24; of leading men of science, 25, 75; necessity of, 174; rationality of, 176; the guide of life, 177.
Faraday's difficulty concerning gravitation, 32.
Ferrers, faith of, 26.
Figurative language, 70.
Fittest, origin of the, 93; does not arise by chance, 94.
Freedom compatible with certainty, 67, 80.

Gas, reservoirs of natural, 128.
Gaudry, M., on the deposits at Santenay, 151.
Gemmules, Darwin's theory of, 46.

Genesis and the higher critics, 135-137, 139; truthfulness of, 139.
Geological time, limitations to, 8.
Geology more than a record of facts, 331.
Gettysburg address, doubts concerning Lincoln's, 193.
Gibraltar, ossiferous fissures on, 153.
Gibson, Mrs., discoveries of, 228.
Gilbert, on the geological hazards of Salt Lake City, 131.
Glacial period and the deluge, 143-165; extent of accumulations during, 144; changes of level during, 145; effects on life, 146 *et seq.*
Gladstone on agnosticism, 199.
God and Nature, chapter on, 62-88.
God keeps control of Nature, 80.
Gomorrah. See SODOM.
Gospels, internal evidence of the early date of, chapter on, 279-327; literary character of, 279; freedom from puerilities, 281; the apocryphal, 282 *et seq.*; freedom from comments, 285 *et seq.*; reflect the general condition of the apostolic age, 300 *et seq.*; not works of imagination, 288; undesigned coincidences in, 289 *et seq.*; profane authorship not claimed, 318; contain no trace of later controversies, 318; or recognition of early Christian schools, 319; or of early Christian customs, 319; or any specific opposition to heathenism, 320; do not use later phrases, 320; or recognize antagonistic heathen institutions, 321; or refer to later historical events, 322; must be contemporary documents, 322 *et seq.*
Grant, General, misrepresented, 195.
Gravitation, Newton's theory of, 28; early objections to, 29; not analogous to other forces, 30; acts in-

SUBJECT AND AUTHOR INDEX. 357

stantaneously, 30; indifferent to all intervening objects, 31; is inexhaustible, 32; Faraday's difficulty, 32; explanations of, 33 *et seq.*; relation of, to design, 90.
Gray, Asa, on design in Nature, 94, 98, 100; on the mysteries of life, 174.
Grenfell discovers the new Logia, 240.
Guernsey, loess on Isle of, 160.

Hamilton, Madam A., 211.
Hamilton, Sir William, on agnosticism, 27.
Harnack, on the date of the Gospels, 326.
Harris, Prof. Rendel, cited, 220, 224, 228, 236.
"Head." See RUBBLE DRIFT.
Hell Gate, excavations in, 10.
Heredity, law of, 42; mysteries of, 49.
Herschel on creation of matter, 5.
Higher critics and Genesis, 135-137; unreasonableness of, 166.
Hill, Rev. J. H., quoted, 228.
Hippopotamus bones at Palermo, 156.
Historic imagination, use of, 213.
Homoeoteluton, 248.
Howorth, Sir William, on deposits of loess, 160.
Huidekoper, cited, 285; on the indirect testimony of history to the genuineness of the Gospels, 317 *et seq.*; quoted, 322.
Human nature, constancy of, 216.
Hunt discovers the new Logia, 240.
Huxley, agnosticism of, 3; robust faith of, 5; on free will, 68; not an automaton, 68; on the benefit of doubt, 184.
Huyghen's opposition to Newton, 29.

Ignorance, inventory of, 2.
Illustrations from explosive compounds, 10; from Two Ocean Pass, 12; from the power of a word, 12; concerning omnipotence, 18; from the Eozoon Canadense, 21; of the complexity of life movements, 56; from the cat, 94; from protective colouring of butterflies, 96, 98; from traducianism and creationism, 104; from a manufactory, 112; from passage of the Red Sea, 121; from the Dead Sea, 125; geological, 130, 325, 340; from Salt Lake City, 131; from the Noachian deluge, 132-165; from the Glacial period, 143 *et seq.*; from legal practice, 178; from insurance, 186; from Lincoln's Gettysburg address, 193; from Madam Hamilton's memory, 211; from early copies of English Bible, 246; from type-setters, 247, 256; from reading between the lines, 256; in proof reading, 258; of amplification, 259; of assimilation, 260; from marginal annotations, 262; from uses of the words "church" and "kingdom," 290 *et seq.*; from "Son of man," 293; from use of words "disciples," "brethren," and "saints," 295; from the issuing of blood and water from the Saviour's side, 296 *et seq.*; from Luke's Gospel, 302 *et seq.*; from chemistry, 329; from astronomy, 330; from geology, 331; from Darwinism, 332.
Immanence, the theory of divine, 66; differs from pantheism, 67.
Immortality of the soul, possible, 14; speculations concerning, 16; credibility of, 16; implications of, 23; blessed, a prize to be won, 188.

Incasement, theory of, 43; 59.
Insufficiency of the world, 82.
Insurance, reason for, 186.
Internal evidences of the early date of the four Gospels, chapter on, 279–327, 341.
Irenæus, testimony of, 202; on Cerinthus, 230; his quotations of the Gospels, 253, 269, 273, 275; on variations of texts, 340.

Jersey, loess on Isle of, 162.
Jerusalem, destruction of, 300, 326; prophecy of the destruction of, 310, 322.
John, Gospel of, genuineness of, 219, 226, 228, 239, 284, 288, 291, 293, 296, 311, 312, 314 et seq.; historical accuracy of, 311 et seq.; discourses in, 317.
Jonah, miracle of, 171.
Jordan, Valley of, 125.
Joshua and the sun's standing still, 169.
Juries, character of, 178; importance of, 179; protection of, 180: charges to, 180.
Justin Martyr, 217, 253; relation to Tatian, 226; relation of, to the Gospel of Peter, 239; New Testament text used, 270 et seq.

Keen, Dr. W. W., on the physical cause of Christ's death, 298.
Kelvin, Lord, on geological time, 8; faith of, 26; humility of, 26; on the constitution of matter, 41.
Kenosis, doctrine of, 165.
Kingdom of heaven contrasted with church, 290 et seq., 320.
Knowledge, power of, 14, 72, 73, 86; more than sensation, 76.

Lake Erie, effect of wind on level of, 123.

Lake Geneva, effect of wind on level of, 124.
Lamarck's theory of evolution, 51, 98.
Language, interpretation of, 112 et seq., 140 et seq., 166, 170.
Latin version, Old, 252, 253, 268, 270, 274.
Le Conte, on the nature of mind and matter, 77.
Leibnitz, opposition to Newton, 29; theory of pre-established harmony, 64.
Lesage's theory of gravitation, 35.
Lewis, Mrs., discoveries of, 228 et seq.
Lewis, Sir G. C., quoted, 211.
Liberty, true, not restricted by the truth, 344.
Life, origin of, 5; continuance of, less mysterious than its origin, 14; mystery of, 42 et seq., 58; Minot's foam theory of, 54; gantlet of, 102; affected by Glacial period, 145 et seq.
Lincoln's Gettysburg address, 193.
Loess, deposits of, 158 et seq.; on the Channel Islands, 160.
Logia, the newly discovered, of Jesus, 240.
Lot's wife, 168.
Luke, accuracy of, 302 et seq.

Man's superiority to Nature, 22, 72, 81, 82, 84, 89; not an automaton, 68, 72, 74, 75; needs the presence of God, 81, 189: limitations of, 83; origin of, 104 et seq.; and the Glacial period, 148; loves the truth. 193.
Manuscripts of the New Testament, oldest, 244, 250, 251; variations in, 245, 258 et seq., 266, 277; causes of variations, 245, 255 et

SUBJECT AND AUTHOR INDEX. 359

seq.; Greek, 250 *et seq.*; classification of, 267.
Marcion, 253; New Testament text used by, 272 *et seq.*
Marginal annotations, 168, 262 *et seq.*
Materialism, incredible, 10, 17.
Matter, origin of, 3; not necessarily eternal, 3; can not produce mind, 4; atomic constitution of, 38; three forms of, 39.
Maxwell, Clerk, discredits materialism, 9; faith of, 26; on Lesage's theory, 36; on the constitution of matter, 41.
Mechitarite convent at Venice, 224, 226.
Mediate miracles, chapter on, 115-171.
Mill, J. S., on the paradoxes of gravitation, 34; on the character of Christ, 336.
Mind can not be produced by matter, 4; moves matter, 11, 13, 73; mysterious relations of body to, 16; unknown capacity of, 22; different from matter, 70, 75, 76 *et seq.*
Minot's theory of life, 54 *et seq.*
Miracles, possibility of, 10, 14; and free will, 71; defined, 84; economy of, 108, 116, 171; mediate, chapter on, 115-171; difficult to invent, 115; difficult to define, 116, 119, 130; doubtful, 118; credibility of biblical, 165; of the sun's standing still, 169; of Jonah, 171; of the resurrection, 190; of Christ's conception, 230 *et seq.*
Moesinger, Prof., on Tatian, 227.
Monism, inadequate, 79.
Müller, Prof. Max, quoted, 224.
Muratorian Canon, 207.
Mysteries, ultimate, 53, 58; no science has a monopoly of, 60.

Napoleon at the Red Sea, 121; tribute to Christ, 349.
Natural selection, inadequacy of, 52, 93, 94, 96, 98, 100; Weismann's criticism of, 52.
Nature, relation of God to, chapter on, 62-88; continuity of, 9; unstable equilibrium in, 10 *et seq.*; man's power over, 13; laws of, violated by free will, 71; under the control of God, 80, 83.
Newly discovered external evidences of Christianity, chapter on, 201-243, 338.
New Testament indorses the Old, 166.
Newton, Sir Isaac, asserts creation, 9; humility of, 26; early views of gravitation, 28, 33, 34; later views, 34; explains gravitation, 33 *et seq.*; religious fervour of, 86 *et seq.*
Norton, Prof. A., quoted, 208, 277, 285.
Nye, Judge, charge to jury, 180.

Obligation, foundation of, 172.
Old Testament indorsed by the New, 166; textual criticism of, 167.
Omnipotence defined, 18.
Origen, 252, 264, 265, 275, 340.
Ossiferous fissures, 151; at Santenay, France, 152.

Pain, liability to, an incidental good, 20.
Palæolithic implements in rubble drift, 150.
Palermo, cave deposits near, 154.
Pangenesis, theory of, 44; obscurity of, 45; incredible, 50, 333.
Pantheism defined, 19, 67.
Paradoxes of science, chapter on, 28-61; concerning the origin of

matter, 3 *et seq.*; the origin of life, 5; endless existence of present order of things, 6 *et seq.*; the continuity of nature, 9 *et seq.*; free will, 11; immortality, 14; omnipotence and the existence of evil, 17 *et seq.*; cause of gravitation, 28 *et seq.*; atomic constitution of matter, 32 *et seq.*; creation out of nothing, 41; the perpetuation of life, 42; the origin of species, 44; pangenesis, 50, 333; Christianity has no monopoly of, 60.

Parker, L. F., on misrepresentations of General Grant, 195.

Parsimony, the law of, 107; of miracles, 108, 116, 171.

Parthenogenesis, Darwin on, 48.

Paul, address on Mars Hill, 223; variation in texts of Epistles of, 275.

Petroleum, reservoirs of, 128.

Peter, Gospel of, 237, 240, 339.

Physiological units, 44; causes of variations, 100.

Pierce, Benjamin, on the future life, 16.

Polycarp, testimony of, 202; on the time of Easter, 216.

Pre-established harmony, 64.

Prestwich on the recent submergence of western Europe, 149–163.

Presumptions in favour of Christianity, 188; force of, 189.

Probability, the guide of life, 177, 185 *et seq.*, 334, 343, 350.

Proof, how constituted, 176, 180, 183, 186, 188, 191, 192, 198; experimental method of, 198.

Proof readers, mental characteristics of, 258.

Protoplasm, properties of, 54.

Providence, special, 84, 119.

Quirinius, census of, 303 *et seq.*

Quotations from Gospels in Church Fathers, 252 *et seq.*

Ramsay, Prof., cited, 303.

Reasonable doubt, 166, 334, 343, 350; judicial charge respecting, 180.

Red Sea, passage of, 121.

Resurrection of Christ the central miracle, 190.

Revised Version of the English Bible, reception of, 215.

Richthofen, Baron, on loess, 159.

Riggs, cited, 255.

Romanes, George J., on agnosticism, 2; on the central argument for theism, 23; on the faith of scientic men, 25; on Weismann's theory of evolution, 51.

Ropes, Prof. J. H., quoted, 242.

Rousseau's tribute to Christ, 348.

Routh, faith of, 26.

Rubble drift in western Europe, 150 *et seq.*, 153, 160, 162.

Saints, use of the word, 295.

Salt deposits of the Dead Sea, 127, 167.

Salt Lake City, geological hazards of, 131.

Santenay, ossiferous fissures at, 151.

Sanday, cited, 272, 274, 285.

Science, paradoxes of, chapter on, 28–61; uncertainties of, 173.

Scientific basis of Christianity, 328 *et seq.*

Scientific thought, limits of, chapter on, 1–27; tendencies of, 85.

Secondary causes, nature of, 68; importance of, 190.

Serapion, Bishop, on the Gospel of Peter, 237.

Shaler, on critical points in Nature, 101.

Shedd advocates traducianism, 105.

SUBJECT AND AUTHOR INDEX. 361

Sinaiticus, Codex, 250; character of, 266.
Sodom and Gomorrah, destruction of, 124 et seq.
"Son of man," use of the phrase, 293 et seq., 320.
Soul, see immortality of, 14; future condition of, 16.
Special providence, 84, 119.
Species, recent destruction of, 146.
Speculation, realm of, 15.
Spencer, Herbert, agnosticism of, 2; philosophy of, 6; definition of evolution. 7; physiological units, 44; on the nature of mind and matter, 79; criticises natural selection, 94, 97; criticised by Darwin, 337.
Statute of limitations, 342.
Steamers, ocean, size of, 134.
Stokes, Sir George, faith of, 26.
Stokes, Prof. G. T., quoted, 223.
Strong, A. H., advocates traducianism, 105.
Stroud on the physical cause of Christ's death, 298.
Sun standing still, 169.
Syriac version, newly discovered, 228 et seq., 324, 338; Curetonian, 229, 235 et seq., 252, 339; Old, 261, 265, 268, 270-272, 339.

Tatian's Diatessaron, 225 et seq., 239, 324, 338; influence of, on texts, 262.
Tait on geological time, 8; faith of, 26; on Lesage's theory, 35.
Taylor, Jeremy, loose quotations of, 219.
Tertullian, 206, 252.
Text, amplification of, how caused, 255, 256 et seq., 259, 262; examples of, 259 et seq., 263 et seq.; purity of, 276, 277.
Textual criticism of the Old Testament, 167.

Textual criticism, the testimony of, chapter on, 244-278, 340.
Thayer, Prof. J. H., cited, 238.
Theism, central argument for, 23.
Theodicy, 17 et seq.
Theodoret on Tatian, 225.
Theophilus of Antioch, 204.
Thomas, Gospel of, 282.
Thomson, Sir W. See LORD KELVIN.
Todhunter, faith of, 26.
Tradition, limits of trustworthy, 209 et seq.; Sir G. C. Lewis on, 211; examples of, 211-214; trustworthiness of, 239.
Traducianism, 104.
Tregelles, cited, 266.
Truth, an element of human nature, 193.
Tulloch, Major-General, on the passage of the Red Sea, 122.
Two Ocean Pass, 12.
Tyndall on the nature of mind and matter, 78.

Uncertainties of specific duties, 172; of science, 173, 191; the spice of life, 175; in everything, 192.
Undesigned coincidences in the Gospels, 289 et seq.
Universe, running down, 7; intelligibility of, 92.

Variations in manuscripts, causes of, 245, 255, 256, 259, 262; instances of, 246, 256, 258, 259 et seq., 262, 270, 272, 277.
Vaticanus, Codex, 251; character of, 266.
Versions, early, 252; Curetonian Syriac, 229, 235 et seq., 252, 339; Egyptian, 252; old Syriac, 261, 265, 268, 270-272, 339; Old Latin, 252, 253, 268, 270, 274.

Weismann's theory of evolution, 51; on ultimate mysteries, 53; on the insufficiency of natural selection, 93, 96, 98.

Westcott and Hort, cited, 257, 268 275, 277.

Whewell on the comprehensiveness of the Creator's designs, 111.

Will, constancy of its action possible, 67, 80; free, 68; relation to miracles, 7; limited sphere of man's, 72.

Wright, Prof. W. E. C., cited, 290.

Xisuthrus and the deluge, 133, 134.

Yellowstone Park, 12.

THE END.

D. APPLETON & CO.'S PUBLICATIONS.

BOOKS BY PROF. G. FREDERICK WRIGHT.

GREENLAND ICEFIELDS, AND LIFE IN THE NORTH ATLANTIC. With a New Discussion of the Causes of the Ice Age. By G. FREDERICK WRIGHT, D. D., LL. D., F. G. S. A., author of "The Ice Age in North America," "Man and the Glacial Period," etc., and WARREN UPHAM, A. M., F. G. S. A., late of the Geological Surveys of New Hampshire, Minnesota, and the United States. With numerous Maps and Illustrations. 12mo. Cloth, $2.00.

The immediate impulse to the preparation of this volume arose in connection with a trip to Greenland by Professor Wright in the summer of 1894 on the steamer Miranda. The work aims to give within moderate limits a comprehensive view of the scenery, the glacial phenomena, the natural history, the people, and the explorations of Greenland. The photographs are all original, and the maps have been prepared to show the latest state of knowledge concerning the region. The volume treats of the ice of the Labrador current, the coast of Labrador, Spitzbergen ice in Davis Strait, the Greenland Eskimos, Europeans in Greenland, explorations of the inland ice, the plants and animals of Greenland, changes of level since the advent of the Glacial period; and includes a summary of the bearing of the facts upon glacial theories. The work is of both popular and scientific interest.

THE ICE AGE IN NORTH AMERICA, and its Bearings upon the Antiquity of Man. With an appendix on "The Probable Cause of Glaciation," by WARREN UPHAM, F. G. S. A., Assistant on the Geological Surveys of New Hampshire, Minnesota, and the United States. New and enlarged edition. With 150 Maps and Illustrations. 8vo, 625 pages, and Index. Cloth, $5.00.

"The author has seen with his own eyes the most important phenomena of the Ice age on this continent from Maine to Alaska. In the work itself, elementary description is combined with a broad, scientific, and philosophic method, without abandoning for a moment the purely scientific character. Professor Wright has contrived to give the whole a philosophical direction which lends interest and inspiration to it, and which in the chapters on Man and the Glacial Period rises to something like dramatic intensity."
—*The Independent.*

MAN AND THE GLACIAL PERIOD. International Scientific Series. With numerous Illustrations. 12mo. Cloth, $1.75.

"The earlier chapters describing glacial action, and the traces of it in North America—especially the defining of its limits, such as the terminal moraine of the great movement itself—are of great interest and value. The maps and diagrams are of much assistance in enabling the reader to grasp the vast extent of the movement."—*London Spectator.*

New York: D. APPLETON & CO., 72 Fifth Avenue.

D. APPLETON & CO.'S PUBLICATIONS.

THE WARFARE OF SCIENCE WITH THE-OLOGY. A History of the Warfare of Science with Theology in Christendom. By ANDREW D. WHITE, LL. D., late President and Professor of History at Cornell University. In two volumes. 8vo. Cloth, $5.00.

"The story of the struggle of searchers after truth with the organized forces of ignorance, bigotry, and superstition is the most inspiring chapter in the whole history of mankind That story has never been better told than by the ex-President of Cornell University in these two volumes. . . . A wonderful story it is that he tells."—*London Daily Chronicle.*

"A literary event of prime importance is the appearance of 'A History of the Warfare of Science with Theology in Christendom.' "—*Philadelphia Press.*

"Such an honest and thorough treatment of the subject in all its bearings that it will carry weight and be accepted as an authority in tracing the process by which the scientific method has come to be supreme in modern thought and life."—*Boston Herald.*

"A great work of a great man upon great subjects, and will always be a religio-scientific classic."—*Chicago Evening Post.*

"It is graphic, lucid, even-tempered—never bitter nor vindictive. No student of human progress should fail to read these volumes. While they have about them the fascination of a well-told tale, they are also crowded with the facts of history that have had a tremendous bearing upon the development of the race."—*Brooklyn Eagle.*

"The same liberal spirit that marked his public life is seen in the pages of his book, giving it a zest and interest that can not fail to secure for it hearty commendation and honest praise."—*Philadelphia Public Ledger.*

"A conscientious summary of the body of learning to which it relates accumulated during long years of research. . . . A monument of industry."—*N. Y. Evening Post.*

"A work which constitutes in many ways the most instructive review that has ever been written of the evolution of human knowledge in its conflict with dogmatic belief. . . . As a contribution to the literature of liberal thought, the book is one the importance of which can not be easily overrated."—*Boston Beacon.*

"The most valuable contribution that has yet been made to the history of the conflicts between the theologians and the scientists."—*Buffalo Commercial.*

"Undoubtedly the most exhaustive treatise which has been written on this subject. . . . Able, scholarly, critical, impartial in tone and exhaustive in treatment."—*Boston Advertiser.*

New York: D. APPLETON & CO., 72 Fifth Avenue.

D. APPLETON & CO.'S PUBLICATIONS.

THE CLAIMS OF CHRISTIANITY. By WILLIAM SAMUEL LILLY, Honorary Fellow of Peterhouse, Cambridge; author of "The Great Enigma," etc. 8vo. Cloth, $3.50.

"A book which has divided attention with Benjamin Kidd's 'Social Evolution.' The author's aim is not that of a theologian, but rather that of what may be termed the student of events; in other words, his book deals with Christianity as a fact in the world's history. . . . In this volume these claims of Christianity are considered, first as regards the two other creeds besides the Christian which claim universality—Buddhism and Islam—and then as affecting and affected by civil society in the middle ages in the epoch of the Renaissance and the Reformation, and in this new age."—*New York Sun.*

THE GREAT ENIGMA. By WILLIAM SAMUEL LILLY. 8vo. Cloth, $4.00.

"This volume is delightfully complete in the whole and in the parts, in form and substance. . . . The author has finished his sentences and his argument, and rounded up his work with an ideal index and a full summary of his line of thought, a very great aid to the ordinary reader in the attempt to master an extended and subtle discussion. He has his reward in the effectiveness of the book, which is a strong, ingenious, and very destructive inquiry into the current atheistic and agnostic philosophies as religions. . . . He makes no extravagant claim for the Bible nor for Christian theology, and he does not lay so much stress on the postulates and conclusions of Christian science or Christian philosophy as the supreme needs and responsibilities of human life. . . . We understand that Mr. Lilly is a Roman Catholic. There is nothing in his book to suggest any Roman limitations to his Catholic faith. He has done great good service to the cause of right thinking and right living."—*New York Independent.*

WHY NOT AND WHY. Short Studies in Churchmanship. By the Rev. WILLIAM DUDLEY POWERS. Second edition. 12mo. Paper, 50 cents.

"'Take heed unto thyself and to the doctrine.' An admirable gentleness and broadness of spirit characterize this little work, whose author is the well-known and much-esteemed rector of St. Andrew's Church, this city. . . . There is not a sentence between the covers which does not breathe of charitableness toward those who hold beliefs other than the writer, and love toward all faith that is earnest and honest, under whatever name."—*Richmond Times.*

WHY WE BELIEVE THE BIBLE. An Hour's Reading for Busy People. By J. P. T. INGRAHAM, S. T. D. 16mo. Cloth, 60 cents.

"Dr. Ingraham has here attempted to give in the categorical form a very condensed summary of the reasons for receiving Holy Scripture. It is impossible, in a work of this scope, to do more than to state dogmatically conclusions and facts. This has been fairly done in the volume. . . . It prepares the ground for honest inquiry, and will enable any one whose general belief has been disturbed to see where the difficulty lies."—*The Churchman.*

"Our author is practical; he does not take up with theories. He has produced a book that pastors and teachers will find of great use. It will be helpful to hundreds of young men, and save them from misconceptions."—*Baltimore American.*

New York : D. APPLETON & CO., 72 Fifth Avenue.

D. APPLETON & CO.'S PUBLICATIONS.

EVOLUTION OF MAN AND CHRISTIANITY. New edition. By the Rev. HOWARD MACQUEARY. With a new Preface, in which the Author answers his Critics, and with some important Additions. 12mo. Cloth, $1.75.

"This is a revised and enlarged edition of a book published last year. The author reviews criticisms upon the first edition, denies that he rejects the doctrine of the incarnation, admits his doubts of the physical resurrection of Christ, and his belief in evolution. The volume is to be marked as one of the most profound expressions of the modern movement toward broader theological positions."—*Brooklyn Times.*

"He does not write with the animus of the destructive school; he intends to be, and honestly believes he is, doing a work of construction, or at least of reconstruction. . . . He writes with manifest earnestness and conviction, and in a style which is always clear and energetic."—*Churchman.*

HISTORY OF THE CONFLICT BETWEEN RELIGION AND SCIENCE. By Dr. JOHN WILLIAM DRAPER. 12mo. Cloth, $1.75.

"The key-note to this volume is found in the antagonism between the progressive tendencies of the human mind and the pretensions of ecclesiastical authority, as developed in the history of modern science. No previous writer has treated the subject from this point of view, and the present monograph will be found to possess no less originality of conception than vigor of reasoning and wealth of erudition."—*New York Tribune.*

A CRITICAL HISTORY OF FREE THOUGHT IN REFERENCE TO THE CHRISTIAN RELIGION. By Rev. Canon ADAM STOREY FARRAR, D. D., F. R. S., etc. 12mo. Cloth, $2.00.

"A conflict might naturally be anticipated between the reasoning faculties of man and a religion which claims the right, on superhuman authority, to impose limits on the field or manner of their exercise. It is the chief of the movements of free thought which it is my purpose to describe, in their historic succession, and their connection with intellectual causes. We must ascertain the facts, discover the causes, and read the moral."—*The Author.*

CREATION OR EVOLUTION? A Philosophical Inquiry. By GEORGE TICKNOR CURTIS. 12mo. Cloth, $2.00.

"A treatise on the great question of Creation or Evolution by one who is neither a naturalist nor theologian, and who does not profess to bring to the discussion a special equipment in either of the sciences which the controversy arrays against each other, may seem strange at first sight; but Mr. Curtis will satisfy the reader, before many pages have been turned, that he has a substantial contribution to make to the debate, and that his book is one to be treated with respect. His part is to apply to the reasonings of the men of science the rigid scrutiny with which the lawyer is accustomed to test the value and pertinency of testimony, and the legitimacy of inferences from established facts."—*New York Tribune.*

"Mr. Curtis's book is honorably distinguished from a sadly too great proportion of treatises which profess to discuss the relation of scientific theories to religion, by its author's thorough acquaintance with his subject, his scrupulous fairness, and remarkable freedom from passion."—*London Literary World.*

D. APPLETON & CO., 72 Fifth Avenue, New York.

D. APPLETON & CO.'S PUBLICATIONS.

OUR HEREDITY FROM GOD. Consisting of Lectures on Evolution. By E. P. POWELL. Fourth edition. 12mo. Cloth, $1.75.

"It is written in a simple, homely, fresh, and piquant style, that will engage the interest of every intelligent reader. Even those who have prejudged the matter in debate, if they once begin to read, will find it hard to stop; and when they reach the end, if they do not make an unconditional surrender, they will find that some of their heavy guns are missing, a good deal of their light artillery, and a great deal of their useless baggage of contempt and scorn for doctrines which they did not understand."—*Christian Register.*

"Mr. Powell traces the rise of intelligence and morals out of and above all preceding developments, until he reaches the great questions of God and immortality. As a statement of the process of conviction by which the doctrine of evolution is established for the development of physical life the work is entitled to confidence, and will interest and instruct its readers."—*Boston Herald.*

"An earnest and profound thinker, Mr. Powell is a logical, forcible, and brilliant writer as well. It is safe to say that no one of the very numerous works which of late years have sought to demonstrate the unknowable, unprovable mysteries of which Darwin and Spencer are the chief apostles and enunciators, has done so in more lucid, scholarly fashion."—*New Orleans Times-Democrat.*

"All parts of the book are instructive, and while they instruct they never fail to interest. The driest facts of the evolution problem are made plain, and happily illustrated; but it is in such chapters as close the work that the interest culminates and the purpose of the work is seen. No one will regret owning and reading Mr. Powell's work."—*Boston New Ideal.*

STUDIES IN HEGEL'S PHILOSOPHY OF RELIGION. With an Appendix on Christian Unity in America. By J. MACBRIDE STERRETT, D. D., Professor of Ethics and Apologetics in the Seabury Divinity School; author of "Reason and Authority in Religion." Second edition. 12mo. Cloth, $2.00.

"Professor Sterrett's 'Studies' are well written and careful. . . . If one wishes to know about Hegel on the Philosophy of Religion, there is really no better book than the present. . . . It gives an excellent general view of the Hegelian position."—*London Saturday Review.*

"A book for study and prolonged consideration. No one can read it without receiving much intellectual and spiritual stimulus."—*Bibliotheca Sacra.*

"The American book I hold worthy of a place beside *Lux Mundi.* It gives the logical method which *Lux Mundi* applies in a less technical and more popular treatment. They are *studies* at first hand, . . . earnest and noble, and offer noble aid to thought that would climb the loftiest and most difficult steep of knowledge. The path they trace is clear to the peak."—Rev. R. A. HOLLAND, D. D., in *The Living Church.*

"Dr. Sterrett is far more than a slavish expositor. . . . We cordially commend it as giving to the general reader a valuable idea of the great German's method in philosophy, as well as initiating him into the latter's treatment of some of the most important departments of human thinking."—*London Literary World.*

"Dr. Sterrett has given to the elucidation of Hegel those literary and critical abilities which make his book a valuable contribution to theology. No one can read it without profit. Dr. Sterrett is a helpful guide. He is careful, honest, frank, and scholarly."—*The Standard of the Cross and the Church.*

New York: D. APPLETON & CO., 72 Fifth Avenue.

D. APPLETON & CO.'S PUBLICATIONS.

A WASHINGTON BIBLE-CLASS. By Gail Hamilton. Large 12mo. Cloth, $1.50.

"The author of this book needs no introduction to American readers. But we will venture to say that she has never before shown greater brilliancy, intellectual grasp, and critical acumen than in this collection of papers, which were originally read in Washington last winter, before a Bible-class composed of prominent women of that city. As we have already intimated, this book will be sternly criticised by many; but in freshness of analysis it takes its place as one of the most important of the more recent contributions to biblical literature."—*New York Tribune.*

"That these lectures are interesting, even entertaining—that, more than that, they are stimulating and suggestive—need hardly be said. They are by Gail Hamilton; that is enough. It is a book of fragments, interesting, entertaining, stimulating, suggestive, and useful, but still of fragments."—*Christian Union.*

"She has at least one merit—she is never dull. Whether her readers agree with her or not, they are interested. The volume gives the reader a very clear idea of the religious discussion of the day, and marks the wide divergence from the older teachings of theology."—*Chicago Inter-Ocean.*

"The whole book is overflowing with fresh, often original thought, and with deep, devout feeling, and the style is crisp, pungent, occasionally caustic, but always firm, confident, and compelling attention if not convictions."—*Chicago Times.*

"That the volume is fresh, bright, and sparkling, goes without saying, and it will be enjoyed by those who have kept abreast of the result of modern biblical criticism, and will be found deeply suggestive and profitable by those who have not."—*Boston Traveller.*

THE HOPE OF THE GOSPEL. By George MacDonald, author of "Unspoken Sermons," "Robert Falconer," etc. 12mo. Cloth, $1.25.

"George MacDonald began life as a preacher; and always, whether in sermon or story, he is a preacher yet. He is also one of the most fervent of preachers. . . . In respect to simplicity, vitality, and directness of style, these sermons might be studied with special profit."—*Advance.*

"These sermons are marked by that same broad and all-embracing charity which has characterized the writer's works of fiction."—*San Francisco Evening Post.*

"In homely language, which is a sure means to touch the heart, the author delivers his message, direct and plain as an every-day duty, but winged with the fervor of truthful utterance."—*Philadelphia Ledger.*

MORAL TEACHINGS OF SCIENCE. By Arabella B. Buckley, author of "The Fairy-Land of Science," "Life and her Children," etc. 12mo. Cloth, 75 cents.

"A little book that proves, with excellent clearness and force, how many and striking are the moral lessons suggested by the study of the life history of the plant or bird, beast or insect."—*London Saturday Review.*

"This is a charming little book, and may be commended to those who are anxious to know how far the acceptance of the latest and most uncompromising scientific theories is consistent with a belief in God and in personal immortality. . . . The book is admirably written, and is full of accurate knowledge clearly and simply stated. Every thoughtful and sincere reader must acknowledge its value and charm."—*Charleston News and Courier.*

New York: D. APPLETON & CO., 72 Fifth Avenue.

D. APPLETON & CO.'S PUBLICATIONS.

AN IMPORTANT WORK.

***J*ESUS CHRIST**: *A History of Our Saviour's Person, Mission, and Spirit.* By PÈRE DIDON, O. P. With an Introduction by His Eminence JAMES, CARDINAL GIBBONS. Edited by Rt. Rev. BERNARD O'REILLY, D. D.: D. Lit. (Laval). Profusely illustrated with Maps, Photogravure reproductions of Celebrated Paintings by the Old Masters, and Woodcuts of Scenes in the Holy Land, engraved from Sketches made by our own Artists.

Complete in Two Large Octavo Volumes of about 500 pages each, handsomely bound in Extra Cloth, with embellished cover. Price, in box, $7.50. Sold only by subscription.

The original edition of Père Didon's great work in the French language has already reached a sale of more than TWENTY EDITIONS. Not in many years has a similar book been published that has attracted more attention abroad, or been received by the foreign reviewers with such enthusiastic and unstinted praise. The work of Père Didon is commended to all—Roman Catholics or Protestants—as being one of the most powerful and intensely interesting contributions to Ecclesiastical Literature that have appeared in recent years.

"Most heartily do we congratulate the author on his having sought to render attractive and pleasing for the cultivated public of our day the life of Our Lord Jesus Christ, without either changing or abbreviating the text of the Gospels. People in France had become most unreasonably infatuated with the 'German critical science.' We must, therefore, feel grateful to Père Didon for the patience he has had to read the lucubrations of the German professors, and for his having made the acquaintance of the German universities. This fact gives great weight to his testimony in the estimation of an immense number of readers, who, deeming that this Life of Christ is on a level with the exigencies of 'contemporary criticism,' will thus read without prepossession this beautiful work, all irradiated with the pure light of the Gospel."—*Revue Bibliographique et Littéraire.*

"To write for those who believe, is well; but to write for those who do not believe, or who are troubled with doubts—who are either indifferent or hostile—is much better. These are the persons who will be attracted and captivated by Père Didon's 'Jesus Christ.'"—*Le Gaulois.*

"This work, so long and carefully prepared and so much spoken of in advance, has had from its first appearance a splendid success. This success is well deserved. Polemics, the refutation of rationalistic criticism, take up a relatively small place, and the author is to be warmly congratulated thereupon. A Life of Christ, in accordance with the views of such critics, would have been read by but a small number of persons. The broad and imposing plan on which Père Didon conceived his work will secure to him daily thousands upon thousands of readers. The literary form given to the book is worthy of the subject. The diction is elevated, like the thoughts it clothes."—*Revue Bibliographique Universelle.*

New York: D. APPLETON & CO., 72 Fifth Avenue.

D. APPLETON AND COMPANY'S PUBLICATIONS.

*C*YPRIAN: *His Life, his Times, his Work.* By Edward White Benson, D. D., D. C. L., sometime Archbishop of Canterbury. With an Introduction by the Rt. Rev. Henry C. Potter, D. D., LL.D., D. C. L., Bishop of New York. 8vo. Cloth, $7.00.

"It is indeed, in every sense—historical, theological, ecclesiastical, biographical, and personal—a singularly edifying book. . . . A noble and touching literary monument."—*London Times.*

"On the whole, and with all reservations which can possibly be made, this weighty volume is a contribution to criticism and learning on which we can but congratulate the Anglican Church. We wish more of her bishops were capable or desirous of descending into that arena of pure intellect from which Dr. Benson returns with these posthumous laurels."—*London Saturday Review.*

"Dr. Benson exhibits a strong individuality. His style is rugged and picturesque, occasionally sprinkled with strange words, but always impressive and intense. He had naturally a passion for the exact truth; and his scholarship was accurate, thorough, and unwearied in its efforts to get to the foundation of things. The book will attract attention, will well repay perusal, and will prove highly suggestive."—*London Athenæum.*

*A*NNALS OF WESTMINSTER ABBEY. By E. T. Bradley (Mrs. A. Murray Smith). With 150 Illustrations by H. M. Paget and W. Hatherell, a Preface by Dean Bradley, and a Chapter on the Abbey Buildings by J. P. Micklethwaite. Royal 4to. Cloth, $15.00.

"An excellent history of Westminster Abbey."—*London Athenæum.*

"Not a few books have been written about the Abbey, but for historical completeness and accuracy, as well as for typographical and artistic finish and tastefulness, the present volume must bear away the palm."—*The Critic.*

"Of the many books that have been written on Westminster Abbey, none that is in so condensed a form as is this one will be found more enjoyable or give greater satisfaction."—*New York Times.*

"By a clear, simple, continuous narrative and a vivid presentation, the author makes far away times and personages seem near and real, and comes on down the long, interesting historic line of sovereigns who have been crowned and married and buried in Westminster. . . . Interesting and charming."—*Chicago Times-Herald.*

D. APPLETON AND COMPANY, NEW YORK.

D. APPLETON & CO.'S PUBLICATIONS.

THE BEGINNERS OF A NATION. A History of the Source and Rise of the Earliest English Settlements in America, with Special Reference to the Life and Character of the People. The first volume in A History of Life in the United States. By EDWARD EGGLESTON. Small 8vo. Cloth, gilt top, uncut, with Maps, $1.50.

"Few works on the period which it covers can compare with this in point of mere literary attractiveness, and we fancy that many to whom its scholarly value will not appeal will read the volume with interest and delight."—*New York Evening Post.*

"Written with a firm grasp of the theme, inspired by ample knowledge, and made attractive by a vigorous and resonant style, the book will receive much attention. It is a great theme the author has taken up, and he grasps it with the confidence of a master."—*New York Times.*

"Mr. Eggleston's 'Beginners' is unique. No similar historical study has, to our knowledge, ever been done in the same way. Mr. Eggleston is a reliable reporter of facts; but he is also an exceedingly keen critic. He writes history without the effort to merge the critic in the historian. His sense of humor is never dormant. He renders some of the dullest passages in colonial annals actually amusing by his witty treatment of them. He finds a laugh for his readers where most of his predecessors have found yawns. And with all this he does not sacrifice the dignity of history for an instant."—*Boston Saturday Evening Gazette.*

"The delightful style, the clear flow of the narrative, the philosophical tone, and the able analysis of men and events will commend Mr. Eggleston's work to earnest students."—*Philadelphia Public Ledger.*

"The work is worthy of careful reading, not only because of the author's ability as a literary artist, but because of his conspicuous proficiency in interpreting the causes of and changes in American life and character."—*Boston Journal.*

"It is noticeable that Mr. Eggleston has followed no beaten track, but has drawn his own conclusions as to the early period, and they differ from the generally received version not a little. The book is stimulating and will prove of great value to the student of history."—*Minneapolis Journal.*

"A very interesting as well as a valuable book. . . . A distinct advance upon most that has been written, particularly of the settlement of New England."—*Newark Advertiser.*

"One of the most important books of the year. It is a work of art as well as of historical science, and its distinctive purpose is to give an insight into the real life and character of people. . . . The author's style is charming, and the history is fully as interesting as a novel."—*Brooklyn Standard-Union.*

"The value of Mr. Eggleston's work is in that it is really a history of 'life,' not merely a record of events. . . . The comprehensive purpose of his volume has been excellently performed. The book is eminently readable."—*Philadelphia Times.*

New York: D. APPLETON & CO., 72 Fifth Avenue.

D. APPLETON & CO.'S PUBLICATIONS.

JOHN BACH MC MASTER.

HISTORY OF THE PEOPLE OF THE UNITED STATES,

from the Revolution to the Civil War. By JOHN BACH McMASTER. To be completed in six volumes. Vols. I, II, III, and IV now ready. 8vo. Cloth, gilt top, $2.50 each.

". . . Prof. McMaster has told us what no other historians have told. . . . The skill, the animation, the brightness, the force, and the charm with which he arrays the facts before us are such that we can hardly conceive of more interesting reading for an American citizen who cares to know the nature of those causes which have made not only him but his environment and the opportunities life has given him what they are."—*N. Y. Times.*

"Those who can read between the lines may discover in these pages constant evidences of care and skill and faithful labor, of which the old-time superficial essayists, compiling library notes on dates and striking events, had no conception; but to the general reader the fluent narrative gives no hint of the conscientious labors, far-reaching, world-wide, vast and yet microscopically minute, that give the strength and value which are felt rather than seen. This is due to the art of presentation. The author's position as a scientific workman we may accept on the abundant testimony of the experts who know the solid worth of his work; his skill as a literary artist we can all appreciate, the charm of his style being self-evident."—*Philadelphia Telegraph.*

"The third volume contains the brilliantly written and fascinating story of the progress and doings of the people of this country from the era of the Louisiana purchase to the opening scenes of the second war with Great Britain—say a period of ten years. In every page of the book the reader finds that fascinating flow of narrative, that clear and lucid style, and that penetrating power of thought and judgment which distinguished the previous volumes."—*Columbus State Journal.*

"Prof. McMaster has more than fulfilled the promises made in his first volumes, and his work is constantly growing better and more valuable as he brings it nearer to our own time. His style is clear, simple, and idiomatic, and there is just enough of the critical spirit in the narrative to guide the reader."—*Boston Herald.*

"Take it all in all, the History promises to be the ideal American history. Not so much given to dates and battles and great events as in the fact that it is like a great panorama of the people, revealing their inner life and action. It contains, with all its sober facts, the spice of personalities and incidents, which relieves every page from dullness."—*Chicago Inter-Ocean.*

"History written in this picturesque style will tempt the most heedless to read. Prof. McMaster is more than a stylist; he is a student, and his History abounds in evidences of research in quarters not before discovered by the historian."—*Chicago Tribune.*

"A History *sui generis* which has made and will keep its own place in our literature."—*New York Evening Post.*

"His style is vigorous and his treatment candid and impartial."—*New York Tribune.*

New York : D. APPLETON & CO., 72 Fifth Avenue.

www.ingramcontent.com/pod-product-compliance
Lightning Source LLC
Chambersburg PA
CBHW030405230426
43664CB00007BB/758